THE DESCENT PROTOCOL

THE DESCENT PROTOCOL

Governance at Depth

DARLENE WATERS-COLON

Blue Depth Press
Charleston, SC
thedescentprotocol.com

First Edition

Hardback ISBN: 979-8-9954178-0-4
Ebook - EPUB ISBN: 979-8-9954178-1-1
Paperback ISBN: 979-8-9954178-2-8
Hardback (Premium Color Edition) ISBN: 979-8-9954178-3-5

Cover and Interior Design: Ian Koviak

Printed in the United States of America

Library of Congress Control Number: 2026912721

Disclaimer:
This book is intended for informational and educational purposes only. While the author has made every effort to ensure the accuracy of the information contained herein, the content reflects the author's views and experience and should not be construed as legal, tax, or professional advice. Readers should consult appropriate professionals for guidance specific to their individual circumstances.

ACKNOWLEDGEMENTS

This work was not created in isolation. While the perspective and conclusions are my own, the depth behind them was shaped by experience, challenge, and the people who have influenced how I see, question, and ultimately define governance.

To those I have worked alongside throughout my career—across industries, across borders, and often under pressure—you have been the proving ground for these ideas. The lessons embedded in these pages are not theoretical. They were earned.

To the leaders and peers who challenged assumptions, asked better questions, and refused to accept surface-level answers—you sharpened my thinking in ways that made this work possible.

To those who supported this process more quietly—through encouragement, patience, and space—you made it possible to sustain the discipline required to complete this work.

To my husband, Ed—your steady support throughout this process has meant more than I can fully express.

To my daughter, Ashley, whose encouragement helped move this work forward when I questioned the premise and needed clarity.

To my son, Joshua, and my granddaughters, Emma, Avery, and Madison—your love, laughter, joy, and unwavering support have carried me through more than you will ever know.

A special acknowledgement to Michelle Stokes, whose leadership and perspective have been both grounding and elevating. Your willingness to engage, challenge, and support this work has been meaningful in more ways than can be fully expressed here.

To Bill Ansley, for believing in me early in my career and setting me on a path that would ultimately lead here.

My sincere appreciation to Steven Rigolosi for his editorial expertise, thoughtful guidance, and commitment to helping strengthen the structure, clarity, and flow of this work.

And finally, to those operating in complexity—leaders, advisors, and practitioners navigating risk, responsibility, and consequence—this work is for you.

—Darlene Waters-Colon

FOREWORD

Governance Before Pressure Accumulates

By Michelle Stokes, Vice-President, Canadian Society of Customs Brokers

In both enterprise governance and scuba diving, the most dangerous moments are not marked by disruption, but by calm conditions that mask accumulating pressure.

Most failures of governance do not begin with error; they begin with assumptions.

Over the course of my career, I have watched capable organizations staffed by experts, supported by controls, and guided by good intentions encounter consequences they never believed they were creating. In nearly every case, the problem was not negligence or a lack of technical competence. It was something quieter: exposure accumulating beyond recognition because governance had never been engineered to account for how deeply conditions had already shifted.

That is why this book matters.

Darlene Waters-Colon has spent her entire career in customs, working where trade risk actually lives: in the trenches of multinational enterprises managing global governance across jurisdictions, business units, and regulatory regimes. She is also a certified diver, trained to operate in environments where pressure increases invisibly, where early conditions feel familiar, and where safety depends on preparation completed long before descent begins.

Customs governance, perhaps more than any other regulatory domain, mirrors those conditions.

Goods continue to move while interpretations are debated. Revenue grows while assumptions persist. Controls perform while exposure compounds. Silence is mistaken for safety, and because consequence rarely arrives at the moment risk is created, organizations can descend gradually, feeling confident and capable but unaware of how much pressure has already been absorbed into their structure.

Darlene does not treat this situation as a technical problem. She frames it as an enterprise problem.

In *The Descent Protocol*, governance is not defined by activity, reporting, or process maturity. It is defined by posture: the deliberate position leadership takes in relation to the exposure it allows to accumulate. Activity demonstrates effort. Governance determines whether depth is entered deliberately or assumed unconsciously.

This framing matters because it challenges how organizations typically understand governance. Too often, effectiveness is inferred from activity: controls that operate, reports that remain clean, and professionals who respond competently when questions arise. Those indicators suggest stability. They do not, on their own, confirm that exposure is being deliberately governed as it accumulates.

This book refuses the comforting fiction that governance failures occur only when controls are absent or compliance breaks down. Instead, it examines the more uncomfortable truth that some of the most significant exposure to unanticipated costs imposed by government customs authorities develops inside organizations that are operating precisely as designed.

Boards do not need to understand tariff codes, origin determinations, or value calculations. Instead, they need recognition. They need to know when exposure has become financially material, when reassessment last occurred, who owns systemic positions, what assumptions remain valid, and whether recognition thresholds were triggered appropriately. Without that awareness, oversight becomes reactive by default, forced to operate under compressed timelines, narrowed options, and externally dictated pace.

One of the most important insights in this book is deceptively simple:

Ownership without authority is surveillance. Ownership with authority is governance.

Darlene shows how trade exposure migrates logically across organizations—toward finance when tariffs shift, toward legal when enforcement tightens, and toward supply chain when disruption dominates. Each shift makes sense and yet, without deliberate anchoring at the enterprise level, ownership fragments.

The result is not chaos; it is delayed recognition.

What makes this work especially powerful is its relevance during periods of success. Organizations rarely misjudge depth during crisis. They misjudge it when growth is steady, controls appear sound, and performance reinforces confidence. Expansion accelerates. Methodologies stabilize. Assumptions harden. Exposure becomes normal. Structural limits are crossed quietly.

By the time pressure demands attention, ascent is no longer deliberate. It is dictated.

This book is not a warning against ambition. Expansion is not treated as recklessness, and expertise is not questioned. Instead, *The Descent Protocol* asks whether governance has been deliberately engineered for the depth at which the enterprise is already operating.

Through parallel concepts found in the principles of diving, such as predive assessment, descent protocol, depth recognition, escalation authority, and controlled ascent, Darlene reframes governance as architecture rather than response. She challenges leaders to move beyond assurance and toward visibility—not more reporting, but structural clarity.

That shift is subtle; it is also transformative. Because once leadership understands that stability does not equal safety, governance ceases to be assumed. It becomes deliberate.

This is not a book about compliance. It is a book about survivability at scale.

For leaders responsible not just for performance but also for durability, *The Descent Protocol: Governance at Depth* offers a discipline drawn from environments where pressure is respected, limits are defined, and depth is never mistaken for safety.

TABLE OF CONTENTS

LIST OF FIGURES

PREFACE

Over time, leaders begin to notice the same questions appearing in different forms, not as overt problems or moments of failure but as subtle signals embedded in the way decisions are framed, what is escalated and what is not, and how responsibility is described when outcomes remain stable and reconsidered when they do not.

Across organizations, the environments differ—industries change, regulatory frameworks shift, and operating models evolve—yet the underlying pattern remains consistent.

Work is performed at a high level, supported by experienced teams, defined processes, and established controls. From both the outside and the inside, these conditions create a clear and persuasive signal of maturity.

And yet, certain questions persist, not about whether the work is being done correctly, but about how decisions hold together over time, particularly as they extend beyond the context in which they were first made.

Questions begin to emerge around ownership and consequence—who ultimately owns a position once it scales beyond its original application, at what point a decision transitions from local to structural, and when responsibility for execution evolves into responsibility for exposure.

These questions are rarely asked directly; instead, they surface gradually, often only when conditions change, when scale increases, or when assumptions that once held begin to shift in ways that make prior decisions more consequential than they originally appeared.

In global trade, those moments tend to arrive with clarity as the interaction between regulation, scale, and time makes accumulation visible in ways that are difficult to ignore, but the pattern itself is not unique to trade. It exists wherever decisions are made within systems that expand faster than the structures designed to govern them.

This book does not attempt to improve execution through additional activity, but to define the structure through which execution is governed, making visible how organizations arrive at positions that are reasonable, defensible, and well-managed in isolation, yet behave differently as they scale. It also explains what must change when governance is designed to evolve with that accumulation.

The ideas that follow are drawn from experience, but they are not limited to it; they reflect a consistent observation that the most consequential exposure is rarely created through isolated error, but instead forms through continuity.

Over time, I found that the language used to describe these patterns often fell short, relying on static terms to explain dynamics that were anything but static, until the comparison to diving began to clarify what traditional frameworks did not—that conditions change as depth increases, that pressure alters behavior even when nothing appears visibly different, and that stability depends not on effort, but on design that anticipates those changes before they are felt. From that point forward, the work requires not only a different structure but also a more precise language to describe it, one that reflects how exposure forms, how governance responds, and how organizations move—often without recognizing it—from surface conditions into depth.

INTRODUCTION

Why Depth Matters

In large organizations, exposure rarely announces itself; instead, it accumulates through decisions that are reasonable in isolation, technically sound, and often made by experienced professionals operating with good intent. Exposure expands gradually through repetition, scale, and time until it becomes embedded in systems, processes, and assumptions that appear stable precisely because nothing has yet required them to be reconsidered.

From the surface, these conditions are difficult to distinguish from control because work remains visible, controls function as designed, reports remain clean, and teams respond quickly when questions arise, creating a steady flow of assurance that risk is being managed. And in many respects, it is.

What is less visible is how management behaves as conditions change.

Management resolves issues as they emerge, but governance determines how exposure accumulates before those issues become visible. The distinction between the two becomes meaningful only when scale increases, regulatory posture shifts, or a single point of challenge forces the organization to evaluate its decisions not transactionally but structurally. At that point, the question is no longer whether individual decisions were defensible, but whether the enterprise deliberately governed how those decisions were allowed to scale.

This book examines that moment, not as an isolated event but as the predictable outcome of systems that were never designed to operate under the conditions they ultimately reached. It explores how capable organizations—well-resourced, experienced, and disciplined in execution—arrive at material exposure without ever believing they took a risk. It also examines how governance quietly yields to execution as authority remains static while exposure evolves and how confidence, reinforced by performance, delays the instinct to reassess.

To understand this progression more precisely, a different lens is required.

The conditions under which exposure accumulates in complex organizations behave less like linear growth and more like descent, where movement into greater scale and complexity alters the environment itself, changing the relationship between visibility, control, and consequence in ways that are not immediately apparent from the surface.

The model used in this book is drawn from deep-sea diving, not as metaphor for illustration but as a structural parallel for how systems behave under increasing pressure.

In diving, conditions at the surface bear little resemblance to those at depth. Visibility changes, pressure increases, movement requires adjustment, and decisions that feel inconsequential near the surface carry materially different consequences as depth increases—not because the diver has changed, but because the environment has.

Most importantly, depth does not create risk on its own. Instead, it changes the conditions under which risk must be managed, and without deliberate adjustment, the same behaviors that felt stable at the surface become misaligned at depth.

Organizations operate under similar conditions.

As they expand across jurisdictions, increase transaction volume, and embed interpretive decisions over time, they do not simply grow—they move into environments where exposure behaves differently, where what was once localized becomes interconnected, where what was once manageable becomes cumulative, and where execution alone, no matter how capable, is no longer sufficient to maintain alignment.

At shallow levels, execution absorbs variation effectively, but at greater depth, structure begins to matter more than activity, design begins to matter more than effort, and governance—if it has not evolved deliberately—begins to fall behind the exposure it is meant to control.

This is why the distinction between managing risk and governing exposure is central to this book's arguments. While risk can be addressed transactionally, exposure accumulates structurally, and the systems designed to manage one are not necessarily sufficient to govern the other.

This book is not a manual for improving execution through additional controls or activity. Rather, it defines the structure through which execution is governed, making visible how organizations arrive at positions that are reasonable, defensible, and well-managed in isolation, yet behave differently as they scale. It also explains what must change when governance is designed to evolve with that accumulation.

While the examples throughout these pages are grounded in global trade—where the interaction between regulation, scale, and time makes accumulation particularly visible—the conditions described are not unique to that domain and exist wherever decisions are made within systems that expand faster than the structures designed to govern them.

This book is written for those responsible for that reality—leaders who must answer for exposure they did not personally create, executives who rely on signals that may not fully reflect structural risk, and professionals who manage complexity daily but recognize that execution alone cannot define the limits of acceptable exposure.

What follows is not a checklist, but a structure—a way of understanding how governance behaves as conditions change and how it must be designed if it is to remain aligned with the exposure it governs, because when exposure is finally measured, the question is rarely how it formed, but why it was allowed to continue.

PROLOGUE

The Assessment

The assessment covered one year.

The amount was $10 million.

It was issued by a single customs authority following a routine review. There was no allegation of fraud and no claim of concealment. The valuation methodology had been documented, applied consistently, and previously defended without objection.

On its face, the matter appeared technical. A disagreement over interpretation, a recalibration of methodology. The kind of issue that global trade functions encounter and resolve as part of ordinary operations.

But the number on the page did not exist in isolation.

The statute permitted review for five years.

The valuation methodology had not been developed for a single transaction, a single shipment, or even a single market. It was embedded in process. It governed how value was declared across product lines, over time, and at scale.

It had been applied across seventy-six countries.

Import activity under that methodology was continuous, not episodic. The $10 million represented one jurisdiction, one year, and one regulatory interpretation. It did not represent the structural footprint of the decision.

The figure was measurable. The architecture behind it was not.

If one year in one country produced that level of exposure, what would seven years produce? If one authority challenged the methodology, then how would others respond? If the interpretation shifted in one jurisdiction, then what did that imply for the seventy-five others operating under the same logic?

The issue was no longer whether the position could be argued. It was whether the enterprise understood the cumulative risk it had allowed to scale.

The methodology had endured, but governance review had not.

No one had intended to accumulate exposure. The valuation approach had been adopted thoughtfully, supported by analysis, and implemented by experienced professionals. It had functioned without disruption. Entries were filed. Goods were moved. Audits were completed. Questions were answered.

The organization had managed trade risk, but it had not governed its accumulation.

"The organization had managed trade risk. It had not governed its accumulation."

In the executive discussion that followed, the framing shifted. The assessment itself was significant, but it was not the true concern. The concern was structural.

The valuation approach was not local. It was systemic.

If exposure was recalculated in one jurisdiction, then the logic would not stop at a border. The same methodology, applied consistently and embedded in process, meant that the implications extended well beyond the initial assessment.

The question was no longer whether the organization could defend a technical position. The question was whether it could demonstrate that the design behind that position had been deliberately governed as it scaled.

The assessment was not the beginning of the problem. Instead, it was the moment the structure became visible.

What changed was not the effort. What changed was the implication.

The assessment itself was significant—but it was not the true shock. The shock was what the assessment forced the organization to confront.

If this position could be challenged here, what did it mean elsewhere? If this methodology was no longer accepted under one regulatory interpretation, how stable was it globally? If one country forced a re-evaluation, what exposure had quietly accumulated across dozens of other countries?

This was not a company operating in a handful of markets. It imported continuously, systematically, and at scale—across more than seventy jurisdictions. Decisions made in one place did not stay local. They echoed.

What had been experienced internally as a well-governed response suddenly appeared, in aggregate, as a fragile global posture.

And no one could point to the moment where leadership had deliberately chosen that posture.

At the executive level, the conversation shifted. The question was no longer whether the company could defend its valuation methodology. It had done that—repeatedly. The question became whether the organization could absorb the consequences if that defense failed elsewhere, or if it succeeded in one jurisdiction and failed in another.

This was no longer about technical correctness. It was about exposure. Not theoretical exposure, not hypothetical risk, but exposure that could now be modeled, quantified, and extrapolated across the enterprise.

A single-country assessment became a lens through which the entire global operating model had to be examined.

At this moment trade risk reached the board. Not because it was technical, but because it had become structural.

From the outside, this period would later be reconstructed differently.

Regulators would not focus on the sophistication of the controls or the reasonableness of the arguments. They would focus on persistence, patterns, and how decisions endured even as conditions changed.

They would ask questions the organization had not asked itself:

- Who reassessed the risk as it scaled?
- When did governance re-engage after urgency subsided?
- What forum reconsidered whether the posture still made sense?

The absence of clear answers would matter more than the original dispute.

This was not a failure of intent. It was a failure of design.

This book begins before that meeting with corporate executives.

The question is not how this happened—it's how it went unnoticed.

As organizations expand in complexity, governance must evolve with equal precision. Without that alignment, exposure grows in ways that are not immediately visible. What is required is not more oversight—but a fundamentally different kind of design.

The progression shown here is not random. It reflects a pattern—one that is more clearly understood through a different lens.

The conditions under which organizations scale, accumulate exposure, and operate under increasing complexity mirror the conditions of deep-sea diving, where movement into greater depth alters visibility, pressure, and control in ways that are not immediately apparent at the surface.

Figure 1: The Assessment ($10M Moment)

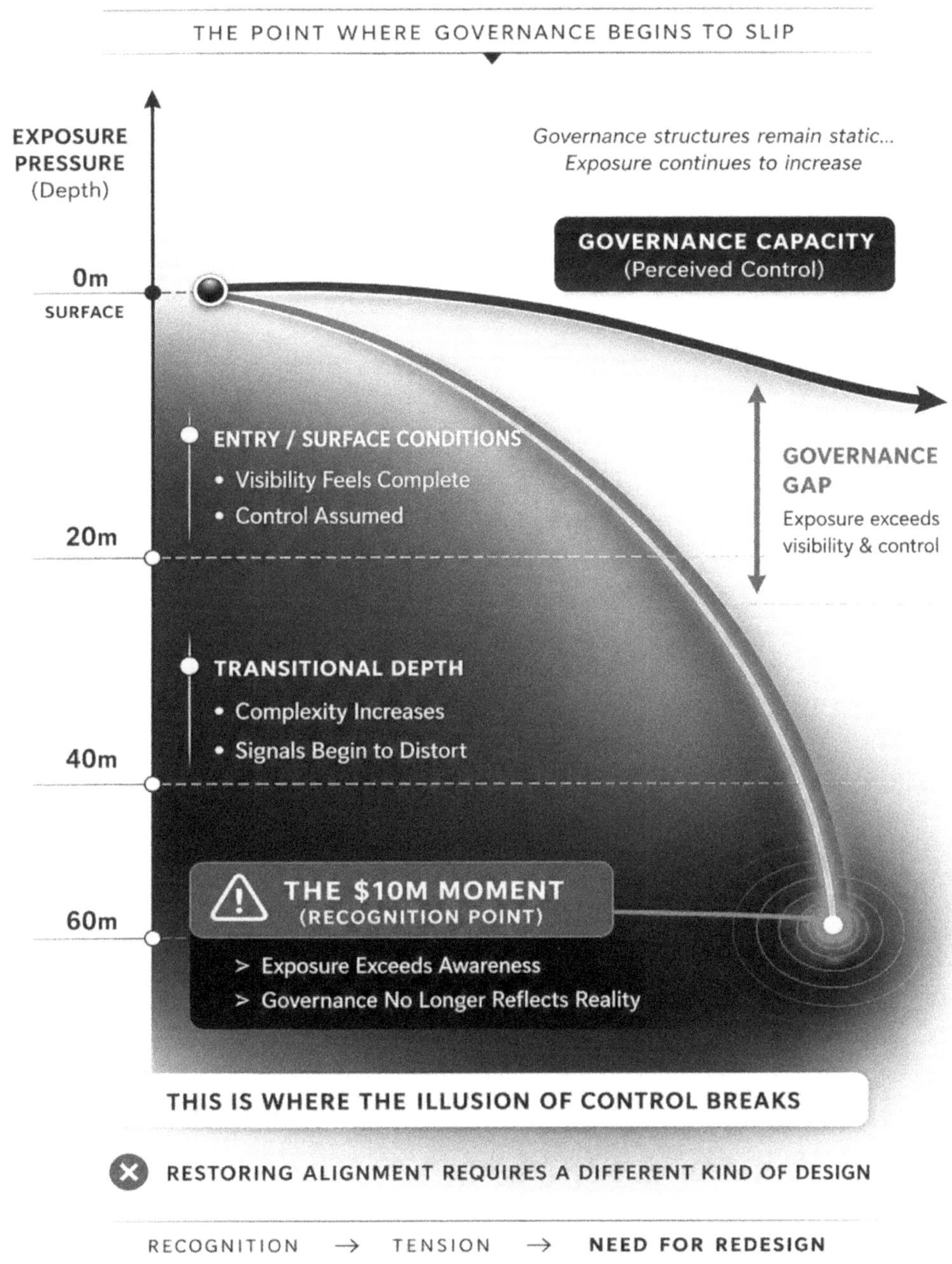

The structure that governs this progression is introduced in Chapter 2, where the conditions of depth are examined in greater detail. What matters here is understanding how misalignment begins.

Figure 1 illustrates the moment described above—the point at which a contained issue begins to reveal a broader structural condition, where exposure extends beyond the immediate assessment and into the way decisions have accumulated over time.

Organizations move through the stages shown in Figure 1 as complexity increases, and success depends on whether governance evolves with that movement—or falls behind it.

The following chapters examine what happens when that alignment is lost—and what is required to restore it.

CHAPTER 1

The First Few Feet

A diver does not enter the water without a plan.

Before descent begins, experienced divers review the conditions that determine whether the dive can be conducted safely. They check their equipment. They study the environment. They decide how deep they intend to go and how long they will remain there. They establish a path and an ascent strategy before the first movement downward ever begins.

These steps form what divers call a dive plan—a protocol designed to ensure that descent happens deliberately rather than accidentally.

Organizations rarely apply the same discipline when operating inside complex regulatory systems. They enter environments that are deep, dynamic, and cumulative without first specifying how exposure will be governed as it scales. It is at that point that movement into complexity begins to take on the characteristics of descent, where conditions change in ways that require a defined structure to navigate them.

The first few feet of a descent rarely feel dramatic or unfamiliar. At the water's surface, conditions often appear calm. Light still reaches the diver, movement remains easy, and the surface is still visible above. The environment feels stable enough to navigate without concern. Air still feels close, and the surface still appears within reach.

Nothing in those early moments suggests that conditions are beginning to change. But experienced divers know that the surface rarely reveals the pressure that begins to build below it.

Organizations experience the same illusion. You are still near the surface when the first signals appear.

From inside the organization, nothing feels broken. The company has invested heavily in trade expertise. It has designed internal controls, documented methodologies, and established escalation pathways. When ambiguity arises, guidance is sought. Prior rulings are requested. Responses are timely and professional. Positions are reviewed and defended. Regulators have reinforced the belief that the organization is operating within the bounds of reasonable care.

There is no complacency. Instead, there is confidence. Confidence forms when activity is visible, when processes function, and when challenges are met without disruption. It creates stability and shapes decision-making. It lowers the instinct to reassess structural assumptions because nothing appears unstable enough to require changes.

So, when a regulatory challenge emerges—one adjacent to positions that have already been defended successfully—the response follows a familiar pattern. Trade professionals assemble documentation. Controls are activated. Precedent is cited. Arguments are refined and resubmitted. Leadership is reassured that the issue is being handled appropriately.

From the inside, this is evidence of maturity. It feels like governance at work.

But governance and activity are not the same thing. Activity demonstrates effort. Governance defines posture—the deliberate position an organization assumes in relation to the exposure it allows to accumulate.

> *"Activity demonstrates effort.*
> *Governance defines posture."*

At the surface, movement creates the impression of control. The water shifts. Equipment adjusts. Signals are exchanged. You are busy managing conditions. But unless you equalize, pressure accumulates quietly. You can remain close to air and still be under force.

Organizations behave the same way.

Work can be continuous. Controls can operate. Reports can remain clean. Silence can persist. But none of these conditions confirm that exposure is being deliberately governed as it scales. They confirm only that execution is functioning within its current tolerance. This book is about how capable organizations—staffed by experienced professionals, supported by controls, and guided by good intentions—arrive at that moment when governance no longer reflects the reality of the exposure it carries, without ever believing they took a risk.

It is about how governance quietly yields to execution under sustained pressure. How temporary decisions become institutionalized. How precedent replaces periodic reconsideration. How expertise absorbs variance before leadership ever sees it. How trade risk, which tolerates deferral so well, becomes the ideal environment for governance to erode.

The assessment makes these consequences visible, but the structure that produced them formed long before the assessment took place.

No one set out to accumulate exposure. The valuation approach had been adopted thoughtfully, supported by analysis, and implemented by experienced professionals. It had functioned without disruption.

Risk was being managed, but exposure was compounding.

Equalization in governance does not mean panic. It does not mean halting operations at the first sign of ambiguity. Instead, it means deliberate reconsideration as exposure scales. It means reassessing ownership as decisions embed across jurisdictions and time. It means confirming that escalation authority matches the structural depth at which the organization is operating.

In the first few feet, that work is rarely urgent. It is simply necessary.

When organizations lose sight of discipline—when activity substitutes for architecture—they can descend for years without feeling strain. They remain close enough to the surface that confidence feels justified.

Until pressure reveals itself.

SECTION I

Surface Signals: The Comfort of Visible Control

Trade compliance produces visible evidence of effort. Classifications are issued and reviewed. Import entries are filed and liquidated. Licenses are obtained, tracked, and renewed. Brokers submit reports. Volumes are reconciled. Exceptions are logged. Dashboards show error rates trending downward, filings submitted on time, and remediation items closed within defined windows. Periodic audits confirm that procedures exist and are being followed as designed.

From the surface, this level of activity signals control, and from a leadership perspective, this visibility matters. It signals attention. It signals investment. It signals discipline in a technical and operationally complex domain. In enterprises where executives must rely on summary information to oversee specialized functions, visible activity offers measurable proof that something is happening.

And in many cases, something *is* happening. Work is being done. Issues are being resolved. Professionals are exercising judgment. Systems are operating. But visible activity does not automatically equate to governance.

At the surface of the water, movement is constant. The current shifts. The boat drifts slightly. Divers adjust their equipment. Signals are exchanged. You are engaged in activity that creates a sense of control. But surface motion does not reveal subsurface pressure. You can remain close to air and still be under force.

Organizations function the same way.

Activity can remain steady while exposure accumulates quietly beneath it. Execution absorbs variance. Expertise compensates for design gaps. Reporting structures capture transactional accuracy. As long as performance remains stable and regulators remain silent, nothing compels leadership to ask whether the architecture itself requires recalibration.

Visible activity is persuasive because it mirrors how organizations are structured to manage complexity. Work is divided into functions. Specialists are assigned ownership. Performance metrics are defined. Deviations are tracked. Remediation is documented. Accountability is framed in terms of throughput and accuracy.

This model is highly effective for execution, but it is less reliable for governing accumulated exposure across time and geography.

Governance requires less visible, less easily summarized elements: clarity of ownership across boundaries, consistency of decision-making under changing conditions, and deliberate reconsideration of positions as scale increases. It requires evidence that judgment is exercised within an intentional architecture rather than through informal accommodation.

These qualities are not easily captured in dashboards. Instead, they are revealed only when pressure demands explanation. Until pressure demands explanation visible activity supplies comfort. Comfort reduces inquiry. And reduced inquiry delays equalization.

Consider a multinational enterprise operating across dozens of jurisdictions, each with its own trade team. The structure appears disciplined. Regional compliance managers oversee execution. Local professionals manage classifications, valuation, and origin determinations. A central function provides policy guidance and coordinates training. Reporting rolls upward monthly. Error rates are low. Brokers are evaluated. Internal audits confirm that processes exist and operate as designed.

From the executive tier, the function appears stable, even mature. There is no evidence of neglect. The teams are engaged. Leadership receives regular updates. When questions arise, answers are precise and confident. The absence of disruption reinforces belief in structural soundness.

The assumption becomes natural: If something material were wrong, it would surface through one of the reporting channels already in place.

This is where visible control begins to substitute for governance. Each regional team operates competently within its own boundaries. When regulations are ambiguous, experienced professionals apply judgment. When systems do not align perfectly with operational realities, workarounds are developed to prevent delays. When escalation feels disproportionate to perceived risk, issues are resolved locally rather than elevated.

These decisions are not concealed. They are pragmatic, and they are often well reasoned. Over time, they become normalized. Normalization is subtle. It does not announce itself as risk. It presents itself as efficiency.

But normalization without architectural oversight introduces variance.

Dashboards will not reveal whether similar interpretive scenarios are handled consistently across regions. They will not show whether escalation thresholds differ based on local culture, commercial pressure, or leadership style. They will not reflect when reliance on individual expertise has quietly replaced reliance on structural design.

The system appears functional because individuals are compensating for ambiguity. Indeed, execution can be excellent while governance remains underdeveloped. This distinction is rarely visible in calm conditions.

Leaders learn to trust the signals presented to them because those signals have proven reliable in other domains. Stable metrics reinforce confidence. Clean audit results confirm that controls operate as intended. External advisors benchmark programs favorably against industry peers. Regulators remain silent. Over time, repetition converts these signals into assurance.

Assurance becomes expectation, and expectation becomes institutional belief. Board conversations follow a familiar rhythm. Trade compliance is apparent in enterprise risk reviews. Indicators remain green. Error rates are low. Escalations are minimal. When asked whether emerging concerns exist, the responsible parties provide accurate responses within the required time frame. Nothing material is failing. Controls function. Monitoring continues. The conversation moves on.

This is not negligence. It is rational response to stable indicators. But dashboards measure defined errors. They do not measure cumulative exposure.

Audits confirm that controls function as designed. They do not confirm that the design remains appropriate as the enterprise expands across jurisdictions, increases import volume, or embeds interpretive positions over multiple fiscal years.

Regulatory silence suggests that positions have not yet been challenged. It does not confirm that those positions have been deliberately reauthorized as scale increases.

The most consequential trade decisions frequently occur in areas that dashboards do not capture: interpretive judgments about valuation methodology, origin qualification under evolving free trade agreements, transfer pricing alignment with customs declarations, and exception handling that gradually becomes standard practice.

These decisions rarely generate immediate disruption. Instead, they accumulate quietly. Capability can mask accumulation. Strong operational management can delay governance engagement precisely because it resolves friction before leadership feels structural pressure.

The result is a paradox: The more skilled an organization becomes at managing trade risk transactionally, the longer it can postpone governing it systemically.

In diving, in the first few feet of descent, nothing feels urgent. The surface remains visible. Air feels accessible. Adjustments are easy. There is margin. That proximity to safety reduces the instinct to reassess. You continue downward because nothing compels you to pause.

In enterprises, proximity to stability creates the same effect. Revenue growth reinforces confidence. Clean audits reinforce comfort. Minimal enforcement activity reinforces belief in resilience. Leaders infer that structural depth remains manageable because performance indicators remain steady.

But depth does not announce itself with disruption. Instead, it compounds through scale, duration, and repetition. A valuation approach applied consistently across seventy jurisdictions embeds more deeply each year. An origin interpretation repeated across product lines becomes institutionalized. A workaround adopted in one region spreads informally to others. Each decision may be defensible. Together, they create structural layering.

Visible activity proves that work is being done, but it does not prove that exposure is being deliberately governed as it accumulates.

Equalization at this stage does not require alarm. It requires disciplined inquiry:

- Who owns systemic exposure as it scales?
- When are sustained positions formally reconsidered at the enterprise level?
- At what thresholds do executives review performance and procedures?
- Is escalation authority insulated from performance pressure?
- Are interpretive dependencies stress-tested against changing enforcement climates?

If those questions are not answered early—while proximity to the surface still provides margin—the organization may descend for years without sensing strain. By the time pressure becomes unmistakable, equalization becomes reactive rather than deliberate. And reactive governance always consumes more margin than disciplined governance at the surface.

The comfort of visible control is understandable, but visible control may be an illusion.

SECTION II

Drift Begins: Why Smart Organizations Miss It

One of the most counterintuitive realities of trade governance is this: The organizations most vulnerable to systemic failure are often the most capable.

They are well resourced. They hire experienced professionals. They invest in systems, advisors, and training. They benchmark against peers. They respond quickly when challenged. They resolve disputes without escalation. They pride themselves on having moved beyond basic compliance.

From the outside—and often from the inside—they appear disciplined and mature, and that appearance is precisely what delays governance.

Smart organizations do not miss governance failures because they underestimate trade risk. They miss them because they overestimate what competence can compensate for. Competence can produce strong outcomes, but it does not, by itself, produce aligned architecture.

When design is not explicitly revisited as exposure scales, structure begins to drift even as performance remains strong.

This is the expertise paradox. In capable organizations, difficult issues rarely reach crisis stage. Experienced professionals absorb ambiguity. They interpret regulation pragmatically. They identify workable solutions. They resolve friction before it escalates to executive attention.

Each successful resolution reinforces the same belief: "We have this under control."

What leadership does not see is that governance has quietly shifted from structure to reliance. That is, the organization is no longer governing exposure through deliberate architecture. It is governing through people.

As long as those people remain in place—and as long as conditions remain stable—the system appears resilient. But resilience built on individuals is not structural resilience. It is continuity disguised as control.

This dynamic is common in mature organizations, where strong trade teams become institutional stabilizers. They are consulted early. They are respected. They are efficient. When operational leaders face ambiguity, they call someone they trust. An experienced professional weighs in. A judgment call is made. A shipment moves. The outcome is acceptable. Nothing breaks.

Each of these moments feels like evidence of maturity. Over time, however, informal resolution replaces formal reconsideration. Decisions that might once have required executive review are handled locally. Escalation becomes discretionary rather than defined. Cross-regional alignment depends on relationships rather than mandate. Documentation reflects execution, not structural reassessment. As judgment expands, architecture remains static.

This is not recklessness. It is operational confidence. But operational confidence does not equal governance discipline.

This pattern becomes even more pronounced when smart organizations absorb friction quietly. When issues arise, they are handled without noise. Internal review identifies gaps. Advisors are consulted. Adjustments are made. External inquiries are answered competently. Because disruptions are resolved before becoming public failures, leadership rarely feels urgency. The absence of visible disruption becomes evidence of structural soundness, creating a subtle feedback loop.

Because issues are resolved effectively, governance architecture is not revisited. Because governance is not revisited, reliance on expertise deepens. Because reliance deepens, architecture becomes less visible. Eventually, escalation thresholds are shaped more by confidence than by design.

This is where exposure begins to accumulate—not because decisions are unreasonable but because they are not periodically re-evaluated at the systemic level.

Another dynamic is at work, too: Maturity becomes a shield. Organizations that have invested in compliance infrastructure assume that early design decisions remain appropriate as scale increases. Policies exist. Training programs are active. Audits occur regularly. Advisory relationships are established.

Several questions may arise: Why revisit foundational governance questions when the program has functioned well for years? Why slow execution to reconsider ownership? Why introduce structural friction when performance indicators remain positive?

All of these questions are rational. They are also questions that allow drift.

In the first few feet of descent, nothing demands a pause. The surface remains visible, and air feels accessible. You do not experience strain severe enough to force recalibration.

In enterprises, growth conditions perception the same way. Revenue expands. Geographic footprint widens. Volume increases. The trade function keeps pace operationally. Success reinforces confidence that the current model scales.

But governance does not scale automatically. It must evolve deliberately. When it does not, one of the most dangerous assumptions is that longevity equals structural adequacy. Years without catastrophic failure create institutional comfort. Teams become seasoned. Processes feel tested. Prior disputes that were navigated successfully become reference points.

Survival becomes evidence, but survival under prior conditions does not guarantee resilience under expanded exposure.

Scale alters physics. Exposure that was once compartmentalized becomes interconnected. Interpretive decisions that once affected one jurisdiction now ripple across dozens. Transfer pricing positions intertwine with customs valuation. Origin determinations influence multi-year sourcing strategy. Geographic concentration increases quietly.

What once felt like discrete operational choices becomes structural dependency. If governance architecture does not evolve alongside that interconnection, then the organization begins operating at greater depth but with only surface-level oversight.

This shallow level of oversight is rarely visible during success. It becomes visible only when pressure intensifies. At that point, the distinction between managing risk and governing becomes impossible to ignore.

Risk management focuses on identifying and resolving discrete issues.

Governance focuses on ensuring that the decision-making system remains appropriate as exposure scales.

Risk management is reactive and episodic.

Governance is structural and continuous.

Smart organizations excel at risk management, but they often delay governance. Because risk management can remain effective for long periods, governance engagement appears unnecessary.

Ironically, the stronger the operational team, the longer an organization can descend without sensing strain. Capability absorbs early pressure but does not eliminate it.

Without deliberate architectural recalibration—ownership clarification, escalation discipline, threshold reauthorization—exposure compounds beneath stable performance. By the time pressure becomes visible at the enterprise level, decisions are embedded, positions are entrenched, and recalibration is no longer proactive.

Any process that is not proactive is reactive. And reactive governance consumes margin quickly.

Smart organizations do not miss governance because they are inattentive. They miss it because they are competent. Competence buys time, but it does not substitute for structure.

SECTION III

Normalized Descent: How Confidence Becomes Institutionalized

Confidence in a trade compliance program does not arrive abruptly.

It accumulates.

In the early stages of a program, decisions are scrutinized carefully because they are new. Policies are debated because they are still forming. Roles are clarified because accountability has not yet settled. Governance questions surface naturally—not because leaders are cautious, but because the architecture is still being constructed.

During this phase, escalation is frequent. Interpretive positions are documented with precision. Ownership boundaries are explicit. Leadership is actively engaged because the system has not yet normalized its assumptions.

Over time, that scrutiny fades. What once required discussion becomes routine. What once felt provisional becomes accepted. Early design decisions—made under specific commercial pressures, leadership priorities, and regulatory interpretations—begin to harden into default practice. Eventually, they are no longer remembered as choices. They are inherited as structure.

This is how confidence becomes institutionalized. And this is where structural drift begins.

Institutionalization does not look like risk. It looks like maturity. Processes feel settled. Reporting cycles feel predictable. Escalation pathways feel familiar. The trade function is no longer building its program—it is running it. New leaders inherit policies that appear established and stable. Historical decisions are rarely revisited because they have been operating without visible negative consequences.

Design becomes invisible, and invisible design is rarely reexamined. What began as an intentional choice becomes an unquestioned norm. A valuation methodology adopted years ago under one regulatory interpretation becomes embedded across jurisdictions without periodic enterprise-level reconsideration. An origin determination approach, once validated, becomes assumed. A transfer pricing alignment decision solidifies because it aligns operationally and financially.

Each decision remains defensible, and together they form structural dependency. Institutional confidence strengthens this effect. When performance remains strong and external disruption is minimal, leaders internalize a belief: "The system works."

That belief reduces appetite for architectural reconsideration. Escalation thresholds drift subtly upward. Issues that once required executive decisions are resolved at lower tiers. Documentation focuses on compliance with established procedure rather than examination of whether the procedure remains appropriate. Confidence shifts from vigilance to assumption.

In the first few feet of descent, equalization is frequent and deliberate. The diver is attentive. Adjustments are constant. But as depth increases gradually without discomfort, vigilance can relax. Movement feels stable, breathing feels controlled, and the environment appears manageable.

Institutional confidence produces the same effect. Stability conditions perception, reducing the instinct to pause.

Institutionalization is reinforced by another factor: personnel continuity. When key experts remain in place for years, knowledge becomes concentrated. Informal judgment patterns solidify. Escalation becomes relational rather than structural. Leadership relies on individuals rather than on architecture. This system works—until it does not.

If expertise is the primary stabilizing mechanism, then transitions in the team increase exposure to risk. A retirement, a role change, or an acquisition can destabilize interpretive consistency quickly. What felt governed through familiarity reveals itself as governed through memory.

Governance that depends on memory is fragile, but governance that depends on architecture endures.

Institutionalization also affects how organizations interpret silence. If a methodology has operated for years without enforcement challenge, it begins to feel validated. Silence is interpreted as acceptance. Acceptance is interpreted as stability. Stability is interpreted as durability.

But regulatory silence is not structural endorsement. It is absence of review. When conditions change—enforcement intensity, interpretive guidance, geopolitical alignment—positions that once felt stable can be reframed rapidly. The longer they have operated without deliberate reconsideration, the more deeply they are embedded.

Such institutional confidence can transform repetition into certainty, but certainty reduces scrutiny. Reduced scrutiny increases exposure sensitivity.

Another force is at work, too: time. Exposure becomes defined by duration, not by volume. A valuation position applied consistently over seven years accumulates differently than one applied for seven months. An origin determination embedded in sourcing strategy for a decade carries structural consequence beyond transactional compliance. Geographic concentration that increases incrementally each fiscal year eventually narrows strategic flexibility.

Institutionalization masks this accumulation: Because change is gradual, it feels manageable. Because performance remains stable, it feels justified. Because no external force interrupts it, it feels safe.

But depth compounds quietly through time, which is why governance cannot rely solely on operational excellence. Governance must periodically interrupt comfort. It must deliberately reconsider sustained positions. It must reauthorize interpretive dependencies at the enterprise level. It must evaluate concentration not as isolated data points but as systemic exposure.

Unfortunately, institutionalization resists interruption. It frames reconsideration as unnecessary friction and encourages continuation rather than recalibration. But continuation without periodic architectural review converts confidence into vulnerability.

The most consequential governance failures do not begin with error. They begin with unexamined continuity. An approach that once made sense remains in place long after the conditions that justified it have changed. Escalation pathways remain static even as exposure scales. Ownership remains implied rather than redefined. Nothing appears broken until pressure reveals depth.

By the time leadership recognizes that exposure has accumulated beyond prior assumptions, architecture is entrenched. At that point, recalibration requires structural adjustment rather than routine review. And structural adjustment under pressure consumes margin.

Confidence institutionalized without governance discipline does not protect the enterprise. It delays recognition.

That delay is where exposure compounds.

SECTION IV

Managing Risk versus Governing Depth

Most organizations believe they are governing trade risk because they are actively managing it.

They respond to regulatory change. They correct errors. They remediate findings. They adjust procedures when necessary. From an operational standpoint, all of these activities feel responsible, disciplined, and controlled.

But activity is not architecture.

Managing risk and governing risk are not interchangeable activities, even though they are often treated as such. One reacts to conditions as they surface. The other defines how exposure accumulates before pressure reveals it. One stabilizes individual movements. The other determines how far descent is authorized in the first place.

The distinction is subtle at the surface, but it becomes decisive at depth.

Managing risk is episodic. It responds to events. A classification error is identified and corrected. A license gap is closed. A broker issue is escalated and resolved. Each response reinforces confidence that the system is working. Leadership sees problems being handled and assumes the structure itself must therefore be sound.

What is rarely examined is whether those responses are occurring within a deliberate governance framework—or simply as a series of competent reactions. Competence can scale exposure just as effectively as negligence if it is not aligned with enterprise risk tolerance. This is how management becomes the default model.

Trade compliance in many enterprises evolved as an operational function. Its objective was to keep goods moving within regulatory bounds. When rules changed, procedures were updated. When discrepancies surfaced, they were corrected. The function matured through responsiveness, not through architectural design.

Responsiveness feels like control, and it does not require structural reconsideration. At shallow depth, this model works well. Frequent correction feels like vigilance. Adjustments are visible. Signals are clear. Recovery is easy. The organization can point to motion as proof of discipline.

At sustained depth, though, repeated correction without trajectory monitoring does not protect the enterprise. It merely maintains local stability while systemic exposure accumulates. A diver can feel steady moment to moment while descending beyond planned limits if no one is monitoring aggregate depth against authorization.

Management stabilizes position. Governance monitors trajectory.

"Management stabilizes position. Governance monitors trajectory."

Consider a global organization with decentralized trade execution. Regional teams manage imports and exports based on local regulations and business realities. Central policy exists, but interpretation is largely delegated.

A new product is introduced. It does not fit neatly into existing classifications. The regional team evaluates the options, applies judgment, and selects an approach that appears reasonable. The product moves.

Months later, another region introduces a similar product. A different team, operating under different commercial pressures, reaches a slightly different conclusion. The outcome is also reasonable. The product moves.

No alarms are triggered. No errors are flagged. From a management perspective, risk has been handled appropriately in both cases.

From a governance perspective, something else has occurred: Two materially similar decisions have been made differently, without a shared framework, without documented rationale, and without clear ownership for alignment. Each decision is defensible in isolation. Together, they define posture. And posture accumulates.

Depth is not determined by a single movement. It is determined by aggregate descent.

Governance would not necessarily have required identical outcomes across regions. It would have required intentional decision architecture. It would have required clarity around who determines when interpretation rises to enterprise significance. It would have required documentation standards tied to exposure sensitivity. It would have required visibility thresholds that elevate divergence before it hardens into precedent.

Governance is not the act of correcting outcomes after divergence occurs. It is the act of defining ownership before divergence compounds.

In diving, no descent begins without agreed parameters: maximum depth, bottom time, air reserve threshold, ascent trigger. These boundaries do not eliminate adjustment. Instead, they define the limits within which adjustment is permitted. Without them, even experienced divers drift.

In enterprise systems without defined thresholds, escalation triggers, and exposure ceilings, competent teams drift collectively. When divergence finally surfaces under scrutiny, the question is no longer whether individual decisions were reasonable. It is whether the enterprise ever deliberately owned the posture into which those decisions accumulated.

At that moment, management feels insufficient, and leadership is forced into reconstruction rather than governance.

The structural difference between managing risk and governing risk becomes visible only when pressure reframes the conversation. Risk management handles issues as they arise. Risk governance defines exposure *before* issues aggregate. Risk management can be delegated to capable teams. Risk governance requires enterprise authorization.

At shallow depth, the two appear similar. At sustained depth, the difference determines survivability.

Boards often misinterpret signals once complexity has scaled and exposure has accumulated beyond the level at which it is actively governed. They see remediation cycles closing. They see audit findings addressed. They see compliance dashboards reflecting activity. They interpret motion as evidence of governance.

But governance is not measured by how efficiently problems are fixed. It is measured by whether exposure was deliberately designed.

If depth increases without architectural authorization, management excellence can accelerate descent rather than contain it. That acceleration does not feel reckless. It feels productive, efficient, and successful—until the organization is asked to explain why it descended that far.

That is the moment when the difference between risk management and risk governance becomes unmistakable.

At that point—when exposure has accumulated beyond the level at which it is actively governed—nothing appears broken. Decisions are being made, controls are functioning, and leadership believes it understands the risks involved. But something has already begun to shift—quietly and without recognition.

The issue is not failure. It is misalignment—visible in Figure 2 as the point at which perceived governance capacity begins to diverge from operational exposure, and the system enters a state of compression.

Figure 2: Pressure Reveals the Illusion (Governance Compression Curve)

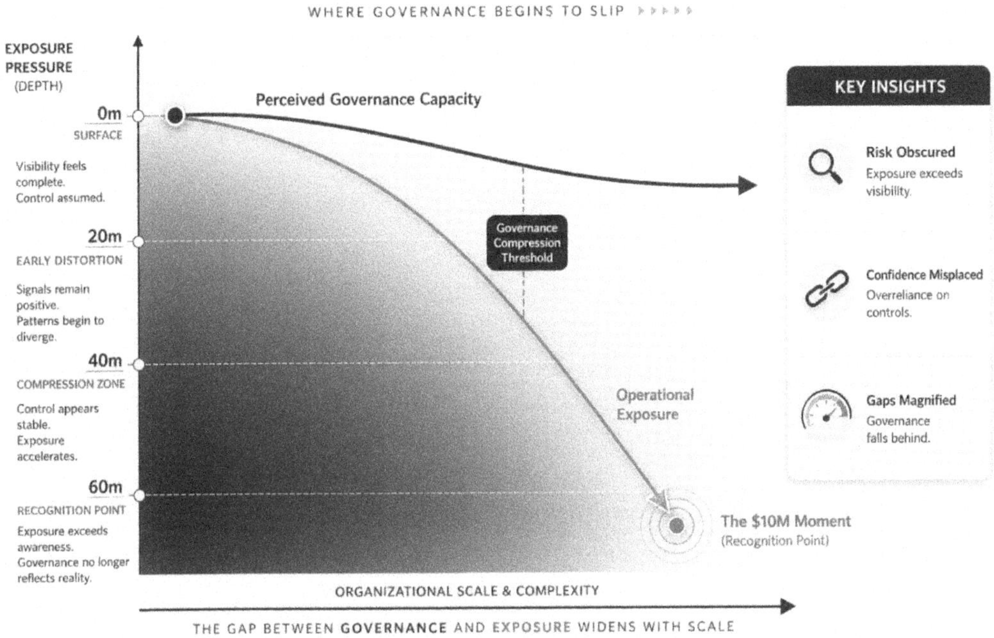

This figure illustrates the point at which perceived governance capacity begins to diverge from operational exposure, creating a state of compression in which control appears stable while risk continues to accumulate. The structure that governs this progression is introduced later; for now, what matters is understanding how misalignment begins.

Once this compression begins, it rarely corrects itself. As Figure 2 shows, organizations continue to operate as though governance still reflects reality, even as exposure moves beyond its reach. And because the early signals are subtle, they are often dismissed.

By the time the gap becomes visible, it is no longer small.

SECTION V

Pressure Reveals the Illusion

The illusion of control rarely collapses in an instant. Instead, it fractures, little by little.

Most organizations do not realize they have been operating on management rather than governance until the environment reframes the conversation for them. The trigger is often external: a regulatory inquiry, a focused audit with expanded scope, a transaction subjected to unexpected scrutiny, a geopolitical shift that casts familiar activity in a different light.

Sometimes the trigger is internal: a system implementation that surfaces inconsistency, a restructuring that exposes interpretive variation, the departure of a key individual whose institutional memory quietly held the architecture together.

What changes first is not the data. It is the tone of the room. Questions arise:

- How was this decision made?
- Why does Region A treat this differently than Region B?
- Who approved this interpretation—and on what basis?
- Where is the documentation that shows this was deliberate?

The volume of prior activity that once felt reassuring becomes irrelevant. Dashboards that once signaled stability cannot answer ownership questions. Audit results that once provided comfort cannot demonstrate why posture existed. Historical silence offers no evidence of intentional design.

At that moment, illusion is exposed. The organization discovers that what it trusted as evidence of control cannot withstand structural scrutiny.

The cause is rarely incompetence. The teams involved are often capable, diligent, and well-intentioned. Decisions were made thoughtfully. Issues were addressed responsibly. Problems were not ignored.

What is revealed instead is absence of architecture. The organization has managed risk effectively, but it has not governed how that risk accumulated.

The shift is abrupt because exposure that accumulated gradually is now being evaluated in compressed time. Years of decentralized judgment are suddenly viewed as a collective posture. Variations that were once tolerated as local nuance are reframed as systemic inconsistency. Interpretive assumptions that felt stable under operational conditions are stress-tested under an enforcement lens.

This pressure reveals depth. When equalization has been occurring informally—adjusted instinctively but never anchored to a plan—descent continues quietly. The diver may feel stable. Breathing may feel controlled. The surface may still appear close enough to touch.

Then pressure reframes the body. If equalization has not been deliberate, descent cannot continue safely.

Enterprise systems behave similarly. Exposure that accumulated comfortably under favorable conditions becomes uncomfortable when examined collectively. Leaders discover that what felt like flexibility was actually fragmentation. What felt like responsiveness was actually absence of threshold. What felt like oversight was actually reliance on trust.

The first meeting under scrutiny often carries quiet shocks. In attendance are senior leaders who have never previously discussed trade methodology in enterprise terms. Materials are assembled quickly. The objective is no longer operational explanation. It is structural defensibility.

At first, the conversation follows familiar patterns. Data are presented. Processes are described. Teams explain how decisions are made locally. Confidence still lingers. Then the questions narrow:

- How do we know this approach is applied consistently?
- Who determined this action was within enterprise risk tolerance?
- When was this posture last formally reviewed?
- Where is the documentation that shows executive authorization?

The room grows quieter. The realization settles that recovery now depends less on technical correctness and more on whether leadership can demonstrate deliberate ownership.

People recognize that the answers are distributed across regions, across teams, and across years. Decisions were competent but not centralized. Judgment was applied but not aggregated. Variations were accepted but not reconciled.

No one acted irresponsibly. The system simply never required those answers to exist in one place.

This is where illusion fully dissolves, and the organization understands that management competence cannot substitute for governance architecture. It sees that activity masked accumulation. It recognizes that success postponed interrogation.

The most destabilizing part of this moment is not regulatory pressure. It is internal recognition. Leaders confront the difference between believing they were in control and demonstrating that control structurally existed.

The difference is not rhetorical. It is evidentiary. Illusion collapses not because the enterprise failed to act, but because it never formally defined how far it intended to descend.

Confidence gives way to exposure awareness.

Management yields to the necessity of governance.

Depth is no longer abstract. It is measurable. And once measured, it demands response.

SECTION VI

The Cost of Reactive Oversight: Governing After the Descent

When governance is absent, oversight becomes reactive by default. Issues are examined only after they surface. Decisions are scrutinized only when questioned. Documentation is assembled retroactively. Accountability is reconstructed rather than designed.

Reactive oversight is not evidence of leadership indifference. It is evidence of architectural delay.

Organizations rarely intend to defer governance. More often, they assume that management discipline is sufficient until proven otherwise. As long as outcomes remain stable, there is little incentive to interrogate the structure beneath them.

Escalation mechanisms exist. Reporting flows. Audit cycles close. The system appears intact.

But when scrutiny reframes posture, the organization discovers that it must now demonstrate not only what it did but also explain how it authorized descent.

This is where reactive oversight emerges.

The shift is subtle at first. Approval thresholds are lowered. Controls are tightened quickly. Escalation becomes more frequent. Reviews expand in scope. What was once handled informally now requires formal documentation.

Under these conditions, the organization is not demonstrating governance. It is attempting to recreate governance under pressure. That distinction matters.

Governance that is embedded early functions quietly. It clarifies ownership before decisions diverge. It defines documentation standards before exposure accumulates. It establishes escalation triggers before thresholds are crossed.

Governance that is introduced late feels restrictive. It constrains movement that once felt fluid. It interrupts momentum. It demands justification for practices that previously required none.

This is why reactive oversight often feels punitive—even when no one intends it to be. Teams experience it as loss of autonomy. Leaders experience it as friction. Executives experience it as distraction from strategy. But the discomfort is not caused by reactive oversight itself. It is caused by introducing architecture after depth has already been reached.

In diving, ascent is safest when it is planned before descent begins. If depth limits are exceeded without preparation, correction becomes complicated. Decompression requirements extend. Margin narrows. Options diminish. Movement must be slower and more deliberate.

Reactive oversight operates under similar constraints. Once exposure has accumulated without structured governance, reconstruction consumes energy. Time is diverted from forward strategy to retrospective defense. Leaders become involved in operational details. Relationships strain as accountability is reassigned retroactively. Confidence erodes—not because the organization was careless, but because it cannot demonstrate deliberate design when it matters most.

Boards recognize this shift immediately. The questions change from "Are we compliant?" to "Who owns this posture?" From "Was this reasonable?" to "Was this authorized?" From "Did we follow procedure?" to "Who defined the boundaries?"

The discussion moves from operational sufficiency to enterprise survivability.

Reactive oversight does not simply increase workload. It also compresses margin.

When oversight arrives late, every adjustment is made within narrowed flexibility. Strategic pacing may be disrupted. Integration efforts may stall. Expansion plans may pause. Market messaging may require recalibration.

The cost is not only regulatory exposure. It is also optionality.

Organizations that embed governance early retain authority over timing. They recalibrate deliberately. They adjust before pressure dictates terms. They preserve margin. Organizations that rely on reactive oversight adjust under compression, and compression amplifies consequence.

The most dangerous misconception at this stage is believing that reactive oversight itself constitutes governance maturity. Tightened controls, expanded reviews, and increased documentation may create the appearance of discipline. In reality, they signal that governance architecture is being assembled after exposure has already hardened.

Governance cannot be retrofitted easily because posture is cumulative: Interpretive decisions embed into financial models. Supply-chain structures align with assumed tariff treatments. Tax positions intertwine with valuation methodologies. Strategic commitments rely on regulatory stability.

Once embedded, change is no longer incremental. It is structural.

This is why governance must exist before it is needed—not because failure is inevitable, but because depth changes how exposure behaves.

Reactive oversight is not a governance strategy. It is a recovery posture. And recovery at depth is always more complex than discipline at the surface.

Recovery at depth requires slowing the system in ways that disciplined governance at the surface never would. Decisions that once felt routine must now be examined collectively. Interpretations that evolved gradually must now be reconciled under scrutiny. What once functioned comfortably within operational tolerance must now withstand enterprise explanation.

At this moment leadership recognizes that depth was reached long before anyone intended to descend.

From inside the organization, the movement never felt dramatic. Each decision had context. Each adjustment had rationale. Each interpretation appeared reasonable at the moment it was made. But depth is not defined by individual movements. It is defined by accumulation.

And accumulation rarely announces itself while the surface still feels close.

Chapter 1 began with the first few feet of the dive—where pressure signals quietly begin. It moved through confidence, institutionalization, management default, and the exposure of illusions. It ends here, with the recognition that without deliberate governance architecture, success can carry an enterprise deeper than intended.

Governance at depth is not about preventing descent.

It is about defining it.

"Governance at depth is not about preventing descent. It is about defining it."

CHAPTER 2

Designing for Depth

A diver does not reach depth safely by accident.

Before descent begins, the diver must understand the conditions that will shape the dive itself—how buoyancy will behave, how weight must be distributed, and how the body will respond as pressure increases. Strength is irrelevant without calibration. Movement alone cannot stabilize the descent.

Depth responds only to design.

> *"Depth responds only to design."*

At the surface, buoyancy feels like safety. In the first few feet of a dive, the water still carries you. Movement is easy. Control feels intuitive. Minor corrections produce visible results. Confidence builds quickly because the environment is forgiving.

But depth does not negotiate with confidence. It responds only to structure.

Divers do not descend safely because they swim harder. They descend because their buoyancy is calibrated. Weight is distributed deliberately across their frame—not to burden them, but to stabilize them. Without ballast, they float. With too much weight concentrated in one place, they tilt, overcorrect, or drop faster than intended.

Their strength does not matter. The physics of diving respond only to structure.

Now apply this metaphor to organizational behavior. In calm water, execution is often enough. Teams perform. Metrics trend upward. Recognition follows excellence. Leadership interprets visible competence as structural strength.

But buoyancy is not the same as stability. When pressure increases—through scale, complexity, regulatory scrutiny, or accumulated exposure—execution alone cannot control descent. What appeared stable at the surface begins to reveal its imbalance. Weight was either never distributed, or it was strapped to the wrong limb.

Compliance carries too much. Audit carries too much. One executive carries too much.

Or no one carries it at all.

The organization may still be swimming—even swimming well—but the design beneath the movement was never calibrated for depth. And when instability appears, leadership often misdiagnoses the symptom. They call for

- more training.
- more controls.
- more reporting.
- more effort.

But effort does not correct misallocated ballast. Design does.

Design determines whether a system can descend intentionally—or whether it will be forced downward by pressure it failed to anticipate.

Chapter 1 examined what happens in the first few feet. This chapter asks a harder question:

Was the system designed to go deeper?

Most organizations believe governance exists because someone owns compliance. There is a trade team. There is a policy. There is reporting. There are escalation pathways. There is documentation. There are controls.

From the outside, and often from the inside, this looks like governance. But it is not governance. It is management.

Chapter 1 explained how confidence at shallow depth masks structural drift. It showed how competence can delay recognition, how exposure compounds quietly, and how reactive oversight compresses margin when governance is introduced too late.

This chapter addresses the important question:

If management is not governance, then what is?

Governance is not the presence of a function. It is the deliberate design of ownership at depth.

The assessment described in the prologue did not reveal incompetence, reckless behavior, or ignored warnings. Instead, it revealed something far quieter: design silence. Execution had been assigned. Oversight had been assumed. But governance—the authority to define, reassess, and realign enterprise exposure as it scaled—had never been structurally engineered.

The problem at the center of most systemic trade failures is not lack of effort. It is the belief that because someone is responsible for compliance, governance must therefore exist.

However, responsibility for activity is not the same as ownership of posture. And when responsibility for activity and ownership of posture are conflated, exposure compounds.

Depth is not created by one decision. It emerges from decisions made within architecture that was never designed to carry them.

Designing for depth requires something most organizations never formally do: They must separate execution responsibility from exposure ownership, and they must architect decision rights to evolve as risk evolves.

Because systemic risk is rarely the result of bad decisions. It is the result of decisions that were never deliberately governed as they multiplied.

SECTION I

Authority at Depth

Most organizations treat governance as something that can be assigned.

A function is named. A leader is appointed. Responsibilities are documented. Oversight is added to the agenda. From an organizational perspective, this feels like progress. Accountability has been established. A box appears on the chart. A role appears in the system.

In global trade, this assumption is particularly persistent. Trade compliance already exists as a function, so governance is often layered onto it by default. If the function performs well—files accurately, corrects errors, manages audits, reports upward—governance is assumed to follow naturally.

It does not.

Governance is not a function. It is an institutional capability. Confusing the two is one of the primary reasons well-run programs fail under pressure.

Functions are attractive containers for accountability because they are visible and measurable. They have budgets, headcount, reporting lines, performance indicators. When something goes wrong, there is a place to look and someone to ask. This model works well for execution. It does not work for governing exposure at depth.

Governance does not reside where work is performed. It resides in how decisions are structured, constrained, escalated, and preserved over time. Those mechanics cut across regions, functions, and reporting lines. When governance is treated as a functional responsibility, it becomes dependent on influence rather than authority.

The function may recommend, advise, or escalate, but it cannot redesign how decisions are made elsewhere in the enterprise. This is how governance quietly becomes optional.

Delegation compounds the problem.

Most global trade programs are built on a reasonable premise: Execution must be delegated. Regions understand local regulations. Local teams respond faster. Decentralization allows the business to move. No serious organization disputes this logic.

The fallacy lies in assuming that delegating execution also delegates ownership of posture.

In practice, accountability remains centralized while decision-making becomes distributed. Regional teams interpret ambiguity, resolve friction, and apply judgment close to the work. Enterprise leadership retains ultimate accountability for exposure. Between those two realities sits a structural gap.

When conditions are stable, that gap is invisible. When pressures increase it becomes exposed.

Without design, the organization relies on professional judgment to bridge the space between distributed decision-making and centralized accountability. Experienced teams compensate for ambiguity. Local leaders make reasonable trade-offs. Decisions are made with good intent and operational awareness.

"Professionalism can compensate for design silence for years. But professionalism is not governance."

Professionalism can compensate for design silence for years. But professionalism is not governance. Professionalism relies on people, while governance relies on architecture. At depth, architecture matters more than effort. Architecture answers questions before pressure forces them into the room:

- Who is authorized to interpret ambiguity—and under what conditions?
- When similar facts lead to different conclusions, who owns alignment?
- When speed conflicts with regulatory posture, how is priority determined?
- When judgment is applied, how is rationale preserved so it survives turnover, scale, and scrutiny?

If these questions are not answered by design, they will be answered by circumstance.

Circumstance is rarely chaotic. More often, it is reasonable. Reasonable decisions accumulate into posture, and posture accumulates into depth.

When governance is embedded, decisions remain repeatable even as staffing changes. When it is absent, outcomes depend on who is in the room, who feels comfortable escalating, and who carries institutional memory forward informally. That distinction is invisible when performance is strong, but it becomes decisive when scrutiny intensifies.

When governance is treated as a role rather than a system, responsibility concentrates while authority remains diffuse. A leader may be accountable for compliance outcomes without possessing the structural authority to shape how exposure is created elsewhere in the enterprise.

Escalation becomes subjective. Documentation becomes selective. Alignment becomes relational rather than structural.

None of these dynamics signal failure. In fact, they often coexist with high-performing programs and experienced teams. That is precisely why they persist.

The organization believes governance exists because someone is responsible for it. In reality, governance exists only to the extent that decision-making has been designed to function without reliance on individual heroics.

A role can manage outcomes. Only architecture can govern them at depth.

SECTION II

Descent Without Design

Many global trade programs fail not because they are poorly run, but because they are exceptionally well executed.

Operational excellence produces results. It creates confidence and reassures leadership that risk is being managed competently and efficiently. In mature organizations, that confidence is often earned—it is built on years of experience, strong technical capability, and consistent delivery under pressure.

The problem is not excellence. The problem is mistaking excellence for design.

Most trade programs are architected to execute well. They are structured to file accurately, respond quickly, correct efficiently, and pass audits consistently. Metrics are tracked. Issues are escalated. Controls are documented. Roles are assigned. Processes are mapped. Performance is reported upward with clarity. From the outside, and often from the inside, this looks like governance.

But there's a vital difference: Execution describes what happens, while governance determines how decisions hold together when conditions change.

Execution is visible.
Design is structural.

Execution produces outcomes.
Design defines durability.

Execution keeps the system moving.
Design determines how deep it is allowed to go.

Operational excellence masks governance gaps in predictable ways. It substitutes people for architecture, consistency for structural resilience, and experience for deliberate authority. As long as the same individuals remain in place and the external environment remains stable, the system appears strong. It moves efficiently, absorbs ambiguity, and resolves friction quietly. The absence of disruption is interpreted as evidence of structural soundness, and that interpretation is where miscalibration begins.

Execution can compensate for weak design for years. Experienced professionals reconcile inconsistencies before they escalate. They interpret regulation pragmatically and align with commercial priorities without losing regulatory awareness. They know how far they can push before triggering scrutiny.

That competence stabilizes the system. It does not define it.

Without design, execution becomes a form of borrowed resilience. The organization relies on judgment rather than architecture to maintain coherence across regions, reporting lines, and evolving regulatory conditions. That reliance feels efficient because it works—until conditions change faster than informal coordination can absorb.

Consider how most organizations explain their trade program:

- They describe policies.
- They describe controls.
- They describe escalation pathways.
- They describe audit frequency.
- They describe error rates.

All of these elements reflect execution, not governance.

Very few describe how decision rights evolve as exposure changes, how ownership shifts when tariff sensitivity increases, how interpretive authority shifts as regulatory enforcement intensifies, or how enterprise-level risk tolerance translates into operational thresholds before ambiguity is encountered.

Execution answers the question "How do we handle this?" Design answers the question "Where does this belong?" This difference becomes visible when exposure scales.

A classification decision applied consistently across one product line is execution. When that classification begins affecting tariff exposure across multiple jurisdictions with materially different enforcement profiles, the question is no longer whether the classification is technically defensible. Instead, the question becomes whether ownership of that exposure remains appropriate at the same decision tier.

Execution continues to function, but design determines when authority must be elevated to address what execution alone can no longer contain.

The same dynamic applies to valuation. Regional teams may apply established methodologies consistently and accurately. Entries move efficiently. Audits conclude without material findings. Adjustments are handled professionally when they are needed.

But as intercompany pricing structures evolve, as assists and royalties accumulate across years, as import volume expands into jurisdictions with higher tariff sensitivity, the enterprise exposure attached to valuation methodology shifts.

Execution may remain strong, but without design, authority does not shift with exposure. This lag is invisible in calm conditions, but it becomes decisive under pressure.

Origin determinations follow the same trajectory. When sourcing patterns are stable and enforcement posture is predictable, local application of origin rules functions effectively. But when trade remedy exposure increases, when preference programs carry material financial consequence, or when geopolitical shifts alter enforcement priorities, origin decisions become enterprise-level exposure drivers.

Execution answers whether the rule was applied. Design determines who owns the consequences as scale changes.

In programs built primarily for execution, decision architecture remains static even as risk multiplies. Authority stays where it was originally placed because nothing forces reconsideration. Escalation occurs when someone feels uncomfortable, not when structural criteria require it. Alignment depends on informal coordination rather than predefined thresholds.

This system works while exposure remains within historical bounds. It falters when those bounds expand.

Operational excellence delays recognition because it absorbs early signals of misalignment. Experienced professionals sense friction and resolve it before it becomes visible. They negotiate trade-offs quietly. They align across regions informally. They compensate for architectural silence.

Leadership sees stability, but it does not see dependency.

The system depends on memory and continuity. It depends on judgment exercised consistently by individuals who understand both regulatory nuance and organizational culture.

Dependency is not the same as durability. Durability requires design. In turn, design requires explicit categorization of decisions before they are made. It demands defining which decisions alter enterprise exposure materially and which do not. It necessitates setting thresholds that trigger elevation not because someone feels uneasy, but because exposure metrics dictate it. It calls for preserving rationale at the moment of decision so that years later the enterprise can demonstrate deliberate ownership.

Execution focuses on performance.

Design focuses on survivability.

The more mature and efficient a program becomes, the easier it is to assume that its architecture is equally mature. Stability reinforces confidence. Consistency reinforces trust. The absence of friction reinforces the belief that exposure is controlled.

But governance is not measured by how well a system performs under familiar conditions. It is measured by whether authority, ownership, and escalation were deliberately structured to evolve as exposure evolved.

Execution excellence does not create systemic risk. Instead, it obscures the rate at which systemic risk compounds. That is why so many well-run programs are surprised when scrutiny reframes their decisions at scale. They were managing effectively. They were performing well. They were correcting issues promptly.

They simply never redesigned decision rights as exposure deepened.

SECTION III

Designing the Descent

Depth is never accidental. A controlled descent begins before movement.

Divers do not simply drop beneath the surface and hope for balance. Instead, they confirm readiness. They look to their dive partner and establish alignment. They scan the environment for a reference point—an anchor line, a fixed structure, something stable against which they can measure their descent. They ensure their regulators are secured. Their instruments are active, and their systems are functioning before pressure increases.

Only when they have ensured that their systems are in place do they release air.

Programs designed to govern are not built to rely on excellence as a substitute for structure. They do not assume that experienced professionals will instinctively recognize when escalation is warranted. They do not assume that informal coordination will sustain alignment across regions and reporting lines. They do not depend on institutional memory to preserve the reasoning behind decisions that may carry enterprise implications years later.

Instead, they make design choices explicit before exposure demands them.

Execution specifies how work is performed.
Design specifies how authority is structured.

Execution clarifies responsibility.
Design clarifies ownership.

Execution manages issues.
Design governs exposure.

Execution keeps the diver moving.
Design determines the depth of the descent.

In programs built to govern rather than merely operate, core trade decisions are categorized before they are executed. Authority is defined before discretion is exercised. Ownership is clarified before exposure scales. Escalation thresholds are embedded before divergence occurs. The question shifts from "Who handles this?" to "Where does this decision belong?"

That shift is subtle in stable conditions. Regional expertise is still valued, and local judgment is still applied. Commercial velocity is not unnecessarily constrained. Execution still occurs close to the work. But the architecture surrounding those decisions is deliberate rather than assumed.

Design does not eliminate discretion. Instead, it defines where discretion lives, where it must be constrained, and where it must elevate.

These definitions are rarely documented explicitly in execution-focused programs, where decisions are handled efficiently, ambiguity is resolved professionally, and alignment is maintained informally.

But without design, the boundaries of discretion remain fluid. Fluid boundaries function when exposure is modest, but they strain when exposure multiplies.

Consider how design alters classification governance.

In execution-driven programs, classification authority is assigned to qualified professionals. They apply technical rules consistently, correct errors, and manage challenges.

In programs designed for depth, classification decisions are differentiated by impact before they are made. Routine classifications may remain local within defined parameters. Classifications that materially alter tariff exposure, trade remedy risk, or preference eligibility are architected differently. They are elevated not because someone feels uncertain, but because the organization has predefined materiality triggers.

The design question is not simply "Who can classify?" It is "Which classifications alter enterprise exposure, and who owns that alteration?"

Valuation requires similar structural clarity.

Execution-focused programs apply valuation methodologies consistently. Entries move efficiently. Adjustments are made when necessary. Audit responses are managed professionally.

Design-oriented programs distinguish valuation decisions by systemic consequence. Assists, royalties, transfer pricing adjustments, post-import pricing mechanisms, and intercompany structures are treated as enterprise exposure drivers. Ownership of valuation methodology is clarified upstream—often across trade, tax, and finance—and preserved as a governance decision rather than rediscovered during audit.

Uniform application is not the objective. Consistent ownership is.

Origin determination follows the same architectural logic. Execution applies rules correctly within operational workflows. Design clarifies which origin determinations carry enterprise-level exposure, particularly where duty preference reliance, trade remedy applicability, or geopolitical shifts alter risk sensitivity.

Execution applies origin.

Design governs how origin decisions accumulate across supply chains and time.

Tariff exposure monitoring illustrates this difference. Programs built around execution track entries, corrections, and audit outcomes. Programs built around design track exposure concentration, monitoring how tariff impact shifts with volume, how enforcement posture alters tolerance thresholds, how previously immaterial determinations become material as commercial reliance deepens.

Design does not require constant intervention. It requires predefined triggers. Structural moments occur when exposure—not error—changes how authority must function.

Across classification, valuation, origin, and tariff exposure, design-oriented programs share a common characteristic: Decisions are categorized by consequence, not convenience. Ownership shifts when exposure shifts. Rationale is preserved as part of the decision itself, not reconstructed after scrutiny begins.

Governance hubs, risk tiering frameworks, and internal control architectures operate quietly within this structure. Their purpose is not to prescribe outcomes, but to make decision logic visible, durable, and transferable beyond individual memory.

The result is not more process. It is less ambiguity.

Operational excellence still matters. Execution still occurs close to the work. But the organization is no longer relying on individuals to compensate for structural silence. The program carries the weight it was designed to carry.

Judgment is expected, but within defined bounds.

Authority is clarified, not inferred.

Reasoning is preserved, not assumed.

These requirements remain understated in calm conditions. They become decisive when exposure is questioned collectively rather than transactionally.

Design does not slow descent.

It defines it.

Designing for depth is not a matter of adding control. It is a matter of building structure that can carry increasing exposure without distortion.

As organizations expand, the demands placed on governance do not increase evenly.

Instead, they accelerate—placing pressure on decisions, escalation, and oversight in ways that cannot be managed through incremental adjustment.

What is required is not reaction, but design: a deliberate progression that aligns governance to depth before compression begins to take hold. Figure 3 introduces that structure—The Descent Protocol™—and the progression through which governance must evolve as depth increases.

Figure 3: The Descent Protocol™ (Governance at Depth Framework)

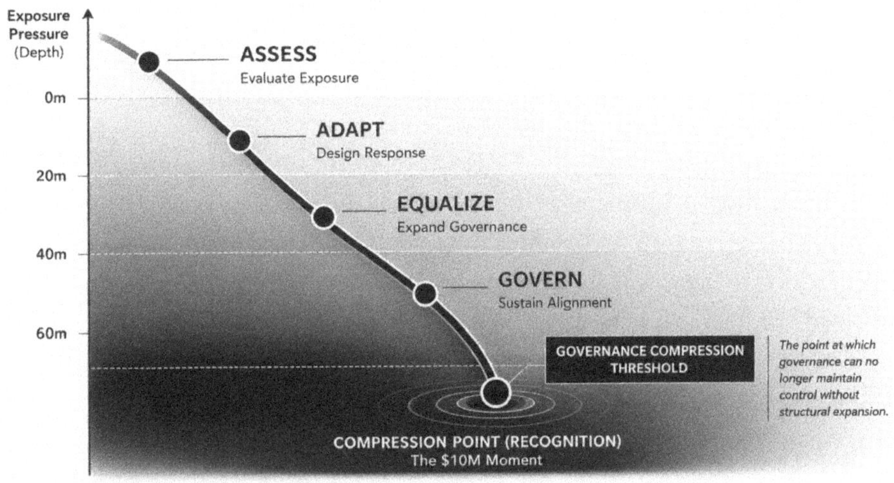

As exposure pressure (depth) increases, governance must evolve through a deliberate progression. Each stage introduces new structural demands. When those demands are anticipated, governance carries the descent. When they are not, governance reaches the compression point.

This figure illustrates how governance must evolve as organizations move into increasing depth and complexity. As exposure pressure increases, effective governance requires progression from initial assessment to adaptation, deliberate expansion of authority, and ultimately enterprise-level oversight. Each stage represents a shift in how decisions are evaluated, escalated, and governed as conditions change. The governance compression threshold marks the point at which control cannot be maintained without structural expansion, reinforcing that governance must be designed to evolve before pressure makes that evolution unavoidable.

This progression is not theoretical. Whether they recognize it or not, organizations move through these stages as complexity increases. The key question is whether governance is designed to move with that progression—or left to adjust after misalignment has already begun.

As Figure 3 shows, each stage introduces a different set of structural demands. When those demands are anticipated, governance carries the descent. When they are not, governance begins to lag, setting the conditions for compression, drift, and eventual failure.

SECTION IV

When Architecture Carries the Descent

The distinction between execution and design becomes most visible not during error, but during stress.

I have seen organizations face simultaneous pressure across regions—not because controls failed, but because conditions diverged. Regulatory posture tightened in one geography. Commercial urgency intensified in another. Interpretive clarity shifted in a third. Tariff sensitivity changed unexpectedly. Enforcement emphasis recalibrated without warning.

In execution-driven programs, effort increases. Experienced teams move quickly. Issues are resolved locally. Escalations occur informally. Leaders are briefed selectively. Documentation expands. The system appears responsive.

And often, it is. But responsiveness is not the same as governed authority.

Pressure does not test competence. It tests architecture.

At depth, skill keeps you stable. Only design keeps the descent survivable.

In programs designed for depth, pressure does not immediately disperse outward to regional resolution. Instead, predefined pathways activate. Decision rights shift according to exposure, not convenience. Escalation occurs because structural criteria require it, not because someone feels uncomfortable.

Regions provide analysis, but enterprise governance owns consequence. Trade-offs are surfaced deliberately rather than negotiated informally. Rationale is documented contemporaneously rather than reconstructed later. Authority is exercised in a defined place, by defined actors, under defined thresholds.

None of this slows execution unnecessarily. Instead, it stabilizes it.

When design carries the weight, decisions do not depend on who is most confident. They depend on architecture that anticipated divergence.

This difference becomes even clearer when exposure scales across time.

Consider a valuation methodology that has operated quietly for years. It is technically defensible and applied consistently. It passed prior audit cycles without material dispute. Under stable tariff conditions, its enterprise consequences appear manageable.

Then tariff rates increase materially in key jurisdictions. What was once immaterial becomes financially significant, affecting the organization's earnings. What once sat comfortably within regional authority now carries enterprise-level consequence.

In execution-driven programs, authority often remains where it was originally placed. Regional teams continue applying the long-established methodology. Escalation occurs only when challenges arise. Enterprise leadership may not revisit ownership until scrutiny forces reconsideration.

In design-oriented programs, authority was never static. Rather, decision rights were structured to elevate automatically when exposure metrics crossed defined thresholds. Ownership shifts not because someone senses danger, but because architecture requires it.

Design recognizes that authority must evolve as exposure evolves. Without that recognition, authority lags exposure. Lag is invisible in stable conditions, and under pressure, lag becomes risk.

This dynamic appears repeatedly across trade functions. A classification approach embedded in sourcing strategy begins to affect remedy exposure at scale. An origin determination methodology intersects with shifting geopolitical enforcement priorities. A tariff position that once had minimal impact becomes embedded in the cost structure through repeated application at scale, creating financial dependence on an outcome that was never intentionally governed. Each of these developments is incremental.

Execution handles each increment effectively.
Design evaluates cumulative effect.

Execution asks whether the rule was applied correctly.
Design asks whether ownership of the decision remains appropriate given scale.

When architecture is deliberate, these questions are answered before external pressure forces them into visibility. With a deliberate architecture in place, the organization does not scramble to assemble rationale. It does not debate authority in real time. It does not discover that escalation thresholds were never clearly defined. Instead, it demonstrates continuity of ownership.

Continuity is the mark of governed exposure. It does not eliminate risk, but it makes risk intelligible.

When design carries the weight, leaders are not surprised by how decisions accumulated across functions, scaled over time, and shaped the exposure the organization ultimately carries. They can trace decision logic across time and demonstrate that authority shifted as exposure shifted. They can show that rationale was preserved deliberately rather than reconstructed defensively.

In other words, the system does not rely on persuasive explanation. It relies on architecture.

This is where the difference between performance and governability becomes unmistakable. Performance may remain strong in both execution-driven and design-oriented programs, but governability exists only where architecture was intentional.

Design does not prevent descent. It ensures that descent remains authorized, and authorization survives scrutiny.

SECTION V

Comfort at the Surface: Why Excellence Delays Recognition

Operational excellence does more than stabilize a system. It also conceals its architectural limits.

Experienced trade professionals resolve ambiguity before it becomes visible. They understand regulatory nuance and recognize enforcement patterns. They know where flexibility exists and where it does not. They negotiate commercial pressure without abandoning compliance discipline. They reconcile regional variation informally and anticipate audit questions before they are asked.

This competence creates stability. In turn, stability creates confidence. And confidence delays scrutiny.

From an executive perspective, the absence of disruption is interpreted as evidence of structural strength. Issues are addressed before they escalate. Reporting remains consistent. External interactions are managed professionally. The program appears disciplined, mature, and resilient. What leadership does not see is how much resilience is borrowed from individuals rather than embedded in design.

Execution excellence allows organizations to compensate for structural gaps quietly. Judgment substitutes for defined thresholds. Relationships substitute for authority pathways. Institutional memory substitutes for documented rationale. Informal alignment substitutes for structured decision architecture.

As long as the same people remain in place and conditions remain familiar, the system holds. That holding pattern feels like governance, but in reality it is continuity. And continuity is fragile.

The fragility is rarely visible because excellence absorbs early signals of misalignment. When exposure increases incrementally, professionals adjust informally. When enforcement posture shifts subtly, teams recalibrate quietly. When commercial initiatives accelerate activity, trade teams work harder rather than question authority structures.

Effort increases, but architecture remains static.

Static architecture explains why mature programs are surprised when scrutiny reframes their decisions collectively. They were not inattentive. They were not reckless. They were performing well. They were correcting issues promptly. They were passing audits. They simply never redesigned decision rights as exposure deepened.

Excellence postpones architectural interrogation because it makes friction disappear before leadership feels it.

In the first few feet of descent, equalization is frequent and instinctive. For the diver, movement remains comfortable. The surface remains visible. There is no immediate pressure to reassess maximum depth. As descent continues smoothly, vigilance can relax, not as a result of negligence but because stability conditions perception.

Enterprises experience a similar conditioning effect. When trade functions operate efficiently year after year, the organization internalizes the belief that its structure must be sound. Longevity is interpreted as validation. Survival under prior conditions becomes evidence of durability in the future.

But durability is not measured under identical conditions. It is tested under altered conditioned.

Excellence also distorts feedback signals. Because competent teams resolve issues early, few problems reach enterprise visibility. Escalation is rare. Major disruptions are infrequent. Leadership may conclude that enterprise exposure is modest because enterprise-level discussions are limited.

In reality, limited escalation may reflect local absorption rather than limited exposure. The stronger the professionals, the less visible the structural gaps, and that invisibility creates dependency.

Programs become reliant on individuals who know how to navigate ambiguity instinctively. Decision logic resides in conversations rather than systems. Authority boundaries are understood implicitly rather than defined explicitly. Thresholds are recognized culturally rather than architected structurally.

This system works—until it doesn't.

The reason it worked for so long is operational excellence, which creates managerial comfort. Goods move across seventy-six countries without interruption. Entries are filed. Classifications are defensible. Audits close without escalation. The dashboard remains green. From the executive level, the system seems not only stable but also mature.

Comfort settles in, but comfort is not proof of structural integrity. It is proof that pressure has not yet exceeded the system's compensatory capacity.

Exceptional teams can absorb friction for extended periods of time. They resolve classification disputes before they escalate. They adjust valuation methodologies before inconsistencies surface. They build workarounds where design was silent. They protect the organization from the visible consequences of architectural gaps. And because they succeed, leadership sees affirmation.

Recognition flows toward performance. Performance becomes evidence. Evidence becomes belief. And belief becomes inertia.

The more excellent the execution, the less incentive there is to examine design. This is where operational excellence becomes deceptive—not because it is flawed, but because it conceals fragility.

Pressure does not disappear. It redistributes, accumulating in decisions that were never structurally integrated. It settles into assumptions that were never stress-tested. It compounds quietly across jurisdictions, supply chains, and regulatory regimes.

The organization remains comfortable—until it isn't.

Depth rarely feels dangerous until the diver realizes how far the surface has receded. By the time depth reveals the architectural limits, exposure feels sudden. Leadership often describes the moment as unforeseen.

But depth rarely surprises a well-designed system. It only exposes what comfort concealed.

If governance appears stable only because exceptional people are compensating for structural gaps, then the organization is not well governed—it is well buffered.

And buffers fail when complexity increases and scale accelerates. They fail when regulatory posture shifts. They fail when the individuals carrying the weight burn out, transfer roles, or leave the organization.

A system that requires extraordinary vigilance to remain compliant is not resilient; it is exposed. Leadership may interpret the absence of visible disruption as proof of design strength, but the absence of disruption often reflects the presence of unrecognized strain. When excellence becomes the mechanism that prevents escalation, it also becomes the reason architecture is never questioned. That is not stability. It is deferred recognition of risk. Operational excellence should be celebrated, but it should never be mistaken for architecture.

The most dangerous governance environments are not chaotic. They are high-performing. In chaotic systems, leadership knows instability exists. In high-performing systems, instability hides behind metrics. When excellence absorbs pressure, exposure becomes invisible to the very leaders accountable for it. That invisibility is not protection. It is vulnerability disguised as performance.

Turnover, expansion, regulatory shift, tariff volatility, geopolitical change, or enforcement intensity can all destabilize reliance on informal excellence. When the individuals who held alignment together depart the organization or when exposure scales beyond historical patterns, the organization discovers that it cannot explain its accumulated decisions without reconstructing them.

Reconstruction is not governance. It is recovery.

The irony is sharp: The more effective the execution, the longer the organization can operate without confronting design silence. Excellence buys time. It does not substitute for architecture.

When recognition finally arrives, it often feels abrupt—not because exposure emerged suddenly, but because the organization had not been evaluating exposure structurally. Decisions that were individually reasonable are now examined collectively. Authority that once felt appropriate is now assessed against scaled consequence.

Leadership begins asking a different set of questions. They do not ask whether teams are capable but whether the enterprise ever deliberately designed how authority evolves with risk.

Excellence did not create the vulnerability. It delayed its visibility, and delay at depth narrows margin.

If the professionals who hold this program together leave tomorrow, could the enterprise still demonstrate ownership of its posture?

SECTION VI

The Executive Diagnostic: Who Owns the Descent

For executives, the lesson of this chapter is not that execution must be replaced. It is that execution must be understood for what it is.

Operational strength is not architectural assurance. Strong performance confirms that capable people are managing complexity effectively. It does not confirm that the enterprise has deliberately designed how authority evolves as exposure scales.

The more mature and efficient a trade program becomes, the easier it is to assume that its structure is equally mature. Stability reinforces confidence. Consistency reinforces trust. The absence of friction reinforces the belief that exposure is controlled.

But governance is not measured by how well the system performs under familiar conditions. It is measured by whether decision rights, ownership, and escalation are deliberately structured to adjust as exposure changes.

This distinction is rarely visible in dashboards. Instead, it becomes visible when leaders ask different questions.

Not:
Are we compliant?

But:
Who owns the enterprise consequence of our most material trade determinations?

Not:
Are controls operating?

But:
Do decision rights shift when exposure thresholds are crossed?

Not:
Are issues escalated?

But:
Are escalation triggers defined structurally—or left to discretion?

Not:
Have we had enforcement action?

But:
If scrutiny expanded tomorrow across every jurisdiction where we operate, could we demonstrate deliberate ownership of how exposure accumulated?

These questions comprise the executive diagnostic.

If authority remains where it was originally placed regardless of scale, then governance has not been designed.

If escalation depends on comfort rather than specific criteria, then governance has not been designed.

If rationale must be reconstructed rather than retrieved, then governance has not been designed.

If enterprise leadership cannot articulate how exposure ownership migrates as financial sensitivity increases, then governance has not been designed.

Importantly, design does not require centralizing every decision. It does require defining which decisions change enterprise consequence and ensuring authority evolves accordingly. That evolution must be intentional, because exposure evolves whether leadership wants it to or not.

Delegation without redesign creates a widening gap between responsibility and authority. Execution without structural recalibration creates dependency on excellence. Performance without architectural clarity creates confidence without durability.

These conditions do not signal failure. They signal silence.

Silence at depth does not feel urgent. It feels efficient—until scrutiny reframes the conversation. By the time that reframing occurs, leaders are no longer evaluating performance. They are evaluating governability.

Governability is not demonstrated through volume of activity or quality of execution. It is demonstrated through clarity of design.

An enterprise that can show how authority shifts as exposure shifts does not eliminate risk. Instead, it demonstrates ownership of that risk, and that ownership survives scrutiny.

Chapter 1 explained how exposure accumulates quietly in the first few feet.

Chapter 2 clarified what must exist beneath that surface.

Governance at depth is not accidental. It is engineered. Without design, descent continues. With design, it remains authorized.

"Governance at depth is not accidental. It is engineered."

CHAPTER 3

Drift Without Recalibration

In a drift dive, where divers move with the current rather than swimming against it, the current carries them across the reef while the dive boat follows overhead, tracking their position as they descend.

Movement can feel controlled even when the divers are no longer where they believe they are. They may believe they are holding position while the current quietly moves them away from their original point of entry.

Currents rarely feel dangerous when they first begin to move.

Governance rarely fails at the moment it is designed. Instead, it erodes over time.

"Drift is how erosion hides inside performance."

Drift is the gradual movement of authority and exposure out of alignment while operations continue to appear stable. Drift allows erosion to hide inside performance.

Chapters 1 and 2 examined how capable organizations descend quietly—how execution can replace architecture, how authority can remain static while exposure scales, and how excellence can delay recognition.

However, those chapters did not explain how enterprises continue operating successfully within that misalignment—often for years—without re-engaging governance deliberately. Drift normalizes that misalignment.

Drift does not require error. It does not require neglect. It requires only time, continuity, and the absence of friction.

In global trade, where consequences are delayed and exposure compounds incrementally, drift is not an anomaly. It is the predictable outcome of governance that is never recalibrated as depth increases.

The most capable organizations are often the most vulnerable to drift. Their trade functions are experienced, and their processes are mature. Their leaders are confident. Escalations are rare, and disruption is minimal. From the surface, nothing appears unstable.

But descent does not announce itself loudly. It accumulates through repetition. And when governance design is not revisited deliberately, authority remains where it was first placed—even as exposure multiplies beneath it.

Drift is not a story of breakdown. It is a story of sustained descent without recalibration.

Drift explains how reasonable decisions, made under prior conditions, harden into inherited assumptions under materially different ones. It allows continuity to become misalignment. It shows boards that what appeared stable internally has evolved structurally beyond original intent.

This chapter examines that movement—not as failure, but as physics.

Because drift does not require recklessness. It requires only continuation without reassessment.

SECTION I

Drift as an Organizational Condition

Trade programs rarely fail loudly. Rather, they drift.

They do not collapse under obvious error or unravel through negligence. More often, they continue functioning—efficiently, professionally, and without disruption—while the architecture beneath them becomes increasingly misaligned with the exposure they carry.

Drift is not the result of weak intent. It is the natural consequence of operating in an environment where trade risk evolves faster than governance structure, and where success is measured by continuity rather than governability. It is why capable organizations—staffed by experienced professionals and supported by mature processes—so often encounter exposure they did not believe they carried.

Drift is not failure. It is sustained operation under outdated design. That distinction matters.

"Drift is not failure. It is sustained operation under outdated design."

Drift diving is often described as effortless. Instead of fighting the current, divers allow it to carry them. Movement feels smooth. Distance accumulates without resistance. Energy is conserved. Under calm conditions, drift appears efficient, even controlled. The boat tracks overhead. The reef unfolds predictably. Nothing feels unstable.

That is precisely why it is dangerous.

Currents do not always move only in one direction. Some push horizontally along the reef. Others move vertically, altering depth far more quickly than the diver intended. Divers who believe they are holding at thirty feet can find themselves at sixty before they feel strain. The surface remains visible, breathing remains steady, and nothing feels urgent. But depth has changed.

If the current strengthens unexpectedly, swimming against it becomes physically taxing. Divers may expend energy attempting to return to a planned exit point that is no longer aligned with their actual position. The longer they allow the current to carry them without recalculating, the farther they travel from where they believed they were operating.

Strong currents can sweep divers off course before they recognize how far they have traveled. In low visibility, they may lose contact with their dive partner without realizing it immediately. Sudden directional shifts can alter depth rapidly, leaving the divers adjusting under pressure rather than navigating intentionally. Planning that did not account for environmental conditions becomes insufficient. Communication becomes more difficult. Energy depletes faster.

The divers are still breathing, but their position has changed. Organizations experience the same pattern.

When execution is strong and performance is steady, continuation feels efficient. Energy is conserved by repeating what works. Decision rights remain where they were first placed because nothing appears broken. Exposure accumulates incrementally. Authority does not shift.

Each individual decision may remain reasonable, but the cumulative depth they create may not.

From inside the organization, stability is visible. Metrics remain acceptable. Escalations are rare. The boat still appears overhead. But the exit point may no longer match the depth being reached.

Strong external forces—tariff volatility, enforcement analytics, geopolitical strain, supply-chain reconfiguration—can accelerate exposure faster than governance structure adjusts. Cross-functional alignment can weaken subtly as decisions are made locally under time pressure. Sudden shifts in regulatory interpretation can alter enterprise consequence vertically rather than horizontally. Planning calibrated to prior conditions becomes insufficient under new ones. Escalation becomes reactive rather than anticipatory.

The program is still operating, but position has changed.

> *"The program is still operating.*
> *But position has changed."*

Drift becomes dangerous not because it is chaotic, but because it feels controlled. It is not discovered through operational breakdown. It is discovered when accumulated movement is finally measured against original design assumptions.

Failure implies neglect, error, or misconduct. Drift implies something far more subtle: that a program can move away from its original governance assumptions while still producing acceptable operational outcomes.

From an internal perspective, the program appears stable:

- Entries continue to file.
- Shipments move.
- Audits return manageable findings.
- Internal reviews confirm adherence to documented processes.
- Metrics trend favorably.

Stability, however, reflects absence of friction—not absence of misalignment.

Governance structures are often designed during moments of scrutiny: after an audit, a penalty, an acquisition, or regulatory inquiry. At that moment, ownership is clarified. Escalation pathways are defined. Documentation standards are reinforced. Authority feels intentional.

But an important gap remains. What is rarely designed is a mechanism to revisit the architecture as exposure evolves. Most organizations cannot identify when their governance design was last formally recalibrated—a major oversight because trade risk does not remain static:

- Tariffs shift.
- Volumes scale.
- Product configurations evolve.
- Supply chains reconfigure.
- Enforcement priorities recalibrate.

Yet governance frameworks often remain unchanged. Decision rights remain where they were first placed. Escalation thresholds remain calibrated to historical exposure. Documentation standards reflect prior scrutiny, not current risk sensitivity.

Drift occurs when continuity replaces reassessment. It is not visible internally because nothing appears broken. It becomes visible externally when the enterprise is asked to explain how authority evolved as exposure evolved.

That is the inflection point, and it is where boards begin to engage differently.

Drift is not discovered through operational review. It is discovered when accountability questions surface:

- Who owns the cumulative impact of these decisions?
- When was this methodology last reassessed at the enterprise level?
- How did escalation criteria evolve as tariff sensitivity increased?

These are not technical questions. They are governance questions.

When drift reaches that stage, it is no longer internal misalignment.

It is enterprise exposure.

SECTION II

Reasonable Decisions at Increasing Depth

Drift rarely begins with a controversial decision. It begins with reasonable decisions: A classification approach is adopted that aligns with prior practice. A valuation methodology is implemented that reflects commercial reality at the time. An origin determination framework is built around sourcing assumptions that are stable and defensible. Escalation thresholds are calibrated to historical audit sensitivity.

Each of these decisions is made deliberately and supported by sound reasoning. Each reflects conditions that existed when it was designed.

What changes over time are the conditions—not the logic. Tariff rates increase in key jurisdictions. Product lines expand into categories with different enforcement sensitivity. Volumes scale in markets where regulatory posture is less predictable. Supply chains reconfigure to respond to geopolitical shifts. Trade remedies become more aggressive. Customs authorities invest in data analytics that alter scrutiny patterns.

The original decisions may remain technically defensible, but their enterprise consequence has changed. This is where drift deepens. Without a structured mechanism to reassess authority as exposure evolves, the organization continues applying yesterday's decision architecture to today's materially different risk environment.

Reasonable decisions harden into precedent. Precedent becomes assumption. Assumption becomes inherited design.

Like a diver carried slowly by a current, the organization continues moving while believing it remains where it began.

Inherited design is rarely stress-tested until consequence multiplies. No one re-examines the original reasoning because nothing appears broken. Execution remains strong. Compliance metrics remain within tolerance. External inquiries remain manageable.

From an internal perspective, the program is functioning. From an enterprise perspective, exposure has multiplied beneath a static authority structure.

This is not mismanagement. It is continuation without recalibration.

Drift accelerates when success reinforces stability. Strong operational performance creates confidence in the original design. The absence of enforcement action is interpreted as validation. Longevity is mistaken for durability.

But durability is not measured by time. It is measured by adaptability.

In trade governance, adaptability does not mean constant change. It means structured reassessment. It means asking the right questions:

- When did we last evaluate whether authority over valuation decisions reflects current tariff sensitivity?
- When did we last revisit escalation criteria in light of increased enforcement analytics?
- When did we last examine whether origin determinations now carry materially different enterprise consequence?

These questions are rarely asked in calm conditions. Instead, they are asked when scrutiny reframes exposure collectively rather than transactionally. Drift becomes visible not because something new occurred, but because accumulated decisions are evaluated against present conditions.

Boards rarely scrutinize individual entries. Instead, they scrutinize cumulative exposure. They examine financial reliance on tariff treatments. They assess sensitivity to regulatory shifts. They evaluate whether enterprise risk tolerance is aligned with trade methodology at scale.

If reasonable decisions were never structurally re-evaluated as conditions evolved, leadership discovers that authority lagged exposure.

That lag is drift, and drift at depth is rarely abrupt. It is gradual, comfortable, and reinforced by performance.

Until it isn't.

SECTION III

Acceleration and Exposure

Drift can persist quietly for years under stable external conditions, but it rarely survives acceleration.

Global trade does not operate in a static environment. Tariff regimes shift rapidly. Trade remedies expand and contract. Enforcement priorities intensify. Data analytics alter how customs authorities detect patterns. Political decisions reframe entire sourcing models within weeks. Supply chains reconfigure in response to events outside the enterprise's control.

Acceleration does not create exposure. It simply strengthens the current that was already moving the diver away from the original reference point, and it reveals how much exposure has accumulated under prior assumptions.

For example, an origin methodology that once produced marginal tariff savings can become materially significant when tariff rates increase sharply. A valuation structure that once operated comfortably within historical audit tolerance can attract scrutiny when customs authorities deploy data models that identify systemic pricing patterns. A classification approach embedded across product lines can shift from immaterial to earnings-sensitive when duty rates multiply.

Under stable conditions, incremental change feels manageable. Under acceleration, incremental change compounds. This is where governance design is tested.

Execution can respond to individual inquiries. It can manage discrete audits. It can adjust procedures quickly. It can issue guidance. It can train teams. It can correct and document.

But acceleration requires more than response. It also requires recalibration.

If decision rights were not structured to evolve with exposure, then acceleration forces that evolution abruptly. Authority must be reassigned in compressed time. Escalation pathways must be clarified under scrutiny. Historical rationale must be assembled quickly to explain why methodology remained unchanged as external sensitivity increased. The organization is not merely answering technical questions. It is defending continuity of ownership.

Boards become attentive at this stage not because operations have failed, but because volatility increases enterprise consequence. Financial reliance on trade determinations becomes more visible. Sensitivity analysis expands. Investor messaging intersects with regulatory exposure. Leadership must articulate how trade risk interacts with earnings, supply-chain resilience, and strategic commitments.

Acceleration collapses the illusion that trade governance is purely operational, revealing that trade decisions are enterprise-level commitments embedded in financial structure.

When external volatility rises, the absence of structured reassessment becomes difficult to defend. Leaders cannot rely on historical performance alone. They must demonstrate that authority shifted as consequence shifted.

Acceleration does not wait for governance to mature. Instead, it forces clarity. Programs designed for depth respond to acceleration by activating predefined reassessment mechanisms. Exposure thresholds trigger formal review. Authority migrates according to design rather than urgency. Cross-functional leadership engages because architecture requires it, not because scrutiny demands it.

Programs built primarily for execution respond by working harder: more reviews, more documentation, more meetings, more reactive elevation. Effort increases, but effort without recalibration does not restore margin.

Acceleration compresses the time available for reflection. It exposes where design was static while exposure evolved. It surfaces dependencies that were manageable under calm conditions but fragile under volatility. Compression of time forces recalibration under scrutiny rather than under strategy.

Acceleration does not begin with crisis. It begins with change: A tariff shift is announced. A regulatory interpretation evolves. A jurisdiction signals heightened enforcement analytics. None of these events immediately destabilize operations. The trade function reviews the change, assesses applicability, and evaluates the existing methodology.

In most capable organizations, the initial response is disciplined. The interpretive position is reviewed. Historical precedent is considered. Internal documentation is referenced. Prior audit outcomes are examined. Trade leadership determines whether the existing framework remains defensible under the new conditions.

In many cases, it appears to be.

This is where acceleration hides.

The methodology was built under prior exposure levels. The interpretive logic may still be technically supportable. The documentation reflects consistency. There is no immediate operational disruption. Shipments continue. Entries file. No regulator has challenged the position directly.

From inside the function, continuity feels appropriate. But exposure has shifted. Volumes may have scaled. Product classifications may now represent greater financial sensitivity. The cumulative impact of the interpretive position may now represent a materially different earnings concentration than when it was originally adopted.

The trade function is evaluating technical defensibility, but the enterprise should be evaluating structural exposure.

Acceleration compresses the time available to reconsider architecture. What could have been revisited deliberately under calm conditions must now be evaluated under scrutiny. The stronger the external current, the less margin exists for reflective recalibration.

Trade defends the interpretive position because it was reasonable when adopted. Finance begins modeling sensitivity only after volatility surfaces. Business units continue operating because operational continuity remains possible.

No one is negligent, but the question has shifted.

It is no longer:
Is the position technically defensible?

It becomes:
Was the governance structure recalibrated as exposure scaled?

Acceleration does not create exposure. It reveals how much exposure has accumulated under prior assumptions.

When the external environment changes quickly, organizations discover whether governance design was built for stability—or for depth.

If authority remained decentralized while exposure concentrated, acceleration exposes that lag. If escalation thresholds were calibrated to prior tariff sensitivity, compression makes that calibration visible. If methodology ownership was never revisited at the enterprise level, acceleration forces the question of who now owns cumulative consequence. The program is still functioning, but time has narrowed.

Acceleration is the vertical current in enterprise form. It alters depth faster than authority adjusts. And once that vertical movement is recognized, recalibration is no longer optional. It is urgent.

This is often the moment when enterprise leadership realizes that governance has been treated as operational assurance rather than structural responsibility. Not because something catastrophic occurred, but because conditions changed faster than authority did.

Acceleration is not an unusual occurrence.

It is the norm of modern trade environments.

And environments that accelerate do not tolerate static design indefinitely.

The challenge is not that governance disappears.

It is that governance remains in place while the conditions around it change. What once provided clarity begins to lose relevance as complexity increases.

And without recalibration, that shift goes largely unnoticed.

Figure 4: Drift Without Recalibration (Acceleration & Exposure)

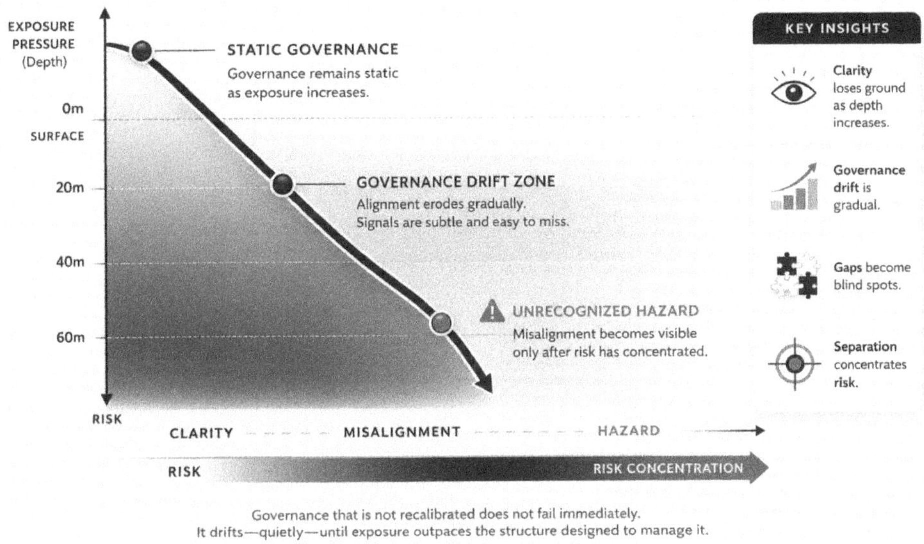

This figure illustrates how governance remains static while exposure continues to evolve, creating a drift zone in which alignment erodes and risk begins to concentrate.

As Figure 4 shows, this transition is rarely acknowledged in real time. Governance remains static while exposure continues to move, creating a drift zone in which alignment gradually erodes without clear signals of failure. Instead, organizations continue to rely on structures designed for a different level of exposure, assuming continuity where there is none. The result is not immediate failure but gradual separation between governance and reality.

That separation is where risk begins to concentrate.

SECTION IV

When Temporary Decisions Become Structural Weight

Governance rarely changes through formal redesign. More often, it shifts quietly through continuation.

A decision is made under specific conditions. It resolves a real issue. It is technically sound and commercially practical at the time. No one views it as permanent. It is simply what made sense in the environment in which it was made.

The organization moves forward. Over time, however, the environment does not remain the same. Volumes increase. Tariff sensitivity changes. Supply chains reconfigure. Enforcement priorities evolve. What once felt appropriately proportionate to the earlier level of exposure may carry materially different consequence under new conditions.

Yet the original decision remains. Not because it was deliberately reaffirmed, but because nothing required it to be revisited. This is how drift becomes embedded.

The decision is referenced as precedent. It becomes part of process. It is absorbed into training, systems, and routine execution. Individuals who understood the original context may no longer be present. The reasoning that once framed the choice fades gradually, while the outcome continues uninterrupted.

Internally, nothing appears unstable. Execution remains disciplined. Metrics remain within acceptable ranges. There is no obvious trigger that forces structural reconsideration.

But governance at depth is not sustained by the absence of disruption. It is sustained by intentional reassessment. For example, a methodology adopted when exposure was modest may carry materially different financial sensitivity when tariff rates increase. An authority structure that functioned appropriately when volumes were limited may no longer align when trade becomes earnings-sensitive. An escalation threshold calibrated under one enforcement climate may lag under another.

When the environment changes, boards do not examine whether a decision was reasonable when it was first made. They examine whether it was revisited as its consequence evolved. They assess whether enterprise leadership deliberately re-evaluated authority as exposure multiplied, or whether prior determinations simply carried forward unchanged.

Temporary accommodations are often necessary in complex environments. What matters is whether they are revisited deliberately once conditions shift. Without that discipline, continuation becomes commitment—not through intent, but through inertia.

But at depth, every temporary adjustment adds weight that must eventually be carried. At depth, inertia carries weight.

Governance requires moments of structured reassessment—not because prior decisions were flawed, but because exposure rarely remains static.

When those moments are absent, the organization does not fail.

It simply descends further than it realizes.

SECTION V

When Depth Is Finally Measured

Drift remains abstract until it is measured.

For years, continuation feels justified. Execution remains disciplined. Internal metrics trend within acceptable variance. Audits do not escalate. Trade leadership maintains confidence in the interpretive framework. Nothing signals instability.

Measurement changes that, not by creating exposure but by aggregating it.

It is the moment the diver finally checks the depth gauge.

When tariff volatility increases or enforcement scrutiny sharpens, the enterprise begins to model cumulative sensitivity. Finance does what finance does:

It quantifies impact. Margin sensitivity is recalculated. Scenario analysis is run. Concentration is mapped across jurisdictions. Interpretive positions are translated into potential financial ranges.

The first reaction is not alarm. It is analysis:

- What percentage of earnings relies on this classification logic?
- How much cumulative value rests on this methodology?
- How concentrated is exposure across specific tariff headings?
- What is the range of variance if interpretation is challenged?

These are measured questions. They are not accusatory, but they are different from the questions that were being asked when drift was still invisible.

The trade function may still believe the methodology is technically defensible. The documentation may be consistent. The rationale may remain intact. But the enterprise is no longer evaluating defensibility alone. It is evaluating magnitude.

Exposure that accumulated incrementally over years now appears in aggregate. What once felt like operational detail now represents material sensitivity. The question shifts from "Can we defend this?" to "Should this level of concentration exist without enterprise-level authorization?"

Silence often follows, not because there is misconduct but because depth has become visible.

When numbers are laid out against earnings impact, the organization recognizes that continuity replaced recalibration. Authority remained where it was first assigned. Escalation thresholds were not revisited as exposure scaled. The methodology was inherited, not reauthorized.

Measurement does not dramatize drift. It clarifies it. And clarity removes comfort.

At this stage, no one argues that the program failed. It did not. It operated exactly as designed.

That is the point. Governance that is never deliberately recalibrated can function effectively while still moving the enterprise beyond its original risk tolerance.

Depth, not collapse, was reached through continuation. When depth is measured, continuation without recalibration is no longer an option. It becomes a requirement.

Recalibration is analytical, structured, and heavy. It marks the moment when governance must shift from assumption to discipline.

Drift can continue for years without visible consequence. Execution remains stable. Teams perform well. Decisions are technically defensible. Exposure evolves incrementally rather than abruptly. Internally, there is little reason to question whether the governance framework beneath those decisions still aligns with the scale of consequence they now carry.

The moment of measurement rarely begins inside the trade function. Instead, it begins when important shifts occur. For example, financial reliance on tariff treatments becomes material to earnings sensitivity. Regulatory volatility intersects with investor expectations. Supply chain concentration becomes a board-level discussion rather than an operational one. A geopolitical shift reframes sourcing exposure in ways that extend beyond customs compliance and into strategic positioning.

At that point, leadership is no longer evaluating individual determinations. It is evaluating cumulative exposure.

Boards do not ask whether entries were filed correctly. They ask how exposure has been structured across time. They look for evidence that authority evolved as financial sensitivity increased. They expect clarity around who owns the enterprise consequence of trade methodology—not only at execution level, but also at strategic level.

The tone of the conversation changes. It becomes less technical and more structural:

- When was this methodology last reassessed in light of current tariff impact?
- How does trade exposure interact with earnings guidance?
- If enforcement posture intensifies, how does decision authority migrate?

- What is our sensitivity to a 5%, 10%, or 25% shift in tariff rate across key jurisdictions? Who owns this analysis?

These questions do not emerge because something has failed. They emerge because consequence has scaled.

Trade determinations that once felt operational now sit directly beneath financial reporting, investor messaging, and strategic planning. The board does not need to understand classification nuance to understand exposure concentration. It does not need to interpret origin rules to recognize earnings sensitivity.

Measurement reframes continuity. What once felt stable internally may now appear static under enterprise scrutiny. What once felt appropriately delegated may now appear insufficiently elevated. What once operated comfortably within historical tolerance may now sit uncomfortably within expanded consequence.

This is not an indictment of the trade function. It is a recalibration of enterprise expectation. Boards are not asking whether trade professionals exercised judgment responsibly. They are asking whether enterprise leadership structured that judgment deliberately as exposure multiplied.

At this stage, the distinction between performance and governability becomes unavoidable. A program may have operated efficiently for years. It may have avoided enforcement action. It may have maintained consistent audit outcomes. None of these indicators alone demonstrates that authority shifted appropriately as financial reliance deepened.

Governability requires evidence of reassessment. It requires clarity about when methodology was revisited. It requires documentation that escalation thresholds were recalibrated when exposure increased. It requires proof that trade risk was integrated into broader enterprise risk mapping—not as an isolated compliance function, but as a structural contributor to earnings and strategic stability.

This is where boards engage differently: not in the mechanics of entries, but in the architecture of ownership. Boards want to know whether descent was recognized and managed deliberately—or whether it simply occurred through continuation.

An enterprise that can demonstrate structured reassessment does not eliminate risk. It demonstrates stewardship. It shows that leadership understood how exposure evolved, and it acted accordingly.

An enterprise that cannot provide that clarity does not necessarily face immediate crisis, but it operates with less room to move. Margin narrows. Strategic flexibility tightens. Time to revisit decisions under stable conditions disappears. Adjustments that could have been made deliberately must now be made under pressure.

Depth, once invisible, becomes measurable. And once measured, it changes the standard.

This chapter has not been about failure. It is about the moment when enterprise governance must catch up to accumulated exposure. Drift does not feel urgent while it is occurring.

Measurement does not create depth. It reveals how far the enterprise has already descended.

"Measurement does not create depth. It reveals how far the enterprise has already descended."

CHAPTER 4

Compression at Depth: When Governance Becomes Visible

Depth often arrives before the diver recognizes it.

In diving, pressure increases gradually as depth increases. Divers rarely feel the change all at once. They can descend farther than they realize before the environment begins to respond differently to the same movements.

At shallow depth, visibility feels generous. Light moves easily through the water. Orientation feels intuitive. The diver can still see the surface overhead, and small variations in position appear inconsequential. Movement feels controlled because the environment has not yet demanded precision. There is margin.

As descent continues, the environment changes, even when the diver does not. Light narrows. Color fades. Contrast sharpens. Distances become harder to judge. Movement that once felt horizontal reveals quiet vertical descent. The margin for error compresses. The same motion now carries different consequences.

Nothing about the diver's intention has changed.

The environment has.

Regulatory scrutiny functions the same way.

Inside the organization, trade decisions accumulate gradually. Classifications are applied consistently. Valuation methodologies remain stable. Origin determinations follow established logic as sourcing evolves. Each decision, viewed individually, appears reasonable within the conditions that existed when it was made.

From the inside, the program feels controlled. But regulators do not experience trade programs from inside the system. They do not inherit internal context. They do not observe the incremental decisions that felt reasonable at the time they were made. They do not rely on institutional memory to explain how today's structure emerged.

They reconstruct patterns: across time, volume, and financial consequence. Where the organization experienced continuity, they evaluate structure. And under that lens, governance either existed—or it did not.

Regulators do not regulate governance directly. They regulate classification, valuation, and origin decisions. Governance becomes visible only when those decisions accumulate exposure across time and scale.

SECTION I

The Regulatory Lens at Depth

Regulatory scrutiny does not begin with the question most organizations expect:

"Did you make a mistake?"

It begins with a different one:

"How did you govern this decision as conditions changed?"

Customs authorities and enforcement bodies review trade decisions across time and scale. They look at how interpretations held up as tariffs shifted, how methodologies persisted as volume increased, and whether decision ownership evolved as exposure grew.

From inside the organization, consistency feels stabilizing. A classification is applied the same way quarter after quarter. A valuation method remains in place through commercial adjustments. Origin determinations follow established logic as sourcing shifts gradually.

Internally, consistency feels disciplined.

Externally, consistency without reassessment feels static.

Internally, consistency without escalation feels comfortable.

Externally, consistency without documented review feels assumed.

What matters under regulatory evaluation is not whether a decision was technically defensible at the beginning. It is whether the organization recognized when its risk profile changed—and acted deliberately. This is the regulatory reframe.

Internally, governance is experienced operationally.

Externally, it is evaluated structurally—through reconstruction of decisions across time, volume, and consequence. Regulators examine how exposure evolved as tariffs increased, as volumes scaled, and as commercial strategies shifted. They evaluate whether governance adjusted as those realities changed. They are reconstructing structure, not intent. When they cannot identify what triggered reassessment, silence becomes meaningful.

Inside the organization, silence often feels reassuring: no expanded audit, no enforcement letter, no challenge to interpretation.

Outside the organization, silence is not confirmation. It is simply the absence of immediate scrutiny.

The longer silence persists under changing conditions, the more regulators focus on whether governance moved at all.

From the inside, the program may have felt controlled.

From the outside, the question becomes: When did governance re-engage?

And if the answer is unclear, margin begins to narrow.

SECTION II

When Silence Attracts Scrutiny

Silence is easy to misinterpret.

Over time, silence begins to feel like confirmation. If something were materially wrong, it would have surfaced. If exposure had reached meaningful scale, someone would have asked.

But silence is not endorsement. It is simply the period before attention concentrates.

The assumption that operations are functioning fully and cleanly becomes embedded quietly. Quarter after quarter, the absence of challenge reinforces internal confidence. Interpretations remain consistent. Documentation practices remain stable. Escalation thresholds remain in their original places. Governance architecture is not formally revisited because nothing has forced the enterprise to revisit it.

Silence becomes operational comfort.

> *"Silence is not endorsement. It is simply the period before attention concentrates."*

In diving, calm water does not mean the diver is stationary. Currents can move quietly beneath the surface while the diver's breathing remains steady and orientation still feels familiar. Water conditions can remain calm even as current builds beneath the surface. A diver may not feel resistance immediately. The boat may still be visible overhead. There is no obvious signal that movement is occurring differently than expected, yet position is changing.

Environmental pressure does not announce itself at once. Rather, it accumulates. The diver continues comfortably—until the environment begins to respond.

Regulatory scrutiny follows the same pattern. Inquiry rarely begins with confrontation. It begins with clarification:

- A request for supporting rationale.
- A question about methodology application across multiple entries.
- A dataset spanning a broader time frame than prior reviews.
- An interest in cumulative value rather than individual transactions.

Each request feels manageable, and the trade function responds. Documentation is assembled. Explanations are provided. Nothing in isolation suggests instability. No shipments are halted. No formal findings are issued. The enterprise remains operational.

Internally, these exchanges are often categorized as routine, but routine inquiry can signal directional focus. The time horizon begins to expand. What was once reviewed quarterly is now reviewed across years. What was once evaluated transactionally is now evaluated structurally. What was once accepted as consistent application is now examined for cumulative consequence.

The questions do not arrive louder. They arrive broader.

At first, the request may focus on a narrow subset of entries—a sampling exercise framed as verification. The trade function responds confidently. Documentation is provided. Rationale is restated. The review closes without formal finding. Internally, the event is logged as resolved.

Months later, another inquiry surfaces, this one expanding the date range. The scope includes additional product lines. The value at issue is larger. The questions now reference prior submissions. The regulator is no longer asking how the methodology works in theory, but rather how it operated in practice across volume.

The tone remains professional, but a pattern is emerging. Leadership begins asking different questions internally. Not whether the interpretation is defensible, but how concentrated reliance has become. The finance group requests updated exposure modeling. Auditors inquire whether reassessment triggers were ever formally defined. The trade function reconstructs historical escalation paths to determine when the issue was last elevated.

The organization is no longer operating on assumptions. Instead, it is operating in reconstruction. Reconstruction happens under scrutiny, not calm conditions—and it is expensive. It requires pulling forward decisions made under different conditions and evaluating them under current sensitivity. It exposes where governance was documented and where it was inferred. It reveals whether authority was intentionally assigned or simply inherited.

Each additional inquiry narrows space—not through accusation, but through accumulation. As inquiries broaden, cross-functional strain appears. Business units resist reopening settled classifications. Commercial teams worry about revenue timing. The legal department assesses disclosure thresholds. The board begins asking whether these signals represents isolated review or systemic exposure.

The trade function remains technically focused, but the enterprise begins to think structurally. That restores mass in a meaningful way.

As exposure increases over time, regulatory attention increases in scope. Not immediately or dramatically, but progressively. Authorities observe patterns before they articulate conclusions. They compare import volumes before they question interpretation. They analyze tariff sensitivity before they challenge classification logic. By the time formal scrutiny appears visible, informal reconstruction has often already begun.

Inside the organization, this shift can feel subtle at first. Requests require more cross-functional coordination. Data must be reconciled across systems. Historical rationales must be retrieved and explained. Decisions made years earlier must be restated under current conditions.

None of this feels like failure. It feels administrative. But it is structural.

Silence was never proof of alignment. It was simply the period before alignment was examined.

When inquiry increases in frequency and scope, leadership begins to sense compression. Not because enforcement action is imminent, but because the organization recognizes that its governance design is now being viewed from outside the narrative that created it.

Internally, consistency felt disciplined.

Externally, consistency now prompts a different question: When did governance formally reassess this exposure?

If that answer requires reconstruction rather than documentation, margin narrows. If escalation thresholds were never adjusted as financial sensitivity increased, margin narrows further. If authority remained in the same place as exposure expanded, questions deepen.

None of this occurs explosively. Instead, it unfolds through accumulation.
Silence did not protect the organization. It postponed scrutiny.

> *"Silence did not protect the organization. It postponed scrutiny."*

And when scrutiny begins, it does not shout. It inquires.

Each inquiry requires reconstruction. Each reconstruction reveals how decisions compounded. And each compounded decision clarifies how governance either adapted or did not.

This is where drift transitions into accountability. Not because regulators assume bad faith, but because depth has become visible beyond the enterprise.

And once depth is visible externally, silence is no longer neutral.

It becomes part of the record.

SECTION III

When Technical Precision Outruns Governance

Trade exposure often accelerates most quietly in the trade engineering group.

In diving, small adjustments that feel insignificant near the surface can produce amplified movement at depth. The diver may feel composed while subtle forces are already changing the diver's position.

Trade engineering behaves in much the same way. Classification decisions are rarely dramatic. Valuation methodologies support commercial efficiency. Origin determinations follow sourcing strategy. Each decision, considered on its own, is technical, rational, and documented. Individually, decisions feel controlled, but collectively they shape exposure.

Trade professionals are trained to engineer defensible positions. They analyze tariff schedules, interpret explanatory notes, review prior rulings, and apply methodology consistently. That discipline protects the organization from careless error, reduces randomness, and builds internal confidence.

But engineering and governance are not the same thing.

Engineering answers the question:

"Can this be supported?"

Governance must answer a different question:

"As scale increases, does this exposure still sit in the right place?"

Those questions are often separated by time. A classification adopted when annual imports were modest may remain in place as volume triples. A valuation approach built under a stable tariff environment may persist as rates increase materially. A sourcing shift made for commercial reasons may alter origin exposure without triggering structural reassessment.

Consider a product line that represented five percent of total imports when a methodology was first adopted. At that level, variance felt manageable. Financial sensitivity was limited, and escalation to enterprise leadership felt unnecessary.

Years later, that same product line may represent thirty percent of total imports. Tariff rates may have increased. Revenue reliance may have deepened. Yet the original decision framework remains in place.

The engineering did not change, but the exposure did.

At shallow depth, the diver may not notice the shift immediately. But as pressure increases, small differences in calibration become consequential.

Consider a classification adopted when tariff rates were modest and import volume was steady. At the time, the financial impact of that classification decision represented a manageable variance within overall margin. The interpretation was reviewed, documented, and applied consistently. No regulator challenged it, and no internal escalation was triggered. The issue was considered stable.

Then tariffs shift. A geopolitical dispute increases duty rates on that product category materially. What had once represented a three percent duty burden now carries a twenty-five percent rate. At the same time, demand increases and import volume grows. The same classification decision that once represented limited exposure now influences a significant portion of earnings.

The interpretation itself has not changed. The environment has.

If the governance structure does not include a trigger to reassess interpretive positions when tariff rates change, the organization continues applying the methodology under dramatically different financial conditions. The trade function may still believe the classification is technically defensible. Documentation may still support the original rationale. But magnitude has altered consequence.

The finance department begins modeling earnings sensitivity. Variance scenarios expand. Questions arise about how much cumulative exposure rests on that single interpretive position. Leadership realizes that the decision was never reauthorized at the enterprise level under the new tariff regime. It was simply inherited.

No one made a reckless choice, and no one ignored data. But the structure did not require reconsideration as exposure expanded. And so reconsideration did not occur.

The first formal recognition of accumulated exposure often arrives through financial modeling rather than regulatory accusation. Earnings forecasts begin to show sensitivity to classification outcomes that were once immaterial. A five-point swing in interpretation now translates into a measurable impact on quarterly performance. What had been a technical determination becomes a financial variable.

As a result, the conversation shifts quietly. The finance department asks whether alternative classifications were ever evaluated under the new tariff rate. Auditors inquire whether a formal reassessment trigger exists when duty burden crosses a defined threshold. The legal department considers whether disclosure language adequately reflects concentration risk. The board reviewing margin compression, asks a broader question: How much of our earnings stability relies on this interpretive position?

The trade function can still defend the analysis, but the enterprise is now evaluating magnitude, not logic. And magnitude requires governance alignment.

The issue is no longer whether the interpretation is technically sustainable. It is whether the exposure attached to it was ever deliberately reauthorized as conditions changed.

That distinction marks the moment when engineering reaches the limits of its mandate.

Governance must now step forward.

If no formal trigger required reassessment as that shift occurred, governance remained anchored to outdated assumptions.

In diving, equipment calibrated for shallow depth behaves differently as pressure increases. Buoyancy shifts, air consumption accelerates, and the body compensates continuously. A diver who fails to recalibrate may not notice these shifts immediately, but the margin for error narrows with each additional foot of descent.

Organizations experience a similar narrowing. Trade engineering continues operating with technical precision. Entries file accurately, and documentation remains organized. Internal reviews confirm adherence to established methodology. Nothing signals operational breakdown.

But exposure accumulates in ways that are not visible transaction by transaction.

As regulatory inquiries expand and financial sensitivity modeling begins, concentration becomes clearer. Commercial teams may begin to see margin sensitivity tied to a single interpretive position. Procurement may question supplier dependencies built on that same assumption. Legal may begin evaluating whether the organization's position can be consistently supported under evolving regulatory scrutiny.

These questions do not challenge competence. They challenge calibration.

If escalation thresholds were defined years earlier and not adjusted as exposure scaled, governance lag is revealed. If ownership remained within a technical function while enterprise sensitivity increased, structural misalignment surfaces. If reassessment was assumed but not documented, reconstruction becomes necessary.

In short: Engineering excellence cannot substitute for governance recalibration. A technically defensible decision, repeated consistently over time, can still represent unmanaged concentration if its magnitude was never reevaluated as conditions changed.

This is where compression becomes real. The organization recognizes that exposure expanded under stable methodology. No one intended to increase enterprise risk tolerance. No one deliberately bypassed escalation. The structure simply did not require reassessment as scale increased.

At depth, small differences become consequential. Minor buoyancy adjustments require greater precision. Air consumption rates matter more. The same movement carries different risk.

So too with trade exposure. What felt immaterial at lower volume may represent significant earnings sensitivity at higher volume. What once required no board visibility may now demand executive oversight. What was managed within a department may now require enterprise ownership.

When engineering outpaces governance, recalibration does not occur gradually. Instead, it occurs under scrutiny. And recalibration under scrutiny is heavier than recalibration under calm conditions.

This is not failure. It is alignment evaluated under conditions that did not exist when the decision was first made.

At depth, decisions are no longer judged only by their technical logic.

They are judged by the consequence they carried as the environment changed.

SECTION IV

Inherited Assumptions at Depth

Every governance structure rests on assumptions:

- Assumptions about materiality.
- Assumptions about likelihood of challenge.
- Assumptions about financial impact.
- Assumptions about who needs to know and when.

At the moment they are formed, these assumptions are usually reasonable. They reflect the scale of the enterprise at that time and the conditions under which the governance architecture was designed.

But as scale increases, assumptions rarely move with it. Exposure levels feel measurable. Financial impact appears bounded. Risk tolerance is discussed within the context of current scale. The structure reflects the enterprise as it exists in that moment.

Less common is a mechanism that requires revisiting those assumptions as scale changes.

Consider an escalation threshold defined at a time when annual duty exposure represented a small percentage of operating margin. Under those conditions, the threshold may have been calibrated appropriately, requiring notification only within the trade function or at a mid-level finance review.

Years later, import volume may have doubled. Tariff rates may have increased. The same threshold may now represent a materially different financial concentration. Yet, because the threshold was never formally reexamined, it continues to govern decision visibility.

No one intentionally concealed exposure. Instead, assumptions hardened quietly over time. The architecture simply did not require recalibration as exposure grew. A classification approach once deemed immaterial becomes foundational. A valuation method once treated as routine becomes earnings-sensitive. A sourcing strategy once viewed as operational becomes structurally consequential.

The organization continues operating within inherited parameters, but scale alters the meaning of those parameters.

At depth, the environment changes even when the diver believes nothing has moved. In diving, small buoyancy adjustments near the surface are forgiving. A diver may drift slightly without consequence. Air supply remains abundant, and depth variance feels manageable.

At greater depth, though, those same adjustments produce amplified movement. Air consumption accelerates, and the environment demands greater precision. What felt negligible earlier now carries weight.

Governance assumptions behave the same way. Thresholds that were reasonable at lower scale may no longer align with enterprise exposure. Escalation paths that once felt sufficient may bypass executive visibility as financial sensitivity increases. Ownership that once fit comfortably within a department may now exceed its mandate.

Unless recalibration is required, assumptions persist. They persist because they are documented, they once worked, and no triggering mechanism required reconsideration.

Over time, persistence becomes structure.

At the time they are formed, these judgments are not casual. They are discussed, and sometimes they are documented. They reflect the best assessment available under then-current conditions.

What makes assumptions dangerous is not their origin. It is their longevity. Over time, the organization forgets that they were assumptions at all, and they become baseline. New personnel inherit them as established doctrine. Escalation thresholds are referenced as if they reflect current exposure rather than historical conditions.

The conversation shifts quietly from "Is this still the right threshold?" to "This is our threshold."

That shift is rarely intentional. It is operational momentum.

As scale increases, assumptions compound quietly. A sourcing shift in one region may increase reliance on a tariff classification that was once marginal. A pricing adjustment may intensify sensitivity to valuation methodology. A commercial strategy designed for growth may concentrate exposure in jurisdictions that were previously secondary.

None of these developments are isolated. They interact. Exposure grows not only in magnitude but also in interconnectedness.

Yet governance assumptions often remain compartmentalized. Escalation thresholds may still evaluate individual decisions rather than cumulative impact. Reporting structures may still focus on transactional compliance rather than enterprise concentration. Authority may remain within the function that engineered the methodology, even as financial sensitivity expands beyond it.

This is how blind spots form: not through negligence, but through normalization.

When something has worked for years, it becomes self-validating. The absence of challenge reinforces the belief that structure is aligned. The organization continues operating within inherited parameters because nothing has required reexamination.

But scale has changed the meaning of those parameters. An assumption about materiality that was reasonable at one revenue level may be untenable at another.

An exposure concentration that once fell below executive visibility may now represent a significant percentage of earnings volatility. A risk tolerance implicitly accepted by a department may not reflect the board's demands at enterprise scale.

The danger is not that assumptions exist. The danger is that they remain invisible.

In diving, depth changes perception gradually. Light fades incrementally, and colors shift subtly. The diver adjusts unconsciously until reaching a point in the environment where recalibration must be deliberate. If the diver assumes conditions remain constant simply because they feel familiar, misjudgment becomes more likely.

Organizations face similar perceptual drift. What feels stable internally may be structurally misaligned externally. What appears immaterial in isolation may represent concentrated exposure in aggregate. What seems operational may carry strategic consequence when measured against enterprise risk tolerance.

Assumptions that are never surfaced remain unchallenged. Unchallenged assumptions become architecture. And architecture determines consequence.

When regulatory scrutiny intensifies or financial modeling reveals concentration, embedded assumptions become visible all at once. Leadership may discover that escalation thresholds were never formally tied to revenue sensitivity, that ownership boundaries were never reevaluated as scale expanded, and that reporting structures reflect historical priorities, not present exposure.

The board does not ask whether those assumptions were once reasonable. It asks whether they remain so. If no mechanism required their reassessment, governance must now respond at depth.

This is where proportional gravity settles. Not because error occurred, but because evolution outpaced review. When regulatory inquiry expands and financial modeling highlights concentration, leadership begins to see assumptions as decisions that were never consciously revisited.

Boards do not ask whether the original threshold was reasonable. They ask when it was last reassessed. They do not question whether trade professionals acted in good faith. They question whether governance architecture evolved deliberately as the enterprise evolved.

In its review, the organization may realize that escalation criteria were defined once and never revisited, that exposure reporting remained departmental even as earnings reliance deepened, and that ownership never formally shifted upward as magnitude increased.

None of these realities indicate misconduct. They indicate stasis under growth, and growth at depth requires recalibration.

When scale exposes inherited assumptions, governance faces a structural test: Continue operating under thresholds defined for a different moment, or redesign the architecture that governs exposure.

At depth, assumptions do not disappear on their own. They harden.

And when they harden, the enterprise eventually confronts them under scrutiny rather than under calm conditions.

That weight is not emotional. It is institutional.

At some point, exposure outgrows assumption. When that happens, governance can no longer rely on inherited thresholds or informal escalation. It requires structure that is deliberately designed to recalibrate as conditions change.

Internal controls are not merely mechanisms for compliance; they are the infrastructure that determines whether recalibration occurs before compression becomes crisis. Without that infrastructure, assumptions persist longer than they should. With it, governance adapts at depth. The next chapter examines how internal controls function not as operational safeguards, but as structural discipline within the enterprise.

CHAPTER 5

Carrying the Weight

In diving, the deeper a diver descends, the more the environment begins to carry weight differently. Pressure increases steadily. Movements that felt effortless near the surface require greater control. Stability depends less on strength and more on how weight is balanced and distributed.

At depth, pressure is no longer theoretical. It is constant and unavoidable.

Whether the diver notices it or not, the environment is now fundamentally different.

At depth, stability depends on how weight is carried.

Divers do not descend safely because they swim harder. They descend safely because ballast is distributed deliberately across their frame. Too little weight and they cannot descend. Too much weight concentrated in one place and they tilt, overcorrect, or drop faster than intended.

Strength does not determine stability. Distribution does.

Organizations behave the same way.

In stable environments, most control frameworks appear sufficient. Policies are written. Procedures are documented. Reviews are performed. Dashboards are distributed. Audits are completed. The system moves, and leadership assumes that governance must therefore exist.

But surface stability does not reveal how weight is carried.

As tariffs shift, volumes scale, supply chains evolve, and regulatory scrutiny intensifies, decisions that once felt operational begin to carry enterprise consequence. Controls that were designed to confirm accuracy must now carry something heavier: the responsibility to signal when pressure is building inside the system.

> *"Controls do not govern exposure.*
> *They reveal where pressure is accumulating."*

Controls do not govern exposure. They reveal where pressure is accumulating. This is where governance becomes visible.

The question is no longer whether controls exist. The question is whether they reveal the pressure that governance must carry—and whether the architecture distributes responsibility in a way that allows exposure to be governed as it grows. Because controls can operate continuously while governance quietly falls behind.

This chapter examines that distinction.

It does not ask whether trade controls are present. It asks whether they function as infrastructure—capable of carrying weight as exposure scales, signaling when reassessment is required, and making trade risk visible beyond the operational layer. In many organizations, the answer is more fragile than leadership realizes.

Controls were built to confirm accuracy.

Governance requires them to carry consequence.

These design objectives are not the same.

At depth, distribution determines stability.

SECTION I

When Controls Exist but Governance Fails

Regulatory scrutiny forces organizations to confront a difficult realization:

Controls can exist. Controls can operate. Controls can pass audit. And governance can still fail.

This realization is destabilizing because it challenges a belief that feels rational. If policies are documented, procedures are followed, reviews are conducted, and audit results are clean, then risk should be governed.

The visible activity supports that conclusion. Evidence exists. Testing confirms operation. Dashboards remain stable.

From inside the organization, nothing appears unmanaged. Yet exposure can accumulate quietly within that structure.

The reason is not negligence. It is design.

Most trade controls were built to confirm accuracy. They answer questions such as:

- Was the entry filed correctly?
- Was the classification applied consistently?
- Was the documentation retained?

These are important questions, but they are not governance questions.

Accuracy confirms that a process operated correctly. Governance determines whether the consequence created by that process still sits in the right place as exposure grows.

Most trade controls are constructed to confirm execution. They verify that classifications are applied as approved. They reconcile declared value to pricing data.

They confirm that origin determinations are documented and supported. They demonstrate that corrections are filed when discrepancies are identified.

Execution asks:
Was the decision applied correctly?

Governance asks:
Has the impact of that decision changed?

When conditions remain stable, the distinction is subtle: A classification that carries limited financial sensitivity remains limited. A valuation methodology aligned with commercial structure remains proportionate. An origin determination tied to a consistent supply chain remains accurate.

Under those conditions, operational control and governance appear aligned.

Depth alters that alignment. Tariffs increase. Volumes expand. Product mix shifts. Sourcing migrates incrementally. Enforcement priorities change. Financial consequence grows.

The original decision may remain technically defensible. The control may continue to confirm correct application. Audit testing may show consistent execution.

But the consequence of that decision is no longer what it was when first adopted.

If no mechanism exists to detect that shift, governance does not re-engage. Nothing breaks, and the system simply continues.

This is the structural vulnerability that most organizations do not see. Controls create reassurance because they generate visible activity. They provide evidence that something is happening. They produce documentation that can be shown. They satisfy audit criteria. They close review cycles. Reassurance becomes mistaken for oversight.

Under regulatory review, however, the evaluation standard changes.

Regulators do not ask only whether controls operated. They examine whether the organization recognized when exposure evolved. They look for evidence that escalation occurred as consequence increased. They evaluate whether ownership shifted appropriately as financial sensitivity grew.

If the record shows consistent execution but no reassessment, regulators conclude that governance did not engage, even when controls were active throughout the period. This distinction explains why enforcement outcomes often surprise organizations that believed they were well controlled.

From the inside, nothing felt neglected. From the outside, the absence of structured reassessment suggests that risk was allowed to mature without oversight.

The difference is not in effort. It is in design intent.

Controls built to confirm accuracy perform well under stable conditions. Controls designed to govern exposure must also detect when stability becomes risk. Without that second layer, trade programs remain operationally disciplined and structurally fragile.

Fragility at depth does not announce itself.

A diver descending through the first several feet may feel composed. Equipment responds as expected. Breathing is steady. The surface remains visible above. Nothing in those first moments suggests instability.

But the body is already compensating. Pressure increases before the diver feels far from safety. Equalization must occur even when the surface still appears close enough to reach. The diver may not perceive danger, yet the environment has changed.

Trade governance behaves in the same way.

In the early stages of exposure growth, nothing feels urgent. Controls operate. Decisions remain defensible. Documentation is intact. Internal reviews conclude without escalation. The system appears calm.

But consequence is increasing beneath that calm. The organization may still be near the surface operationally—entries filed correctly, reconciliations complete, audit cycles stable—yet financial sensitivity, enforcement attention, or regulatory interest may already be intensifying.

If governance is designed only to react to visible disruption, it engages too late.

Governance requires pressure, and pressure is cumulative.

When governance is tied solely to error detection, it overlooks the more dangerous condition: technically correct decisions applied at materially greater consequence than when governance was first adopted.

This is where control effectiveness and governance effectiveness separate.

One confirms that the system is functioning. The other ensures that the system is still appropriate for the consequence it now carries.

SECTION II

Controls Are Signals: Governance as Structure

Most organizations treat controls as safeguards.

If a control exists, leadership assumes risk is contained. If reviews are performed and documentation is complete, confidence increases. If audit findings are minimal, reassurance hardens into belief.

This assumption is understandable. Controls do prevent errors. They do detect discrepancies. They do correct execution. Over time, organizations associate the presence of controls with protection.

But in trade governance, controls do not function primarily as shields. They function as signals, and every control produces information:

- A reconciliation reveals variance.
- A classification review surfaces interpretive tension.
- A valuation adjustment exposes commercial pressure.
- A post-entry correction signals that assumptions are shifting.

Individually, these signals appear operational. Collectively, they reveal movement inside the system.

Governance exists to interpret those signals.

> *"Controls report what happened.*
> *Governance asks why conditions changed."*

Controls report what happened. Governance asks why conditions changed—and whether responsibility for the resulting exposure still sits in the right place.

Every control reveals how an organization thinks about risk. A classification control that verifies the correct tariff code signals that the organization values technical accuracy. A valuation control that reconciles declared value to pricing data signals that the organization values consistency. An origin review that confirms documentation signals that the organization values defensibility.

All of these signals matter. But none of them, on its own, indicates whether exposure is governed as it evolves.

The distinction becomes visible when consequence changes.

If tariffs increase materially and classification controls do not require reassessment, that absence is a signal. If valuation reconciliations continue without questioning whether commercial shifts have altered dutiability, that continuity is a signal. If origin determinations are documented but not revisited as sourcing migrates incrementally, that stability is a signal.

Controls reveal design intent. They reveal whether the organization built its system to confirm correctness—or to detect changing consequence. From inside the organization, these signals are easy to miss. Control reports feel reassuring. Dashboards remain steady. Review cycles close cleanly. Activity continues.

But regulators read controls differently. They are not asking how frequently a control operated. They are asking what that control was designed to surface.

Was it built to confirm that a decision was applied correctly? Or was it built to signal when that decision required elevation?

This is not a semantic distinction. It is structural.

At depth, instruments do not prevent pressure. They reveal it.

A depth gauge does not stop descent. It makes descent visible. An air gauge does not eliminate air consumption. It signals remaining capacity. These instruments do not protect the diver by themselves. Instead, they inform the diver's judgment.

Trade controls function the same way. They do not eliminate exposure. They make exposure legible—but only if they are designed to do so.

When controls are interpreted as safeguards rather than signals, organizations begin to rely on them as proof that risk is managed. But proof of activity is not proof of governance. A system can operate smoothly while consequence grows around it. This is why programs that feel disciplined internally can appear unmanaged externally.

Internally, the signal being read is activity.

Externally, the signal being read is escalation.

If a control never prompts reassessment as financial sensitivity increases, regulators infer that governance did not adapt. If ownership never shifts as exposure scales, regulators infer that accountability remained static. If escalation thresholds were never tied to consequence, regulators infer that risk was allowed to mature silently.

The control itself may have operated perfectly, but the signal it sent was different than intended.

This is where design becomes decisive.

Controls built solely to prevent error generate reassurance. Controls built to surface consequence generate governance.

The difference is not visible during calm conditions, but it becomes visible when pressure increases.

And once pressure increases, regulators examine not only what controls did but also what they were designed to reveal.

The difference is rarely articulated clearly inside organizations. Yet it determines whether trade risk remains manageable as consequence increases.

Operational controls are familiar. They validate classification accuracy. They reconcile declared value. They confirm origin documentation. They test whether procedures were followed. They detect deviations and correct them.

They sit close to the transaction. They are essential. Without them, trade programs collapse under basic error.

Governance controls operate differently. They do not sit at the transaction level. They sit above it. They are not designed to confirm that a decision was applied correctly. They are designed to detect when the context surrounding that decision has changed.

Governance controls ask questions that operational controls do not:

- When does increasing financial sensitivity require reassessment?
- At what point does cumulative exposure trigger elevation?
- Who owns the decision when consequence expands beyond operational tolerance?
- What mechanism forces reconsideration when conditions shift?

These questions are uncomfortable because their answers are not binary. They do not test for correctness. They test for adequacy over time.

Many organizations assume that governance controls exist implicitly. They rely on experienced professionals to recognize when something "feels different." They trust that leadership will engage if risk becomes material. They assume that if escalation is necessary, it will occur.

But assumption is not structure. And at depth, reliance on professional instinct is insufficient.

A diver does not rely solely on feeling to determine remaining air. Instruments exist to provide information before danger is visible. The absence of instrumentation does not eliminate risk. It eliminates early awareness.

Governance controls function as instrumentation. They tie exposure to thresholds. They connect financial impact to escalation pathways. They define when ownership must shift beyond the trade function. They preserve decision logic so that reassessment is not dependent on memory.

Without governance controls, operational discipline can mask structural fragility.

Consider a classification that has been reviewed, documented, and applied consistently for years. Operational controls confirm its accuracy. Audit cycles validate its application. From a process standpoint, the system is stable.

Now tariffs increase materially on that heading. Volumes scale. The financial impact of that classification multiplies.

If no governance control requires reassessment when duty impact crosses a defined threshold, nothing happens. The classification remains correct, and the control continues to validate it.

Exposure grows, but the absence of escalation is interpreted internally as confirmation that no issue exists. Externally, that absence becomes the issue.

Governance controls would behave differently. They would not assume that technical defensibility is sufficient. They would connect tariff sensitivity to reassessment. They would require documentation that exposure was reconsidered under new conditions. They would define ownership at the point where consequence became material.

This does not mean that the classification would change. Instead, it means that governance would be visible.

The same distinction applies to valuation. Operational controls confirm that declared values align with approved pricing models. They reconcile invoices. They test calculations. They document assists and royalties.

Governance controls ask whether the pricing model still reflects how value is created as business conditions evolve. They connect commercial changes to customs exposure. They require reassessment when cumulative duty impact increases.

Operational control validates arithmetic.

Governance control validates relevance.

This layer is often missing because it is harder to design.

Operational controls are rule-based. Governance controls are threshold-based.

Operational controls confirm compliance with what has been decided. Governance controls interrogate whether what was decided remains appropriate.

The first produces documentation.

The second produces accountability.

When regulators evaluate a trade program under scrutiny, they are not impressed by the density of operational controls. They examine whether governance controls existed—whether there were defined triggers for reassessment, whether ownership shifted appropriately as exposure grew, and whether deliberation was preserved when consequence changed.

If that layer is absent, regulators conclude that governance depended on execution alone.

Execution can be excellent. But without governance controls, it is not sufficient.

At depth, structure must anticipate pressure.

It cannot wait for visible failure.

SECTION III

Pressure Points and Governance Response

Depth does not stress every component equally. Some structures hold longer. Some points absorb pressure quietly. Some areas reveal weakness first.

In trade governance, breakdown rarely occurs randomly. It appears in the same places—across industries, across operating models, and across levels of sophistication.

These are not weak programs. They are pressure points.

And pressure points are predictable. Those pressure points are not abstract. They appear consistently within the core technical structures that organizations rely on most heavily—classification, valuation, origin, tariff response, and post-entry behavior—where operational discipline is strongest, and governance is most likely to fall behind.

Classification: Stability That Masks Consequence

Classification is often the most mature element of a trade program. Organizations invest heavily in expertise. Decisions are documented. Databases are maintained. Reviews occur. Audit results are frequently strong.

Stability creates confidence. Over time, classifications stop feeling like active decisions and begin to feel settled. Institutional knowledge forms around why they were adopted. Escalation decreases because technical defensibility feels sufficient.

Operationally, this maturity is valuable. At depth, it can become brittle.

Classification decisions often remain technically stable while their financial consequence changes dramatically. Tariff regimes shift. Product volumes increase. Market exposure scales. What once carried modest duty impact becomes materially sensitive.

The classification itself may not change, but the risk surrounding it does.

If no governance control connects tariff sensitivity or volume growth to reassessment, then classification becomes the first quiet fracture point.

Operational controls continue to confirm correct application. Reviews validate consistency. Documentation remains intact.

From inside the organization, nothing appears unstable.

From outside, exposure has scaled without visible governance re-engagement.

The signal regulators read is not technical error.

It is structural silence.

Valuation: Accuracy That Obscures Drift

Valuation programs are frequently built on disciplined methodologies. Transfer pricing models are documented. Intercompany agreements exist. Reconciliations occur. Controls confirm alignment between customs declarations and financial systems.

Accuracy becomes the measure of success. At depth, though, accuracy is insufficient.

Valuation risk rarely emerges from arithmetic error. It emerges from economic drift—incremental shifts in commercial reality that outpace the methodology designed to reflect it.

Margins adjust. Manufacturing responsibilities migrate. Royalty structures evolve. Cost allocations shift. None of these changes may appear significant in isolation.

Controls continue to confirm that declared values align with approved models. But if no governance control requires reassessment when economic substance evolves—particularly under increased tariff consequence—valuation becomes a pressure point.

The methodology may remain technically defensible, but its relevance may not.

From inside the organization, continuity feels like discipline.

From outside, continuity can appear as inertia.

Origin: Cumulative Change Without Trigger

Origin determinations often begin with rigorous analysis. Production steps are mapped. Substantial transformation tests are applied. Documentation is preserved.

Once established, origin logic becomes embedded across sourcing, logistics, and commercial planning.

At depth, embedding creates risk.

Supply chains rarely change through singular events. Instead, they evolve incrementally. Inputs shift gradually. Assembly steps migrate. Responsibilities move across entities. No individual change appears material enough to demand reassessment.

Operational controls validate that declared origin aligns with established logic.

Governance controls must ask whether cumulative change has altered that logic.

When no trigger ties incremental sourcing evolution to reassessment, origin becomes another predictable fracture point.

Consistency persists.

Alignment drifts.

Regulators reconstruct that drift longitudinally.

Organizations often do not.

Tariff Response: Speed Over Recalibration

Tariff increases introduce compression quickly. Financial consequence becomes visible. Leadership attention intensifies. Commercial urgency accelerates.

In these moments, organizations move quickly because speed is necessary.

Existing interpretations are reused. Mitigation strategies are implemented. Temporary measures are adopted to preserve continuity.

Often, recalibration fails to follow.

If governance does not require reassessment once urgency stabilizes, crisis-era decisions become normalized. What was intended as interim posture becomes sustained design.

Operational controls confirm execution.

Governance remains paused.

Tariffs do not create fragility.

They reveal it.

Post-Entry Behavior: Correction as Substitution

Post-entry activity often signals maturity. Disclosures are filed. Corrections are made. Adjustments are documented.

Operationally, this activity demonstrates responsiveness.

At depth, correction can substitute for governance. But if issues are resolved transactionally without structural reassessment, exposure persists even though compliance appears active.

Repeated correction without redesign becomes a signal—not of diligence, but of delayed oversight.

Interpreting the Pressure Points

These pressure points are not signs of incompetence. They are signs of missing instrumentation.

At depth, pressure accumulates predictably. The diver who knows where equipment fails first checks those points deliberately. Governance requires the same awareness.

Classification, valuation, origin, tariff response, and post-entry behavior are not random vulnerabilities. They are structural inflection points where operational discipline is most likely to substitute for governance.

When governance controls are absent, these are the first areas regulators examine.

Not because they expect failure, but because depth tests them first.

A Pattern of Accumulation

There is a pattern I have seen more than once.

A company maintains a mature classification program. Decisions are documented. Databases are centralized. Reviews occur periodically. Internal audit confirms consistency. The trade function is respected internally for its technical competence.

Then tariff conditions shift, and a classification that once carried modest duty impact now carries significant financial consequence. The product line tied to that classification scales rapidly. Volumes increase. The revenue tied to that tariff heading becomes material to quarterly performance.

Operationally, nothing changes. The classification remains technically sound. The control that verifies application continues to operate. Audit results remain stable. Entries are filed correctly.

From inside the organization, the system appears disciplined.

At the same time, commercial teams adjust pricing strategies to absorb some of the increased duty burden. The finance group models margin impact. Supply-chain managers explore alternative sourcing, but incremental shifts do not cross internal materiality thresholds. Each change feels manageable in isolation.

What does not occur is formal reassessment of the classification's cumulative exposure under the new tariff environment because no defined governance control requires escalation when financial consequence crosses a specific threshold. No structured trigger forces elevation of the decision beyond the trade function. No documentation captures a reconsideration of whether reliance on that classification remains appropriate under materially different conditions.

Years pass, and the cumulative duty impact tied to that heading grows significantly. What began as modest exposure becomes enterprise-level sensitivity.

Then inquiry begins. It does not start with accusation. It starts with data requests. A broader review period. An interest in cumulative value. A request for internal analysis supporting the classification logic.

The trade function responds confidently. Documentation is provided. The technical rationale remains defensible.

But regulators do not evaluate the decision in isolation. Instead, they reconstruct the timeline. They examine when tariffs increased. They review import volumes over multiple years. They calculate cumulative duty paid. They ask when governance reassessed exposure in light of the new consequence.

The answer, in many cases, is uncomfortable: There was no defined moment of reassessment. There was no formal escalation tied to financial growth. There was no documented evaluation of whether the decision, though technically correct, had become materially sensitive at the enterprise level.

The classification was accurate, but governance never moved.

From the company's perspective, nothing had failed. Controls operated, reviews occurred, and documentation existed.

From the regulator's perspective, exposure matured without visible governance engagement.

The difference is not technical error. It is the absence of structural adaptation.

When multiple factors converge—tariff escalation, volume growth, commercial adjustment, incremental sourcing change—exposure compounds quietly. Each factor remains manageable alone. Together, they alter consequence.

Without governance controls that connect consequence to escalation, organizations descend deeper than they realize.

By the time inquiry formalizes, the reconstruction phase has already begun. And reconstruction is always more expensive than recalibration.

> *"Reconstruction is always more expensive than recalibration."*

Escalation, ownership, and visibility are the mechanisms that transform control frameworks from surface structure into load-bearing infrastructure. Without them, governance appears stable—until it is tested.

Trade governance requires the same discipline.

Escalation, ownership, and visibility are not reactive tools. They are structural checks that determine whether exposure remains governable as pressure builds.

In many organizations, escalation activates only when something goes visibly wrong. A shipment is detained. A regulator requests clarification. An audit identifies a discrepancy. At that moment, leadership becomes aware and response begins.

That is event-driven escalation.

Governance-driven escalation is different. It activates when consequence changes, not when correctness fails. It is triggered when tariff sensitivity increases materially, when cumulative exposure crosses defined thresholds, when assumptions persist beyond the conditions in which they were adopted, or when financial impact scales beyond operational tolerance.

Without defined escalation architecture, organizations rely on intuition. Experienced professionals may sense when something feels different. Conversations may occur informally. Concerns may be raised in meetings. But intuition does not scale, and informal escalation leaves no durable record.

At depth, instinct is not sufficient. Instruments are.

Escalation architecture must answer practical questions:

- Who is notified when exposure increases?
- At what financial threshold does review move beyond operational teams?
- What factors force reassessment even when execution remains technically correct?
- Where is deliberation preserved?

If these questions do not have structural answers, escalation becomes episodic rather than systematic.

Ownership presents a similar vulnerability.

Equipment checks do not depend on memory. They depend on responsibility. Someone confirms air supply. Someone verifies connections. Someone ensures readiness before descent. Accountability is explicit because ambiguity under pressure is dangerous.

Trade governance often lacks that clarity. Classification may reside with the trade function. Valuation may sit within the finance or tax group. Origin may be managed regionally. Under stable conditions, this distribution functions adequately. As consequence increases, though, diffusion becomes fragility.

When tariff impact doubles, who owns reassessment? When commercial models evolve under higher duty consequence, who carries accountability? When cumulative sourcing changes alter exposure trajectory, who is responsible for elevating that recognition?

If ownership shifts implicitly rather than deliberately, governance fragments quietly. Responsibility becomes shared, which often means that responsibility becomes diluted.

Regulators do not evaluate participation. They look for identifiable accountability. They expect that as exposure becomes material, ownership becomes visible at the appropriate level.

Ownership must also be durable. Trade decisions often outlive the individuals who made them. Governance that depends on personal vigilance dissolves with turnover. Durable ownership requires that decision logic, reassessment triggers, and escalation pathways survive leadership change.

Visibility is the glue that binds escalation and ownership together. Escalation without visibility is invisible governance. Ownership without visibility is isolated responsibility.

At depth, gauges are monitored continuously—not because something is wrong, but because remaining capacity, orientation, and pressure must be understood before urgency arrives. Awareness is continuous, not episodic.

Trade exposure requires the same visibility.

Boards do not need to understand tariff codes in detail. They need to understand when exposure has become financially material. They need clarity regarding when reassessment occurred, who owns that exposure, what assumptions remain unresolved, and whether escalation thresholds were triggered appropriately.

If that information remains within the operational layer, governance remains local. Local governance cannot manage enterprise-level consequence.

This is where many trade programs fracture quietly. Controls operate. Reviews occur. Corrections are made when necessary. The system appears disciplined. Yet escalation is tied to error rather than consequence. Ownership is implied rather than assigned. Visibility is limited to operational metrics rather than exposure trajectory.

From inside the organization, the program feels managed.

From outside, it appears that governance never truly engaged.

Escalation, ownership, and visibility are not enhancements to trade controls. They are the structural spine that determines whether controls function as infrastructure or documentation.

When designed intentionally, they create confidence grounded in awareness rather than reassurance. They ensure that as pressure increases, governance adapts. They allow exposure to be seen before it hardens.

Without them, organizations descend relying on operational discipline alone.

Operational discipline performs well in calm conditions.

At depth, awareness determines survivability.

SECTION IV

What Boards Need

Boards do not govern trade risk by mastering technical detail. They govern trade risk by ensuring that structure adapts as consequence increases.

This distinction matters.

Most boards receive reassurance. They are told that controls exist, that audits are clean, that reviews occur regularly, and that no material findings have surfaced. Those statements may be accurate. They may reflect diligent operational performance. They do not, by themselves, demonstrate governability.

Boards do not need classification summaries. They do not need valuation spreadsheets. They do not need origin documentation.

What they need is visibility into exposure trajectory—for example, when trade consequence has changed materially, when assumptions were reassessed under new conditions, who owns that reassessment, and whether escalation occurred at the appropriate threshold.

Without that visibility, oversight becomes passive, and passive oversight is not governance.

Governance requires the ability to intervene before consequence hardens. That ability depends on information designed to surface change, not merely confirm stability.

When controls function as infrastructure, boards see movement early. They see exposure scaling. They see when escalation was triggered. They see when ownership shifted. They see where reassessment occurred. They see what assumptions remain open.

They are not burdened with technical detail. Instead, they are equipped with the structural awareness they need. This awareness changes how regulatory scrutiny unfolds.

Regulators do not expect boards to be technical experts. They expect boards to demonstrate that trade exposure was visible at the appropriate level as it evolved. They expect to see evidence that governance engaged proportionately as consequence increased.

Where that visibility exists, scrutiny becomes dialogue. Where it does not, scrutiny becomes reconstruction.

Reconstruction is expensive. It requires explaining why exposure matured without escalation. It requires documenting conversations that were never formally captured. It requires justifying why assumptions persisted beyond the conditions in which they were adopted.

Boards rarely realize that the absence of structured visibility is interpreted as a design choice. If exposure increased materially and the board was never informed, regulators do not assume ignorance. They infer that governance architecture did not require awareness.

This is why control design matters at the board level.

Controls that surface exposure, trigger escalation, preserve accountability, and translate technical decisions into consequence narratives function as infrastructure. Controls that merely confirm execution function as compliance artifacts. This difference becomes visible under pressure.

Boards do not need more reports. They need different signals.

They need to see when trade exposure is becoming enterprise-level risk. They need to understand when reassessment was required—and whether it occurred. They need clarity on who owns the decision when consequence scales.

That is what governance looks like at depth.

When that structure exists, organizations do not avoid scrutiny. They withstand it.

When it does not, confidence collapses at the moment it is tested.

Trade expertise matters. Operational discipline matters. But without escalation, ownership, and visibility designed intentionally, expertise remains local and discipline remains transactional.

Governance requires structure that carries weight as consequence increases.

This is the point in the descent where reassurance is no longer enough.

Structure must hold.

Infrastructure alone does not govern exposure. It creates the conditions in which governance can occur.

The true test emerges when pressure requires decisions in real time—when leaders must choose whether to elevate, reassess, defend, disclose, or redesign under compressed timelines and visible consequence.

Structure determines what is possible.

Judgment determines what actually happens.

At depth, even well-designed infrastructure depends on disciplined leadership.

The next chapter examines what happens when that judgment is tested under pressure.

CHAPTER 6

Decision-Making Under Pressure

Pressure alters how the body responds long before the diver consciously recognizes it. Movements that felt controlled just moments earlier require greater focus. Attention narrows. Decisions must be made more quickly, often with less clarity than the diver would prefer.

Governance behaves the same way under pressure.

Governance is easy to believe in when nothing is forcing it to choose. In stable conditions, trade programs feel deliberate. Decisions move through defined channels. Controls operate. Escalation paths exist. Documentation accumulates. The organization experiences continuity and calls it control.

But calm water is not proof of readiness. At depth, pressure changes how quickly decisions must be made and how much consequence attaches to them. Time compresses. Options narrow. The margin for hesitation shrinks. The question is no longer simply what is technically correct. It becomes "What preserves continuity without amplifying risk?"

In those moments, organizations do not construct governance. They reveal it.

> *"In those moments, organizations do not construct governance. They reveal it."*

Some discover that structure holds and activates proportionately. Others discover that structure bends toward speed. The difference is rarely visible until urgency arrives.

This chapter examines that moment—not the failure of rules or the absence of expertise, but the shift that occurs when pressure forces judgment to accelerate faster than governance was designed to accommodate.

At depth, breathing changes before awareness does.

Decision-making under pressure behaves the same way.

SECTION I

Pressure Reveals Design

Trade programs are not truly tested in steady conditions. They are tested when pressure accelerates decisions faster than governance can comfortably convene.

Under ordinary circumstances, trade decisions unfold methodically. Classification reviews occur within defined cycles. Valuation methodologies are revisited through scheduled governance channels. Origin determinations are reconsidered when sourcing changes are identified. Controls operate predictably, and escalation follows recognizable paths.

Pressure disrupts that cadence. Tariffs shift abruptly. Geopolitical events force rapid sourcing changes. Enforcement priorities intensify without advance notice. Commercial leadership demands immediate clarity on exposure and cost. The time available for deliberation contracts, even as the financial consequence of error expands.

The organization feels the compression.

At depth, compression does not announce itself dramatically. Instead, it alters breathing and narrows peripheral awareness. It increases urgency without always increasing clarity. Judgment begins to prioritize movement over reflection.

Decision-making under pressure follows the same pattern. When urgency increases, organizations default to what is already embedded. They rely on prior interpretations. They reuse precedent. They trust institutional memory. They assume that what was reasonable yesterday remains reasonable today.

This instinct is not reckless. It reflects experience and confidence earned through prior success. But pressure changes the meaning of continuity. A classification that once carried modest financial impact may, under a new tariff regime, become material. A valuation assumption developed under stable commercial conditions may operate differently when margins tighten. An origin determination that once sat comfortably within tolerance may shift significance as enforcement attention intensifies.

If governance has been deliberately designed to recognize these inflection points, pressure activates it.

If governance has been assumed rather than structured, pressure bypasses it.

Audits do not expose this distinction easily. Rather, audits test whether controls function under controlled conditions. They examine whether documented processes are followed and whether execution aligns with expectation.

Pressure tests something else entirely: whether governance adapts in real time.

When trade risk escalates quickly, organizations do not pause to redesign ownership or redefine escalation thresholds. They rely on whatever structure already exists. If escalation criteria were exposure-based before disruption, they remain exposure-based during disruption. If ownership was clear before urgency, it remains clear when urgency intensifies.

If neither existed, pressure does not create them. This is why many trade programs appear robust during audit cycles yet fracture during prolonged disruption. Operational controls continue to validate execution. Documentation continues to accumulate. Activity remains visible.

What may not re-engage is structured reconsideration.

Under pressure, organizations frequently frame decisions as temporary. A classification interpretation is adopted "until clarity emerges." A valuation assumption is carried forward "for the current environment." A sourcing workaround is implemented "to maintain continuity."

These decisions feel reversible, and they are often technically defensible. They are justified by urgency and accompanied by an implicit promise of future reconsideration.

What is frequently absent is a mechanism ensuring that reconsideration occurs. Controls confirm that the temporary decision is being applied consistently. Escalation quiets once immediate disruption subsides. The decision persists because nothing forces it to be reopened.

By the time urgency fades, something has shifted—not through deliberate redesign, but through endurance.

Every organization has a decision velocity. Few have a governance velocity calibrated to match it.

When trade decisions accelerate faster than governance can respond, structure fails silently. Controls keep pace with execution, documentation accumulates, and activity remains visible. What lags is structured pause.

From inside the organization, continuity signals resilience.

From outside, it can signal something very different.

When regulators later reconstruct decisions made under pressure, they do not dismiss urgency. They understand disruption and recognize commercial constraint. What they evaluate is whether governance adapted as consequence increased.

They reconstruct the period longitudinally and ask:

- Who owned the decision as exposure scaled?
- When were assumptions revisited?

- What triggered escalation?
- How was risk tolerance reassessed?
- Where is the record of deliberation under constraint?

Pressure does not excuse governance failure.

It reveals whether governance was designed to withstand it.

SECTION II

The Instinct to Preserve Continuity

Pressure rarely produces chaos. Instead, it produces narrowing.

When disruption enters a trade program, continuity becomes the organizing instinct. Supply chains cannot stop. Customers expect delivery. Financial commitments have already been made. Leaders are not searching for theoretical precision. They are searching for stability.

In the moment, all of this feels responsible.

At depth, narrowing vision is not a sign of failure. It is a physiological response. Attention contracts toward what feels immediately necessary. Peripheral awareness diminishes. The diver focuses on breathing, orientation, and immediate movement.

Organizations behave the same way under sustained pressure. They do not stop managing risk. They reorder it.

This reordering often resembles triage, even if it is never described that way. Risks are sorted instinctively into two categories: those that threaten immediate continuity and those that can be managed later. The risks that halt operations rise to the top. The risks that unfold gradually fall lower on the list. Trade risk lives comfortably in the second category.

Classification sensitivity rarely stops shipments in the moment. Valuation assumptions rarely prevent delivery tomorrow. Origin implications often remain technically defensible in the short term. Tariff exposure accumulates quietly rather than explosively. As a result, trade exposure is deprioritized—not because it is unimportant, but because it does not demand instant resolution.

This is not negligence. It is survival logic.

Under pressure, leaders ask different questions. Instead of asking whether a decision remains appropriate under new conditions, they ask whether it creates friction. Instead of reassessing assumptions, they ask whether execution can continue. Instead of escalating exposure, they ask whether disruption can be avoided.

Controls support this narrowing. They confirm that decisions are being applied consistently. They reassure leadership that nothing has failed. They provide visible evidence that systems remain intact.

Governance, which depends on reconsideration rather than ranking, struggles to assert itself in this environment. Meanwhile, the organization believes it is managing risk responsibly. What it may not recognize is that prioritization is not the same as governance. Governance requires moments of deliberate pause—moments where continuity is questioned rather than preserved.

Under compression, pause feels irresponsible and speed feels prudent.

This is where the shift from deliberate reconsideration to continuity preservation begins.

When decisions are made to protect continuity, they are often framed as provisional. An interpretation is carried forward for now. A valuation approach is maintained while clarity is sought. A sourcing decision is implemented to stabilize operations.

The language is temporary, but the structure rarely is. Unless governance contains a defined return point—a mechanism that requires the organization to step back once stability returns—the provisional decision persists.

Temporary logic becomes standing logic—not because it was affirmed, but because it endured.

The longer triage persists, the more it normalizes. Urgency becomes background noise. The compressed decision-making environment becomes routine. Teams grow comfortable operating within it. Leadership confidence stabilizes, and nothing feels unstable.

From inside the organization, this period is remembered as one of competence and resilience.

From outside, it can appear as something else entirely: a prolonged absence of deliberate reconsideration.

At depth, the body adapts to pressure gradually. Breathing becomes automatic. The sensation of compression becomes familiar. The diver may not consciously register how far descent has continued.

Organizations adapt the same way.

Continuity, once an emergency priority, becomes default behavior.

And governance, if not deliberately reactivated, recedes quietly into the background.

This pattern becomes most visible when organizations face sustained disruption.

A Decision Under Pressure[1]

I have seen this pattern most clearly when organizations enter sustained periods of disruption.

For example, one company believed its trade program was mature and well governed. Prior rulings had been requested, interpretive positions had been accepted, and controls were documented and functioning. Leadership had confidence that decisions were being handled responsibly.

When a new issue emerged—one that appeared adjacent to positions previously defended successfully—the organization responded in the way capable organizations do. It relied on precedent, reusing logic that had held before. Teams assembled documentation quickly, citing prior approvals and technical rationale. Meetings were efficient. Responses were coordinated. Nothing felt improvised.

From the inside, this felt disciplined. No one believed additional risk was being introduced. They were preserving continuity using already-tested decisions.

When regulators questioned the position, the response was immediate and professional. Documentation was refined, arguments strengthened. Leadership was reassured that governance was functioning as designed.

Then the framing shifted. The regulator was not challenging effort or technical reasoning. Instead, the question broadened: Had the organization reconsidered the decision as conditions evolved?

Tariff exposure had increased, volumes had scaled, and enforcement attention had intensified. What had once been proportionate had become materially sensitive.

The organization realized something uncomfortable: It had governed the response. It had never deliberately re-governed the decision itself.

Precedent had become reliance. Reliance had become continuity. Continuity had never been formally re-evaluated.

From the company's perspective, the realization that the decision had never been re-governed felt like surprise.

From the regulator's perspective, it appeared as endurance without structured reassessment.

The difference between those perspectives defined the outcome.

Pressure had not produced a reckless decision.

It had produced a reasonable one that was never deliberately revisited.

[1]Composite example drawn from multiple regulatory engagements.

SECTION III

When Defense Becomes Endurance

Pressure does not usually produce reckless decisions. It produces accelerated ones.

I have seen this effect most clearly in valuation disputes that unfold across years rather than weeks.

A global company operating through related-party transactions believes its valuation methodology is mature and defensible. Transfer pricing policies are documented and aligned with tax. Intercompany agreements are formalized. Assists have been evaluated. Royalties have been addressed. Internal controls demonstrate reasonable care. The methodology has been reviewed previously and sustained without material finding.

From the company's perspective, the structure is sound. Then a customs authority challenges transaction value, asserting that the related-party relationship may influence price.

The organization responds quickly and seriously. Trade professionals assemble comparables. Pricing logic is explained. Arm's-length principles are demonstrated. Internal meetings intensify. Leadership is briefed. External advisors may be consulted. The response is disciplined.

Sometimes the authority accepts the explanation. Sometimes it does not. When the authority insists on adjustment, the organization faces a consequential choice.

Altering valuation methodology globally is not a narrow correction. It affects systems, tax alignment, pricing structures, margins, and contractual relationships. It introduces uncertainty in jurisdictions that have not raised concerns. It creates commercial implications beyond customs.

Maintaining the existing methodology can feel not only defensible but also responsible. As a result, the organization holds its position. Not because it is dismissing risk, but because it believes the position is correct.

Time passes. The dispute stabilizes. Operations continue. Documentation becomes more robust. Arguments are refined. Trade teams grow increasingly adept at explaining the structure. Controls validate consistent application. Leadership regains confidence. Nothing appears unstable.

This is the inflection point.

The organization no longer experiences the methodology as a temporary decision under scrutiny. Instead, it becomes the standing approach—defended when necessary, supported by prior analysis, reinforced by experience.

No formal resolution is adopted to affirm permanence. It simply continues.

At depth, adaptation to pressure feels normal. Breathing stabilizes, movement resumes, and the body adjusts without conscious recognition of continued descent.

Organizations adapt the same way.

What began as a response becomes routine. What was once actively reconsidered becomes quietly assumed. The effort shifts from asking whether the approach should change to refining how it is defended.

This distinction is subtle but consequential.

Defense feels like governance because effort is visible. Meetings occur. Documentation is updated. Experts remain engaged.

Reconsideration requires something different: a deliberate return—a moment where the organization asks, under materially different conditions, whether it would adopt the same approach today.

That moment rarely occurs unless structure forces it.

Years later, when regulators reconstruct the timeline, they do not focus solely on the initial challenge. They map cumulative duty impact. They examine how long the approach endured. They evaluate whether escalation occurred as financial sensitivity increased. They look for evidence that governance re-engaged once urgency subsided.

If that record does not exist, they infer that endurance replaced reconsideration—a conclusion that comes as a surprise to the organization.

From the regulator's perspective, endurance appears as continuity without structured reassessment.

Pressure did not create the risk.

Endurance preserved it.

SECTION IV

The Moment Drift Becomes Visible

Drift rarely announces itself inside the organization.

By the time leadership feels confident in its approach, execution has stabilized. Controls function predictably. Trade teams know how to defend decisions. Responses to inquiry feel measured and professional. The organization experiences continuity and interprets it as stability.

Visibility almost never begins here. Instead, it begins when an external actor reconstructs a pattern the organization never examined as a whole.

Internally, trade decisions are experienced as discrete responses: a valuation inquiry here, a classification clarification there, an origin review in another jurisdiction. Each moment feels bounded and reasonable. Each is addressed with effort and expertise. Each is supported by documentation.

Externally, those same moments are evaluated differently. Regulators do not experience them as isolated events. They reconstruct duration and map repetition. They examine how decisions persisted across time, regions, and shifting conditions. They analyze whether governance re-engaged as exposure evolved.

What they often identify is not technical error. It is endurance without documented reconsideration. This is the moment drift becomes visible.

From inside the organization, this realization can feel jarring. Leaders remember effort. They remember disciplined responses. They remember the context of urgency. They remember the meetings, the analysis, the documentation. What they do not always see is the absence of a deliberate return point.

At depth, a diver may not feel continued descent immediately. The body adapts to pressure gradually. Breathing stabilizes, and orientation feels steady. The environment does not appear dramatically different from a few moments earlier. The descent continues anyway.

Organizations adapt the same way. Continuity feels safe because nothing is visibly failing. Controls validate execution. Audit cycles close without catastrophe. Shipments continue. Duties are paid. Nothing stops the line.

What is missing is a structural pause—a moment where governance deliberately steps back and asks whether the conditions that justified prior decisions still exist.

External review reframes the timeline. Regulators do not ask whether the organization believed it was correct at the time. They ask whether it reconsidered its assumptions as circumstances evolved. They examine cumulative exposure and look for escalation tied to financial growth. They search for documentation showing that governance re-engaged once urgency stabilized.

When that evidence is absent, silence becomes interpretive—not silence as inactivity, but silence as absence of reassessment.

Periods without change are not interpreted as periods without risk. They are interpreted as periods where governance did not require change.

This distinction surprises organizations. Internally, consistency is often viewed as discipline. Externally, consistency without visible reconsideration can appear as rigidity.

The difference lies in perspective.

From inside, the organization made a series of reasonable decisions made under constraint. From outside, regulators see an enduring approach that continued despite increasing exposure and an evolving enforcement climate.

Neither perspective is entirely wrong, but once drift becomes visible externally, the conversation changes. The organization is no longer defending the quality of individual decisions. It is defending the absence of structured re-decision.

What makes this situation more dangerous than it first appears is not the decision itself. Instead, it is the way pressure rewrites language. Under compression, the vocabulary of governance narrows.

"Material" becomes "manageable." "Reassessment" becomes "later." "Escalation" becomes "if necessary."

Risk tolerance does not expand explicitly. It stretches incrementally.

Leaders do not announce that standards are shifting. They describe decisions as pragmatic. They frame continuity as stability. They describe endurance as evidence of correctness. These descriptions are not irrational. They are context-driven.

At depth, the body adapts to pressure so gradually that the diver may not perceive how far descent has continued. The sensation of compression becomes familiar. What once felt intense begins to feel normal.

Organizations adapt in the same way. A decision made under constraint feels temporary. When that constraint persists, the decision feels durable. When the decision endures without visible failure, it begins to feel validated.

The shift from provisional to permanent rarely includes a deliberate moment of affirmation. Instead, it occurs through repetition. And repetition carries psychological weight.

Every time a decision survives scrutiny, confidence increases. Every time a regulator does not escalate further, reassurance grows. Every quarter that passes without disruption strengthens the belief that the original judgment was sound.

The organization does not feel reckless. It feels experienced.

This is precisely where risk hardens.

Because governance was designed to respond to error, not endurance. When risk accumulates quietly, when decisions remain technically defensible, and when disruption does not occur immediately, governance does not experience the urgency that would trigger reconsideration.

The absence of visible failure becomes evidence of alignment.

But endurance is not alignment. It is duration. And duration under changing conditions is where exposure compounds.

This dynamic is dangerous because it produces confidence without recalibration.

The organization believes it understands its risk.

The regulator later evaluates whether the organization understood how its risk evolved.

This is the inflection point where the reader should begin to feel uneasy. Because nothing described here is dramatic, and nothing involves fraud or neglect. Endurance involves reasonable people making defensible decisions under pressure—but never deliberately returning to re-evaluate them once the pressure normalized.

That is how technically correct decisions become structurally fragile.

Not because regulators assume bad faith, but because they are evaluating governability over time.

Pressure did not create the exposure. Duration made it apparent. And when duration becomes the lens, governance is measured not by effort, but by whether it deliberately returned to re-evaluate its own assumptions.

What this often looks like over twenty-four months is not collapse but rather continuity.

Month one begins with disruption: a tariff shift, a regulatory challenge, a sourcing constraint, a commercial deadline. The organization responds with urgency. Teams assemble. Documentation is refined. Advisors are consulted. Leadership is briefed. The objective is stability.

In this first phase, governance feels active. Decisions are deliberate and effort is visible. The organization believes it is managing risk responsibly.

By month three, the immediate disruption has stabilized. The decision made under pressure is now operational. Controls have been updated to reflect the approach. Communication has quieted. The issue is no longer urgent, but it remains present.

At this stage, the organization tells itself a reasonable story: The decision has held. Nothing catastrophic occurred. The approach appears workable, and no one feels compelled to revisit it.

By month nine, the context surrounding the decision has evolved. Volumes may have increased. Financial sensitivity may have expanded. Enforcement attention may have shifted across jurisdictions. The decision remains technically defensible.

It is also now embedded. Systems reflect it. Training reinforces it. Internal explanations have been standardized. What began as a response is now how the organization operates.

The fact that it endured becomes informal evidence of its validity.

By month eighteen, the original urgency that prompted the decision is barely remembered. Personnel may have changed. Leadership has shifted its focus to new priorities. The decision exists not as an active choice, but as inherited design.

No one consciously adopted it as permanent. It simply was not reexamined.

By month twenty-four, cumulative exposure tied to that decision may be materially different from the organization's exposure during the first month. Financial impact has compounded. Regulatory environments have continued to evolve. The organization's commercial footprint may have expanded.

From inside the enterprise, nothing feels unstable. Controls continue to operate. Reviews confirm consistent application. There are no alarms.

From outside, the timeline tells a different story. Regulators do not see month one in isolation. They see twenty-four months of continuity. They map duty impact across that period. They examine whether escalation occurred as consequence increased. They evaluate whether leadership reconsidered the decision once the emergency phase ended. When the record does not show that return, endurance becomes evidence.

This is what makes the dynamic so difficult to detect internally. No single month feels irresponsible. No single decision appears reckless. It is the accumulation across time—under changing conditions—that transforms a defensible response into structural exposure.

The organization remembers urgency. The regulator measures duration.

Those perspectives rarely align.

And the longer duration persists without deliberate reconsideration, the harder it becomes to distinguish confidence from overextension.

This is not collapse. It is descent without recalibration.

And descent without recalibration eventually reaches depth whether the organization feels it or not.

SECTION V

Designing the Return

What separates organizations that endure pressure from those that drift quietly forward is not expertise.

It is design.

Governance that survives compression is not reactive. It anticipates that urgency will distort judgment, that continuity will feel responsible, and that duration will quietly validate decisions that were never deliberately reaffirmed.

It builds a return.

That return is not automatic. It does not occur because disruption fades, because operations stabilize, or because leaders regain confidence. It occurs because governance requires it.

Structural design is the first layer.

Escalation triggers must activate not only when disruption begins, but also when it stabilizes. Exposure thresholds must be tied to financial consequence, not simply error detection. Decisions made under constraint must carry expiration mechanisms—that is, defined moments when they must be revisited, even if nothing appears broken.

Without structural triggers, reconsideration depends on memory. Memory is not durable governance.

Leadership discipline is the second layer.

Under pressure, leaders naturally prioritize continuity. That instinct is not flawed. It is necessary.

What distinguishes disciplined governance is the willingness to re-open decisions once stability returns. That requires asking uncomfortable questions:

- Would we adopt this position today under current conditions?
- Has cumulative exposure altered our risk tolerance?
- Has duration itself changed the nature of this decision?

Answering those questions takes time. It requires slowing momentum deliberately. It also demands leadership willing to risk short-term discomfort in exchange for long-term alignment.

Pressure compresses time. Governance must deliberately create space.

The board expectation is the third layer.

Boards do not need technical detail to govern effectively. They need evidence that reconsideration occurs deliberately and proportionately as exposure evolves. They need to see that decisions made under constraint are not allowed to harden without review. They need clarity regarding who owns that reconsideration. They need documentation that shows when leadership re-engaged, not simply when it defended.

When boards expect that visibility, organizations design for it.

When boards accept continuity as proof of stability, governance remains local.

This is where the descent metaphor becomes unavoidable.

At depth, equipment checks do not end once entry is complete. They continue. Gauges are monitored, air consumption is recalculated, and depth is tracked. The diver does not assume that because the first few minutes felt controlled, the remainder of the descent requires no adjustment.

Governance requires the same vigilance.

The danger is not the emergency moment. It is the period after the emergency, when confidence returns and urgency fades.

This is where many organizations drift downward without noticing.

Designing governance that holds under pressure means institutionalizing the return. It means embedding reassessment as a requirement rather than an option. It means connecting financial scaling to governance engagement. It means ensuring that exposure growth triggers visibility beyond the operational layer.

It also means recognizing that endurance is not validation.

Duration under changing conditions must prompt deliberate re-decision.

Without that discipline, even technically sound decisions accumulate risk quietly. Trade exposure rarely collapses suddenly. Instead, it compounds. And compounding risk, once visible externally, is far more difficult to manage than it would have been earlier.

Pressure does not create governance failure. It reveals whether governance was designed to return.

Organizations that hold under pressure are not those that avoid disruption. They are those that treat disruption as the beginning of a governance cycle, not the end of one.

They respond. They stabilize. And then they deliberately reconsider.

That reconsideration is what separates endurance from alignment.

It is what distinguishes resilience from rigidity.

It is what prevents temporary logic from becoming inherited structure.

And it is what ensures that when exposure finally surfaces—as it inevitably does—the organization is not defending duration, but rather demonstrating deliberate governance.

This dynamic is particularly dangerous because the organization rarely experiences it as risk accumulation. Instead, it experiences it as maturity. The trade function becomes more adept at defending decisions. Documentation improves. Responses to inquiry become faster and more precise. Leadership grows comfortable explaining exposure in consistent language. What once felt fragile begins to feel stable.

Competence increases, and exposure increases with it.

That pairing is deceptive because skill in defense can mask the need for reconsideration. When teams become proficient at explaining why a decision remains defensible, they can unintentionally reduce the likelihood that anyone asks whether it should continue at all. The energy of governance shifts toward preservation rather than reevaluation.

This shift is subtle.

It sounds like confidence. It feels like professionalism. It reads like stability in board summaries. But over time, it produces structural inertia.

Inertia is rarely visible while momentum continues forward. It is visible only when an external force interrupts it.

In trade governance, that interruption often comes through enforcement escalation, multi-year review expansion, or cross-jurisdictional alignment of regulatory focus. By the time these events occur, the internal narrative has solidified. The organization no longer remembers the decision as provisional. It remembers it as justified.

The original constraint fades from memory. The context that made urgency necessary is no longer salient. What remains is the structure that endured.

This is where another distortion enters.

Duration begins to be mistaken for validation: If the decision were materially flawed, it would have failed by now. If regulators were deeply concerned, they would have escalated earlier. If exposure were truly intolerable, we would have seen disruption.

These conclusions feel logical, but they are incomplete. Trade exposure does not behave like operational failure. It does not stop production immediately. It does not announce its compounding impact with visible breakdown. It accumulates in the background, often across fiscal years, leadership transitions, and changing commercial conditions.

What appears stable can be growing more sensitive with every quarter. This sensitivity is not always visible in control reports.

This is where governance requires a different form of courage. Not the courage to defend a decision under pressure, but the courage to reopen a defensible decision when nothing is forcing it to be reopened.

That is a different discipline entirely. It requires leaders to question success. It requires boards to ask whether endurance reflects alignment or simply absence of challenge. It requires trade professionals to say, "We may be correct, but conditions have changed."

Without that discipline, organizations create what appears to be steady ground. In reality, they are descending gradually into deeper exposure.

At depth, descent is not dramatic. It is incremental. The diver may still see light above. The surface may still feel within reach. Orientation may remain intact. But air consumption increases with depth. Margin narrows, and the distance to safety expands quietly.

Trade exposure behaves the same way.

As financial impact scales, as enforcement attention shifts, and as regulatory coordination increases globally, the cost of reversal grows. What could have been recalibrated early becomes expensive to unwind later. What could have been escalated locally becomes enterprise-level risk.

And when the moment finally arrives—when exposure is formally quantified, when scrutiny broadens, when leadership must answer for cumulative duration—the organization is no longer debating a single decision. It is defending a pattern, and patterns are harder to defend than positions because patterns imply governance over time.

This is why designing the return is not optional. It is protective. It prevents endurance from becoming evidence, and it ensures that duration reflects deliberate reaffirmation rather than passive continuation. It transforms governance from reactive defense into active recalibration.

Without it, pressure leaves behind something more dangerous than error.

It leaves behind confidence.

"Confidence without structured reconsideration is the most resilient form of drift."

Confidence without structured reconsideration is the most resilient form of drift. It is quiet, professional, and well-documented. And it is often recognized only when exposure finally surfaces in a form that can no longer be reframed as manageable.

That is the layer beneath pressure: not chaos, not negligence, but steady descent reinforced by competence.

Pressure does not end when the moment passes. It leaves behind the decisions made within it.

Governance is not measured by how organizations respond during disruption. It is measured by whether they deliberately return to those decisions once stability returns.

Without that return, continuity becomes endurance. Endurance becomes structure, and structure quietly carries the organization deeper than it realizes.

That is how exposure matures.

Not through recklessness, but through competence that was never deliberately revisited.

CHAPTER 7

When Confidence Meets Consequence

At depth, the diver may feel composed.

Breathing stabilizes. Movement feels controlled. The descent that once required attention now feels routine. The environment seems understood. Then the diver checks the depth gauge, and suddenly the descent has a number.

> *"Exposure does not become dangerous when a decision is made. It becomes dangerous when it becomes visible."*

Exposure behaves the same way.

Exposure does not become dangerous when a decision is made. It becomes dangerous when it becomes visible.

The prior chapters—on drift, continuity, endurance—have described how risk forms. What has not yet appeared is consequence.

For most organizations, consequence does not arrive as accusation. It arrives as a number. And when that number appears, it reframes everything that came before it.

Until that moment, governance is experienced internally as activity. Decisions are debated, and expertise is applied. Controls function and documentation exists. Positions are defended. Confidence builds because nothing has failed.

Then the number appears: not as theory, not as interpretation, but as quantified exposure. And in that moment, the conversation changes.

This chapter is not about a mistake. It is about the moment when accumulation becomes undeniable—when governance that once felt present is measured against material exposure.

That moment is defining.

It does not merely challenge a technical decision. It reframes responsibility.

Confidence, when untested, feels disciplined.

Confidence, when quantified, becomes something else.

And once consequence enters the room, governance is no longer theoretical.

It is visible.

SECTION I

The Illusion of Contained Risk

For most organizations, trade risk does not feel dangerous while it is forming. Instead, it feels managed.

Decisions are made deliberately. When questions arise, they are answered. When challenges occur, they are addressed. From the inside, the organization experiences trade risk as a series of discrete, technical issues, with each one handled competently by capable professionals.

This creates the powerful illusion that risk is contained because it is understood.

This illusion is reinforced because trade risk rarely announces itself in a way that demands immediate attention. Classifications do not collapse overnight. Valuation methodologies do not fail loudly. Tariff exposure accumulates incrementally. Each decision, viewed on its own, appears reasonable. Each response feels proportionate.

The organization does not experience risk as something growing. It experiences risk as something recurring.

That distinction matters.

When risk is experienced episodically, governance tends to follow suit. Decisions are evaluated individually and responses are scoped narrowly. Escalation occurs when a particular issue appears significant enough to warrant it. Once resolved, attention moves on.

From inside the organization, this feels like discipline. Leaders believe they are allocating attention appropriately. Trade professionals believe they are exercising judgment responsibly. Controls provide reassurance that decisions are being applied consistently. Nothing appears out of control.

What is often missing in this picture is aggregation.

Trade risk is distributed by design. It lives across jurisdictions, products, entities, and time. It does not concentrate itself neatly in one place. As a result, no single decision feels large enough to command sustained governance attention. Exposure forms not through one incorrect choice, but through many defensible ones that endure.

That endurance rarely triggers concern internally. Instead, it often reinforces confidence.

This is why trade risk so often escapes early governance scrutiny. Each decision is evaluated for correctness, but few are evaluated for endurance.

As long as decisions continue to be defensible, escalation feels unnecessary. As long as controls function, governance feels present. As long as operations continue, leadership confidence grows. The organization believes it knows where its risk is because nothing has forced it to see otherwise.

In my experience, this is not a failure of awareness. It is a failure of perspective.

Trade teams are trained to resolve issues. Finance teams are trained to measure outcomes. Governance requires something different: the ability to step back and ask whether a collection of reasonable decisions has quietly become an unreasonable exposure.

Most organizations never ask that question until someone else does, usually unexpectedly.

What follows in this chapter is not a story about a bad decision. It is a story about how good decisions—made under pressure, defended competently, and left unexamined over time—can accumulate into material financial exposure without ever feeling risky along the way.

The illusion does not break when the decision is made.

It breaks when the exposure is finally seen.

SECTION II

Why Exposure Is Discovered Financially, Not Operationally

By the time trade risk becomes visible, it is almost never discovered by the trade function.

Instead, it is discovered financially.

This is one of the most counterintuitive realities of governing trade risk—and one of the reasons it so often reaches senior leadership late. Trade exposure does not usually announce itself through failed controls, stopped shipments, or obvious operational breakdowns. It surfaces when numbers no longer reconcile, when reserves must be established, or when a previously theoretical risk crystallizes into a quantified obligation.

In my experience, this does not occur because trade professionals fail to see risk developing. It is because trade risk accumulates in places that organizations are not structurally designed to watch.

Trade risk does not behave like other operational risk. In fact, most executives are accustomed to risks that announce themselves operationally. For example, production issues disrupt output. Logistics failures delay delivery. Quality problems generate returns. These risks are loud. They trigger immediate response because they interfere with the organization's ability to function day-to-day.

Trade risk behaves differently. Classification decisions do not interrupt shipment flow. Valuation methodologies do not halt production. Tariff exposure does not stop goods from crossing borders. Origin determinations do not break systems when they are wrong—instead, they quietly persist.

As a result, trade exposure grows without generating the kinds of operational signals leadership is trained to respond to. Nothing feels broken.

Because trade risk accumulates silently, it is often the finance function—not the trade function—that encounters it first. This usually happens in one of three ways:

- A reserve must be established for a potential assessment.
- A multi-period exposure is quantified during audit or diligence.
- A regulatory position forces retroactive adjustment.

In each case, the exposure has existed for some time. What is new is not the risk. It is the visibility.

When that moment arrives, leadership is often taken off guard. From their perspective, the issue seems to have appeared out of nowhere. In reality, it has been forming gradually, supported by decisions that were once reasonable, defensible, and made under pressure.

Pressure does not create exposure. Pressure shapes the decisions that allow exposure to persist long enough to become material.

What changes is not the quality of the original judgment.

What changes is the scale.

And once scale is expressed financially, the conversation shifts. What was previously discussed as interpretation, defensibility, or regulatory disagreement becomes expressed as impact:

- Duty owed.
- Penalties assessed.
- Interest accrued.
- Reserve required.

At this point, the organization is no longer discussing whether a position is defensible. It is discussing whether it is affordable.

This shift is often jarring, particularly for leaders who believed risk was being managed effectively. Trade teams may feel misunderstood. Finance teams may feel blindsided. Executives may feel misled even when no one acted improperly.

What has changed is not the quality of decision-making. Instead, the change occurs in the frame through which the decisions are now being evaluated.

What has changed is not the discipline of execution. It is the translation. The exposure has moved from technical language into financial consequence. And when financial exposure surfaces, organizations often interpret it as failure. That reaction is understandable but incomplete.

In most cases I have seen, the exposure did not result from neglect or incompetence. It resulted from endurance without reconsideration. Decisions that were made to preserve continuity under pressure were never structurally revisited once conditions stabilized. Over time, those decisions became position. By the time finance quantified the exposure, governance had already been absent for longer than anyone realized.

This is why executives often ask the wrong question at this stage.

They ask, "How did this happen?"

The more useful question is, "When did this become normal?"

Once exposure becomes financial, governance re-enters forcefully—but late. Escalation accelerates. External advisors are engaged. Documentation is reviewed. Leadership demands answers. Decisions that no longer feel discretionary are scrutinized.

At this point, governance is no longer shaping outcomes. It is responding to them.

This is not a failure of effort. It is a failure of timing.

Governance is most effective before exposure becomes visible—not after.

Governing trade risk is not about arguing that trade risk should always be prevented. That is unrealistic. Instead, it is about recognizing where trade risk becomes visible and designing governance accordingly:

- If organizations wait for operational signals, they will miss it.
- If they rely on control performance, they will overlook it.
- If they assume silence equals stability, they will misread it.

Trade risk reveals itself financially when accumulation finally becomes undeniable. Governance that understands this does not wait for financial discovery to act. Rather, it builds mechanisms that force reconsideration before exposure needs to be booked. That is the difference between governing trade risk and explaining it after the fact.

Yet even in organizations that respond quickly once exposure becomes visible, another dynamic is often present—one that explains why the issue matured before it was ever translated financially.

Inside the enterprise, trade risk frequently feels active, addressed, and professionally managed. Trade professionals are responsive and credible. From the executive perspective, this creates a reassuring narrative: The risk is known, and it is being handled by capable people. In short, risk appears to be in capable hands. But that appearance can obscure something more fundamental: Management is not the same as ownership.

Trade teams manage decisions.
Governance owns position.

That distinction is rarely explicit.

> *"Trade teams manage decisions.
> Governance owns position."*

In most organizations, escalation is triggered by disruption: stopped shipments, missed revenue, system failure, or reputational crisis. In contrast, trade risk rarely triggers disruption. In fact, it tolerates continuity exceptionally well. Goods continue to move, customers are served, and financial results remain stable. Nothing demands immediate executive intervention.

As a result, the organization equates *absence of friction* with *absence of risk.*

From inside the trade function, professionals may recognize that exposure is accumulating. They may understand that a position is increasingly being defended rather than reassessed. They may sense that precedent is doing more work than governance. But without a structural requirement to escalate endurance risk, those concerns remain technical, not executive.

No one is ignoring the issue. No one is failing to act. No one believes they are carrying unacceptable risk. And that is precisely the problem.

Over time, the consequences are predictable. When risk is actively managed but never structurally owned, the absence of disruption begins to feel meaningful. The organization reads continuity as stability and interprets the lack of escalation as reassurance.

Slowly, silence takes on significance it does not deserve. As time passes, that silence begins to feel meaningful. If the position were truly problematic, leadership assumes it would surface. If exposure were truly material, it would be visible financially. If governance needed to intervene, someone would say so. This is organizational logic, not complacency.

But trade risk does not announce its accumulation. It does not trigger alarms as it grows. It does not create urgency on its own. In the absence of an explicit governance mechanism to translate persistence into escalation, silence becomes interpreted as validation.

The organization believes it has equilibrium, but what it actually has is unexamined endurance. Escalation quietly disappears from view, and in hindsight, executives often ask why the issue was not elevated sooner.

The uncomfortable answer is that nothing in the system required it to be. Why? Escalation frameworks tend to focus on

- Deviations from policy.
- Control failures.
- Regulatory findings.
- Operational disruption.

They rarely focus on

- Duration of exposure.
- Repetition of defense.
- Accumulation across jurisdictions.
- Scaling impact over time.

As long as decisions remain technically defensible and controls continue to function, the organization experiences no signal that governance should re-enter the conversation.

As a result, trade risk remains *managed*, but not *owned*. This is why the moment of discovery feels so sudden. Although the exposure did not form overnight, ownership had never been explicitly assigned at the enterprise level.

The result is not chaos. It is a blind spot.

From the executive vantage point, trade risk is often perceived as episodic: an inquiry here, a challenge there, a discussion that resolves itself.

What is not visible is the pattern. No single event seems large enough to merit sustained attention. No single decision feels strategic. And so the organization moves forward, confident that risk is being handled appropriately.

The blind spot is not lack of information. It is lack of aggregation.

Governance does not fail because leaders are disengaged. It fails because no structure forces them to see how many reasonable decisions, sustained over time, have quietly become a material exposure.

By the time that aggregation becomes visible, it no longer belongs to the trade function.

And that is where the following story begins.

Case Example
When Financial Exposure Finally Becomes Visible

For a long time, the organization believed its trade risk was contained. Not because it was complacent, but because it had reasons to believe so. Valuation methodologies had been designed deliberately. Controls were in place. Documentation existed. Prior challenges had been addressed, sometimes successfully, sometimes not—but always thoughtfully. The company had lived with scrutiny before and understood how to respond.

From inside the organization, the position felt disciplined. Trade professionals knew the valuation model intimately. They understood the intercompany structure, the pricing logic, and the controls designed to demonstrate reasonable care. Questions were answered as they arose. When authorities pushed back, the response was methodical. Nothing felt unmanaged.

What no one was actively doing was aggregating the exposure. Each valuation inquiry was handled as its own event. Each customs challenge was treated as jurisdiction-specific. Each tariff increase was absorbed as part of a broader cost structure. The organization experienced these moments as discrete technical issues handled by capable teams.

Over time, the company became very good at defending its position. That confidence shaped how subsequent decisions were made. When one authority questioned transaction value based on related-party influence, the organization responded quickly. Documentation was assembled and comparables were analyzed. Prior reasoning was reinforced. The goal was clear: Defend the methodology without destabilizing a global operating model.

Changing valuation methodology across related parties would not have been a tactical fix. It would have been a structural event with cascading implications for pricing, systems, contracts, tax, and financial reporting. The organization understood that trade-offs existed, and it chose continuity.

At the time, that choice felt responsible. What was less visible was how that decision began to function over time. The initial response hardened into position. Trade teams continued to defend the methodology. Controls validated consistency. Leadership confidence increased as operations remained stable. The question quietly shifted from "Should this change?" to "How do we continue to support it?"

No one formally accepted increased exposure. It simply accumulated.

The moment of visibility did not come from trade but from finance. During a broader financial review—one that aggregated customs assessments, tariff exposure, and valuation impacts across regions—a pattern emerged that had never been visible decision-by-decision. The exposure was no longer theoretical. It was measurable, quantifiable, and material.

What had felt like manageable, jurisdiction-specific issues resolved through expertise and control now presented as a consolidated risk with real financial consequence. A multi-million-dollar assessment (on the order of eight figures) reframed everything the organization thought it understood about its risk position.

The assessment did not arise from a single failure. It was not the result of negligence or ignorance. It was the product of endurance.

From the organization's perspective, this felt deeply unfair. We had acted responsibly. We had invested in expertise. We had documented our reasoning. Nothing about the process felt reckless. We believed the methodology was defensible, and we protected it accordingly. And yet, the outcome suggested something else entirely.

I did not have the authority to change the model, but I had been part of defending it. And during that assessment, defense felt palpably different from ownership. It became clear in hindsight that governance had focused on defending decisions, not on reconsidering position.

At no time had leadership stepped back and asked whether the continued defense of the methodology still made sense as exposure scaled. No governance forum reframed the issue from technical defensibility to enterprise risk. The position endured not because it was re-approved, but because it was never re-examined.

From a regulatory perspective, the story looked different. What the regulators saw was persistence. The same valuation approach applied repeatedly across jurisdictions, despite challenges. The absence of visible reassessment became part of the narrative—not because the original decision was unreasonable but because the organization could not demonstrate when, or how, it had reconsidered the position as circumstances evolved.

This verdict seemed sudden, even shocking. In reality, nothing about it was sudden. The exposure had been forming quietly for years. What was sudden was the aggregation—and the realization that governance had never re-entered the conversation once urgency faded.

This is how trade risk becomes financial risk.

Not through a single bad decision, but through a series of reasonable ones that are never deliberately re-evaluated.

SECTION III

When Financial Exposure Forces the Conversation

For a long time, trade risk can exist without a price tag that commands attention.

Tariffs accrue quietly. Valuation positions persist. Classifications remain unchanged. Exposure grows, but it grows diffusely—spread across entries, jurisdictions, and time. No single shipment feels material enough to escalate. No individual decision appears reckless. Controls continue to validate execution.

Then the exposure is quantified.

In my experience, this is the moment when trade risk stops being an abstract compliance issue and becomes a financial event that the organization cannot ignore.

Sometimes it arrives through an assessment. Sometimes through an audit finding. Sometimes through a reconciliation that was never expected to surface anything meaningful. However it appears, the effect is the same: Accumulated decisions are suddenly converted into a number.

And that number changes everything. The debate moves from defensibility to consequence.

Up until this point, discussions about trade risk often live comfortably within technical teams. Valuation is debated on methodology. Classification is argued through legal notes and explanatory guidance. Reasonable care is demonstrated through controls, documentation, and precedent. These conversations are rigorous, but they remain bounded by expertise.

Once financial exposure is identified, the conversation expands rapidly, and the questions change:

- Instead of "Is this defensible?" leadership begins asking "How did this get so big?"
- Instead of "What is our position?" the question becomes "Who approved this?"
- Instead of "Can we support this?" the focus shifts to "Why didn't we see this sooner?"

It is not that the organization suddenly cares about governance. It is that governance is now attached to material consequence.

In the valuation example discussed earlier, the issue was not that the company lacked controls or failed to respond. The issue was that a defensible position, maintained under pressure, persisted long enough for exposure to scale. When that exposure was finally assessed, it was no longer viewed as a series of reasonable decisions. It was viewed as a single financial outcome. That reframing is powerful.

One of the most uncomfortable truths about trade governance is that exposure is often discovered only after it has matured—not because organizations are negligent but because trade exposure rarely announces itself incrementally. It accumulates in places that do not trigger alarms:

- Tariffs embedded in pricing.
- Valuation adjustments absorbed into margin.
- Classification decisions applied consistently but never re-evaluated.
- Post-entry mechanisms treated as procedural rather than diagnostic.

In many organizations, trade risk is not tracked as exposure. It is tracked as activity: entries filed, controls applied, reviews completed, audits passed. But none of these criteria capture how much risk is being carried forward.

So, when a multi-million-dollar assessment emerges—whether $10 million or otherwise—it feels sudden and abrupt.

In reality, the exposure was not sudden. The visibility was.

Once financial exposure is visible, governance is reconstructed backward. Regulators, auditors, and internal reviewers do not examine decisions as they were experienced in the moment. They examine them as a sequence that led to a quantifiable outcome.

They ask:

- When did this position first emerge?
- How long did it persist?
- When did exposure scale materially?
- Who reassessed the risk as it grew?

If those questions do not have clear answers, the conclusion is not that the organization acted irresponsibly—it is that governance did not keep pace with exposure. At this moment, leadership realizes that what felt like operational resilience was, in fact, unmanaged endurance.

For executives, this discovery can feel disorienting. Trade teams believed they were doing their job. Controls were functioning, issues were being handled, and no one was ignoring risk. Yet the outcome suggests that something systemic failed.

The failure did not lie in execution. Instead, it resulted from the absence of a mechanism to translate technical persistence into financial awareness.

Governance did not force the organization to ask whether continued defense was still appropriate as exposure scaled. It allowed reasonable decisions to continue without re-framing their impact. That is not a technical failure. It is a governance gap. And when that gap is seen clearly, it changes the scale of the question.

What makes the moment of discovery so destabilizing is not the number itself. It is the realization that the number is not bounded.

At first, exposure appears containable. It is associated with a specific country, authority, or challenge. The organization experiences it as a discrete event—serious but localized. Resources are mobilized and advisors are engaged. The issue is framed as something to be resolved.

That framing holds only briefly. As soon as leadership begins asking the next set of questions, the nature of the risk changes.

- If this interpretation holds here, could it hold elsewhere?
- If this methodology is being questioned now, has it always been vulnerable?
- If this structure was defensible under one enforcement position, is it defensible under another?

At this moment, discovery turns existential. What surfaces is not a compliance gap but a structural realization: The organization's global operating model has just been exposed to scrutiny.

And the implications do not stop at exposure. The very features that make global trade programs efficient are the ones that magnify exposure once a position is challenged.

Valuation methodologies between related parties were designed for consistency. They are embedded in systems, contracts, transfer pricing frameworks, and intercompany agreements. They are applied across regions to ensure predictability, scalability, and operational coherence. That consistency works—until it doesn't.

When a customs authority challenges the methodology and prevails, the organization is forced to confront a difficult truth: Consistency does not isolate risk. It replicates it. What was once viewed as a strength—uniform application across jurisdictions—becomes a point of vulnerability. The same logic, the same assumptions, and the same documentation exist everywhere.

The exposure is no longer tied to one shipment, one country, or one dispute. It is tied to a position.

That exposure behaves differently depending on how the enterprise is built.

Related-party trade structures intensify this realization. Because pricing is established within an enterprise rather than negotiated externally, customs authorities often view the relationship itself as suspect. Controls and documentation may demonstrate reasonable care, but they do not eliminate scrutiny. They merely shape the debate.

Once a valuation methodology between related parties is successfully challenged in one jurisdiction, an uncomfortable precedent is created. Other authorities may not need to discover the issue independently. They may simply adopt the reasoning.

At that point, leadership no longer faces the question of whether the methodology is defensible in theory. Instead, it examines whether the organization can withstand the cascading impact if that theory is rejected elsewhere.

For companies importing into dozens of countries, this realization is profound: Exposure does not increase incrementally. It multiplies, and multiplication changes the scale of perception.

At this moment trade risk stops feeling technical and starts feeling systemic. Executives are no longer evaluating the likelihood of success in a single dispute. Instead, they are evaluating scenarios.

- What if another authority takes the same position next quarter?
- What if enforcement priorities shift simultaneously in multiple regions?
- What if tariffs increase while valuation assumptions remain under pressure?

Suddenly, the exposure cannot be addressed by fixing a single issue. The solution requires understanding how the organization would absorb repeated challenges over time.

What once felt like a contained compliance matter now raises questions about financial resilience, earnings volatility, regulatory credibility, and strategic flexibility. The organization realizes it is not reacting to an event. It is confronting a model-level risk.

In hindsight, leaders often wonder why this risk was not apparent earlier. The answer does not lie in a lack of awareness. It lies in a lack of aggregation.

Each decision made under pressure was reasonable. Each response was defensible, each dispute handled competently. Nothing, taken alone, demanded a fundamental rethink.

What was missing was a governance moment that forced leadership to ask whether the accumulation of those reasonable decisions had crossed a threshold.

That threshold is rarely visible from inside the function. It becomes visible only when discovery forces the organization to view its position as a whole. This is why the realization feels abrupt. The risk did not form suddenly, but an understanding of it did. And that distinction is often lost in the moment.

The assessment is the event everyone remembers. It has a number attached to it. It appears in reports. It is discussed in meetings. It is often described as "the problem."

In reality, though, the assessment is rarely the most consequential part. In this case, the multi-million-dollar valuation assessment was not devastating because of its size alone. It was devastating because of what it forced into view.

Once the position was challenged and a financial assessment imposed, the organization could no longer treat the issue as a localized disagreement. What had been framed as a country-specific interpretation suddenly became a global exposure question.

The first realization was immediate and uncomfortable: If one customs authority rejected the valuation methodology between related parties, there was nothing preventing another from doing the same. And the organization did not operate in one jurisdiction. It imported into dozens.

At that moment, the question was no longer "How do we resolve this assessment?"

It became

"What have we just exposed ourselves to globally?"

Boardroom Example #1
When the Number Stops Being the Point

The room was quieter than expected.

The number had already been circulated—a multi-million-dollar assessment tied to valuation. Everyone had read it before the meeting began. No one needed it restated.

The size of the assessment was material, but it was not what unsettled the room. What unsettled it was the implication that the issue extended beyond a single outcome.

Someone finally asked the question no one had wanted to lead with: "If this position was challenged here ... where else does this apply?"

At that moment, the conversation shifted. The assessment stopped being a discrete regulatory event and became a structural one. The issue was no longer only whether the company could absorb the cost. It was whether the valuation model that supported global trade flows was still defensible under increasing scrutiny.

The implications unfolded quickly. If one authority rejected the methodology, others could follow—not because the facts had changed, but because the argument had been exposed. A position once defended quietly had now been surfaced and documented, and it effectively invited comparison.

The company operated in dozens of jurisdictions. The same valuation logic flowed through each of them.

Someone else asked the next question: "What happens if another country takes the same view?"

No one answered immediately—not because the answer was unknown, but because it was suddenly too large to state casually.

I sat there understanding the methodology as well as anyone in the room. I knew why we believed it was defensible. I also knew I did not have the authority to change it. I had helped defend it. Now we were facing legal exposure. Retroactive duties. Financial restatement risk. Operational disruption. Reputational damage. Executive accountability.

This was no longer a discussion about trade compliance. It was about scale. It was about whether the company had visibility into the cumulative risk it had been carrying—and whether governance had ever been asked to weigh that risk deliberately.

The methodology had not changed. What changed was how it was being seen.

But the confidence that had existed before the assessment did not return.

The assessment had started as a single-country issue. It no longer was.

Valuation methodologies between related parties are not designed to be local. They are inherently global by necessity. Systems, transfer pricing structures, intercompany agreements, and pricing logic are built for consistency. That consistency is operationally efficient but governance-fragile.

When a single country challenged the methodology and prevailed, it introduced a new and unsettling possibility: that the same logic could be applied elsewhere, at scale. Suddenly, leadership was not looking at one assessment. They were looking at a map: Seventy-six importing countries. Decades of trade activity. Volumes that varied dramatically by region. Tariff profiles that changed with political and economic shifts.

The assessment raised questions that had never been asked before:

- What if this interpretation spreads?
- What if another authority adopted the same reasoning?

- What if multiple authorities did?
- What if timing aligned poorly—during a tariff spike, a supply-chain disruption, or a period of heightened enforcement?

The financial exposure was no longer linear. It was multiplicative, and multiplication carries consequences beyond dollars.

The second realization followed quickly: The organization could not manage this alone. Trade professionals were deeply knowledgeable and controls existed, but the scope of the exposure had outgrown the function.

External trade attorneys were engaged to assess legal defensibility across jurisdictions. Consultants were brought in to model exposure scenarios. A major financial firm was engaged to quantify potential impact under different regulatory assumptions.

Each engagement added cost—but more importantly, each added perspective. It became clear that the organization was no longer dealing with a compliance question. It was dealing with a balance-sheet risk that required executive interpretation. That interpretation could not be delegated, and responsibility flowed upward.

At the executive level, the conversation shifted again. The question was no longer whether the valuation method was technically defensible. It had been defended before. Instead, the question executives now faced was far more uncomfortable: What level of exposure are we willing to carry if this position is challenged elsewhere?

Trade teams cannot answer this question without output from across the organization. The answer involves

- Financial tolerance.
- Risk appetite.
- Reputational exposure.
- Operational disruption.
- Investor confidence.
- Regulatory credibility.

The assessment forced leadership to confront something governance had not previously required them to quantify: endurance risk. Specifically, how long could the organization sustain this position if it became a recurring challenge rather than an isolated event?

What made this moment profound was not the realization that risk existed—because risk always exists. It was the realization that the organization had crossed an invisible line from defending a position to owning a position.

The valuation methodology was no longer just a trade decision. It had become a strategic choice with global implications. Changing it would be costly, disruptive, and complex. Keeping it carried escalating regulatory and financial risk.

Neither option was clean. Neither was purely technical.

This is where governance is supposed to step in—not to choose the "right" answer, but to frame the decision correctly.

What mattered now was not whether the company could continue to defend the methodology, but whether leadership had consciously decided to accept the exposure that came with doing so.

That is the difference between defending a position and governing it.

This is the moment that separates operational trade management from executive governance.

Before the assessment, the organization believed it was managing risk.

After the assessment, it realized it was carrying risk at scale. And scale changes everything. What had once felt contained now felt systemic. What had once felt defensible now felt fragile. What had once been delegated now demanded ownership.

This is why the real cost is not the assessment. The real cost is the forced reckoning—the moment when leadership must acknowledge that a decision made under confidence, precedent, and operational necessity has become a global exposure with the potential to ripple across the enterprise.

At this moment governance either becomes explicit or proves it never truly existed.

Boardroom Moment #2
When Risk Becomes Ownership

The conversation did not begin with blame. It began with silence.

The numbers were on the screen—not just the assessment, but also the modeled scenarios that followed. Best case, likely case, worst case. What had started as a single country's position was now expressed as potential exposure across dozens of jurisdictions.

No one questioned the competence of the trade team. No one challenged the existence of controls. No one disputed that reasonable care had been exercised.

The discomfort came from something else. For the first time, the question was not "Is our position defensible?" It was "Is this a risk we have knowingly chosen to carry?"

That distinction mattered. Executives around the table began asking different questions—not about valuation mechanics, but about endurance.

- If another authority adopted the same interpretation, how quickly would exposure scale?
- If enforcement priorities shifted, how visible would that exposure become?
- If this position persisted for another year, another three years, what would it mean financially? Strategically? Reputationally?

In that moment it became clear that this decision no longer belonged to the trade function. It was not a compliance issue to be managed. Instead, it was a governance question that required ownership.

Something in the room shifted. The organization had crossed a line—not because the original decision was wrong, but because the consequences were now large enough to demand conscious acceptance at the highest level.

At this moment governance finally entered the conversation.

Not to relitigate the past, but to decide the future. That—more than the assessment itself—was the true cost of waiting.

*"The real cost is not the assessment.
The real cost is the forced reckoning."*

Governance had finally entered the room. Now it would have to stay there.

CHAPTER 8

Equalization

In diving, equalization happens immediately because it must.

Pressure begins the moment descent begins, even when the surface is still visible and the light remains strong. A diver cannot wait until discomfort becomes severe. Equalization is required early and repeatedly. The body does not negotiate with physics. It responds to pressure whether the diver acknowledges it or not.

Equalization cannot be delegated. It cannot be ignored. It is not dramatic—it is disciplined. It prevents injury at depth. It enables further descent safely.

Divers who refuse to equalize do not avoid pressure. They accumulate it.

Trade governance operates under similar physics.

Exposure begins accumulating long before consequence feels material. Volume expands. Geographic reach widens. Sourcing models evolve. Valuation methodologies endure. What once felt contained begins to scale quietly beneath operational stability. Nothing appears broken. Controls function, audits close, and reporting reassures. The surface remains calm.

But depth is not measured by calm water. It is measured by pressure.

Organizations often assume governance exists because activity is disciplined. Expertise is visible, processes operate, and documentation supports interpretation. Leadership receives reports that confirm control. At the surface, this feels responsible.

But governance is not tested at the surface. It is tested as exposure deepens.

Trade exposure does not escalate because organizations lack effort or intelligence. It escalates because decision authority and structural accountability separate gradually over time. Execution continues, and governance becomes implied rather than designed. No one pauses to ask whether the posture the enterprise is carrying today is the posture leadership would consciously choose at current scale.

That pause is equalization.

Equalization in governance is the deliberate act of reassessment before exposure becomes injury. It is the structural requirement that enduring methodologies be reconsidered as volume increases, as enforcement priorities shift, and as consequences grow. It is leadership's responsibility to ensure that depth does not change without awareness.

It is not reaction. It is discipline under descent.

Earlier chapters explained how capable organizations drift, how continuity hardens into endurance, and how exposure becomes visible only when it is finally measured. Chapter 7 revealed what happens when pressure is quantified. This chapter addresses what must occur before that moment.

Equalization is not a crisis response. It is a design principle.

> *"Equalization is not a crisis response.*
> *It is a design principle."*

Without it, even the most disciplined trade programs accumulate pressure quietly until injury forces attention. With it, leadership does not wait for discomfort to escalate. It recalibrates continuously and deliberately as descent continues.

Governance fails not because organizations are careless.

It fails because equalization was never made structural.

And when equalization is absent, descent does not stop.

Pressure simply builds.

SECTION I

The First Signs of Pressure

In diving, the first signals of pressure are rarely dramatic.

A diver is still near the surface. Light remains strong. Movement feels controlled. The boat is visible overhead. Nothing about the environment suggests urgency. And yet the body registers change immediately. Equalization must begin before discomfort escalates. It must be repeated consistently—not because something feels wrong, but because physics demands it.

Governance operates under similar physics.

The earliest signs that accountability and execution have separated are not disruptive. Trade functions operate efficiently. Controls demonstrate reasonable care. Documentation supports interpretation. Internal audits confirm process adherence. Reporting appears stable. From an executive vantage point, nothing appears broken. Everything feels managed.

"But management is not governance."

But management is not governance.

Management ensures that procedures are followed.

Governance determines who owns the exposure created by those procedures over time.

At shallow depth, that distinction feels academic. As scale increases, it becomes structural.

Organizations often assume that governance exists because activity is disciplined, expertise is visible, and trade professionals are credentialed. Escalations occur when regulators challenge positions. Issues are resolved. From the surface, this creates confidence.

But confidence is not equalization. Equalization requires deliberate reassessment—not reassurance.

A valuation methodology may be technically defensible. A classification position may be consistently applied. An origin determination may be supported by prevailing interpretation. None of these decisions are inherently flawed. In fact, they may be entirely reasonable at the time they are made.

Pressure does not begin because a decision was careless. It begins because scale changes consequence.

As markets expand, volumes increase, sourcing models evolve, and enforcement priorities shift, the financial sensitivity attached to those decisions changes with them. What once felt contained begins to carry enterprise weight. What once appeared local becomes systemic. What once required no executive visibility begins to influence margin, capital allocation, and regulatory posture.

If leadership is not deliberately revisiting those positions as scale changes, equalization has already been deferred.

Delegation is often where this separation begins.

Trade governance cannot be delegated. Execution can be assigned. Technical expertise can be hired. Processes can be documented. And controls can be audited. But ownership of cumulative exposure cannot be transferred simply because the subject matter is complex.

Global trade is specialized terrain. It requires disciplined interpretation, operational precision, and constant monitoring. Leadership appropriately entrusts those responsibilities to professionals trained to manage them. Trade teams classify products, determine origin, apply valuation methodologies, oversee brokers, and respond to regulatory inquiry. The machinery functions. Goods move. Findings are addressed.

From the surface, this trade function appears to be governed, but equalization is not about activity. It is about structural ownership.

The question is not whether trade professionals are disciplined. The question is whether leadership has defined when cumulative exposure requires conscious reauthorization.

Without that definition, governance becomes episodic. It activates when challenged and recedes when stability returns. Exposure continues accumulating between those moments.

This accumulation rarely announces itself loudly. It does not disrupt operations or halt shipments. It does not immediately affect revenue recognition. Instead, it grows proportionally with volume and duration. Over time, the enterprise is no longer carrying the exposure it originally approved. Instead, it is carrying an expanded version of it, often without realizing the expansion occurred.

This is the first sign of pressure: accumulation without structural recalibration. Not misconduct, not error, not even negligence.

Across global organizations, a familiar pattern emerges. Trade functions are restructured repeatedly. Reporting lines shift between finance, legal, supply chain, and operations. Titles change. Centers of excellence are formed. Authority is centralized, then redistributed. Each restructuring promises improved alignment. Each addresses a real concern at the time. And yet, the underlying exposure remains largely unchanged.

The repetition is not incompetence. It is an attempt to solve a structural issue through visible movement.

Structure feels actionable. It signals responsiveness. It demonstrates that leadership is paying attention. But restructuring does not equal equalization. Changing reporting lines does not define exposure thresholds. Centralizing a team does not clarify ownership of cumulative risk.

When leadership relies on structure rather than design, equalization is delayed, and pressure continues to build beneath operational stability.

What often goes unexamined is duration.

Decisions in trade are rarely made with a one-year horizon in mind. They are made to sustain operations. They become embedded in systems, reflected in pricing logic, integrated into ERP configurations, repeated across jurisdictions, inherited by new personnel, and carried forward because nothing has forced reconsideration.

Duration compounds exposure. A methodology that was reasonable at $50 million in annual volume is not the same posture at $500 million. A sourcing model implemented before tariff escalation does not carry the same sensitivity after enforcement intensifies. A classification position defended once cannot be replicated across product lines and countries. The decision may not change, but its consequence does.

Equalization requires recognizing when duration and scale have altered the weight of a posture, even if the posture itself remains technically defensible. Without that recognition, organizations operate under historical approval while carrying current-scale exposure.

That gap is rarely visible in reporting.

Reports show activity: findings resolved, audits completed, and training delivered. They rarely show accumulated sensitivity. And accumulated sensitivity is what governance is meant to own. The solution? Executive leadership must move from awareness to structural discipline because governance is not a matter of being informed. It is a matter of deciding:

- Deciding that a methodology will continue.
- Deciding that exposure at current scale is acceptable.
- Deciding that margin compression, if challenged, is tolerable.
- Deciding that reputational impact has been weighed.

Without those deliberate decisions, leadership has not governed. It has observed, and observation is not equalization.

Equalization requires conscious recalibration before pressure forces it, and that recalibration must occur while the surface still looks calm. Because once discomfort becomes obvious, the delay has already compounded.

A governable program behaves differently. It distinguishes clearly between execution and ownership. It defines exposure thresholds that trigger executive review. It revisits enduring methodologies as scale changes. It embeds reassessment into architecture rather than waiting for enforcement to force it.

Equalization in governance is not reactive. It is designed. It requires leadership to ask, at defined intervals: Is this still the position we would choose at this scale? Has financial sensitivity changed? Has regulatory focus shifted? Has geographic reach amplified the consequence beyond what was originally contemplated?

At shallow depth, governance feels assumed. At increasing depth, governance must be deliberate.

Equalization is not dramatic. It is disciplined recalibration under descent.

The first signs of pressure are quiet. They appear as stability and feel like continuity. They look like operational excellence.

Whether leadership responds before discomfort escalates is the difference between controlled descent and injury at depth.

SECTION II

When Movement Replaces Stability

In diving, when pressure builds, equalization must occur through deliberate adjustment, not through erratic movement. A diver who responds to discomfort by swimming faster or changing direction without recalibrating does not relieve pressure. Movement is not equalization.

In many global organizations, trade does not remain structurally stable for long. Instead, it moves. It shifts between finance, legal, supply chain, and operations. It is centralized, then decentralized. It becomes a center of excellence. It is embedded regionally. It is elevated, then absorbed. Each restructuring is logical.

When tariffs shift, trade moves closer to finance. When enforcement tightens, it migrates toward legal. When operational disruption dominates, it settles inside supply chain.

The adjustments are rarely arbitrary. They reflect real pressures. Leadership responds to the issue most visible at the time and aligns trade accordingly. The structure changes to match the perceived risk. In many enterprises, this realignment occurs repeatedly.

This pattern is not confined to one industry or limited to immature programs. It appears in sophisticated global companies with experienced executives and capable trade teams. Every few years, the function moves again—sometimes subtly, sometimes significantly. The reasoning is consistent:

- "We need clearer oversight."
- "We need stronger alignment with cost."
- "We need tighter regulatory control."
- "We need better operational integration."

Each explanation is defensible, but stability remains elusive.

If structure were the solution, repeated restructuring would produce increasing steadiness. Instead, exposure patterns tend to resurface. Regulatory pressure returns, and leadership revisits the function's placement once more.

The organization is active, but the architecture remains unsettled. This repetition is not evidence of failure. It is evidence of search.

When exposure becomes visible, leadership reaches for the most visible lever: structure. Reporting lines are clear. Accountability appears defined. Movement signals intent. In boardrooms, restructuring communicates seriousness. It demonstrates that the issue has been acknowledged and addressed.

Structure is tangible. Governance design is not. It is far easier to move a function than to redesign how exposure becomes visible as it accumulates.

This is where false equalization occurs. Restructuring feels like pressure relief. It creates motion, generates attention, and temporarily sharpens focus. For a period, leadership feels closer to the risk.

But proximity is not recalibration. Equalization requires adjustment to posture, not relocation of responsibility.

The boardroom moment often unfolds quietly. Trade appears midway through the agenda—not urgent, not absent. Metrics are presented. Error rates are stable. Audit findings are manageable. Escalations are described as contained. The slide deck is clean.

Then a director asks a question that feels procedural: "Given the recent regulatory activity, are we comfortable with where trade sits in the organization?"

The discussion that follows is practical. Finance offers cost visibility. Legal emphasizes regulatory interpretation. Supply chain highlights operational integration. Each perspective is valid. The conversation becomes structural.

Eventually, a conclusion forms: "If we align trade under [the chosen function], oversight will improve."

Heads nod. The structure shifts.

The organization experiences relief. Action has been taken.

The unasked questions are more difficult: How will leadership know when posture itself requires reconsideration? What mechanism forces exposure upward before regulators do? Where is the trigger that requires reauthorization of enduring decisions?

Structure can clarify reporting. It does not guarantee visibility into evolving exposure.

Restructuring feels like governance because it reallocates responsibility. But responsibility for execution is not the same as ownership of posture. By posture, I do not mean a single classification or valuation decision. I mean the accumulated position the organization carries—the set of enduring assumptions that shape how trade risk behaves over time.

Moving the function does not automatically redesign how leadership sees accumulation.

A trade program can report into finance and still scale exposure without deliberate review of methodology. It can sit in legal and still operate under assumptions that were never revisited as volumes expanded. It can be embedded in supply chain and still allow regional divergence to accumulate quietly.

Each placement can be justified. Trade intersects cost, regulation, and operations.

What none of them guarantees is executive ownership of evolving exposure.

When organizations restructure repeatedly, they are often attempting to correct visibility through alignment. They are seeking a vantage point from which risk feels clearer. The impulse is rational.

But vantage point is not architecture. Architecture defines how information flows, how escalation is triggered, and how accountability persists when conditions change. Without that design, reporting lines absorb pressure temporarily. Over time, the same questions reemerge.

- Why did this exposure scale without earlier review?
- Why were similar decisions made differently across regions?
- Why was a long-standing position never reconsidered as enforcement intensified?

The answers rarely rest in structure alone.

There is a subtle shift that occurs after each restructuring. Initially, attention sharpens. New leadership reviews existing positions. Reporting becomes more frequent. Escalation thresholds lower. The organization feels disciplined. Governance appears strengthened.

Gradually, urgency fades. Metrics stabilize. Questions diminish. Confidence returns. The new structure becomes familiar. What once required review becomes routine. The organization settles.

Unless governance has been deliberately redesigned, the cycle begins again.

This is the difference between energy and equalization.

Energy is episodic.

Equalization is structural.

Energy intensifies when pressure becomes visible.

Equalization anticipates pressure before discomfort escalates.

Restructuring relies on energy. Governability relies on design.

A governable trade program does not depend on its reporting structure to ensure that exposure becomes visible. It does not rely on the vigilance of a particular executive to maintain alignment. Instead, it embeds reconsideration into its operating logic. It defines when posture must be reexamined. It clarifies who owns accumulated exposure, not just individual decisions.

When that design exists, structure becomes secondary. When it does not, structure becomes the proxy.

This is why job titles change but exposure patterns persist. The organization adjusts roles in search of clarity, but if it does not redefine how leadership engages with evolving risk, the clarity is temporary.

Restructuring is visible. It signals movement and creates a narrative of improvement.

Governance design is quieter. It requires deliberate definition of ownership, escalation, and reconsideration. It does not announce itself through charts. It reveals itself through stability under increasing depth.

Boards rarely intend to chase structure. They respond to the signals available. When exposure surfaces, they ask whether the function is properly positioned. That question is logical, but it is also incomplete. The more foundational question is: Has governance been designed so that exposure cannot accumulate without deliberate leadership equalization?

If the answer depends on structure, stability will remain fragile. If the answer depends on architecture, structure becomes reinforcement, not remedy.

Restructuring may accompany evolution. It may even be necessary at times. But it cannot substitute for equalization. Without deliberate design of how exposure surfaces, how posture is reconsidered, and how accountability endures beyond individuals, structure will continue to carry pressure it was never meant to absorb.

Restructuring addresses visibility at the surface.

Governance addresses ownership at depth.

Until ownership is defined at the leadership level, the organization will continue to search for clarity through movement.

A governable program does not require repeated relocation to regain control. It remains steady because leadership has designed how it equalizes.

And once leadership equalizes deliberately, structure becomes reinforcement, not remedy.

Responding to depth requires more than awareness. It requires deliberate adjustment. Figure 5 illustrates how governance must evolve through equalization as exposure increases, defining the progression required to sustain alignment at depth. As the figure shows, each level introduces a different set of demands.

Figure 5: Equalization (Managed Progression at Depth)

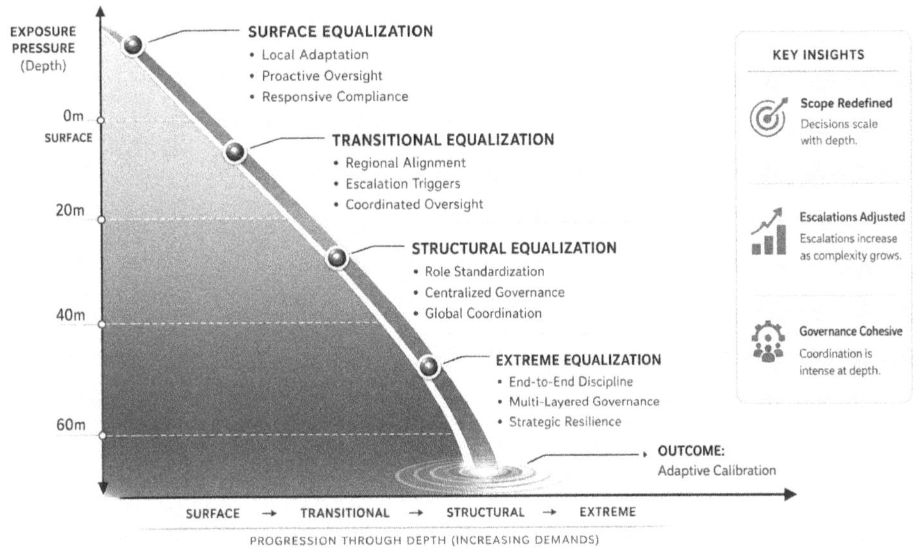

This figure illustrates how governance must evolve through successive levels of equalization as exposure increases. Each level introduces new structural demands—shifting from localized adaptation to coordinated, enterprise-wide oversight—ensuring that governance remains aligned with the conditions it is meant to control.

Organizations that sustain performance at depth are not those that resist this progression, but those that recognize it early and adapt deliberately.

Equalization is not a single action. It is an ongoing discipline.

SECTION III

Distortion at Depth

Design determines whether pressure becomes visible before it becomes consequential.

When governance relies on structure alone, visibility depends on where the function sits. When governance is designed deliberately, visibility depends on how exposure accumulates, regardless of placement.

That distinction becomes most apparent at the board level because boards rarely lack information. They lack accumulation.

Most boards believe they have visibility into trade risk. They receive reports and review audit summaries. They see metrics trend over time and approve policy frameworks. They are briefed when disputes arise.

From the vantage point of governance, all of this appears responsible. But the board's information is incomplete. The distinction lies in the difference between reporting and visibility.

Reporting communicates activity.

Visibility reveals accumulation because trade compounds.

Boards are shown how trade performs at a surface level. Error rates trend downward. Controls operate as designed. Regulatory inquiries are addressed. Findings are remediated. These indicators are valuable. They confirm discipline and demonstrate management. They reassure leadership that operational mechanisms function as intended. But reassurance is not the same as awareness.

Operational metrics answer the question "Is the system working?"

Governance must answer a different question: "What position is the system creating as it scales?"

Those are not interchangeable inquiries.

Distortion at depth emerges when performance substitutes for posture. Stable dashboards create cognitive comfort. Comfort reduces inquiry. Reduced inquiry narrows discussion to visible friction. Over time, leadership becomes deeply informed about trade events.

It remains less informed about cumulative trade position.

The organization is not uninformed. It is underinformed.

This distortion is not accidental. It reflects how most governance systems are constructed.

Board oversight is traditionally designed around deviation—variance from expectation, breach of control, financial restatement, regulatory citation. Governance activates when something moves outside defined boundaries. What remains inside those boundaries is interpreted as controlled.

Trade exposure, however, does not always announce itself through deviation. It compounds through repetition.

A defensible methodology applied across expanding volume increases cumulative impact without ever breaching procedural discipline. A classification approach may remain technically consistent even as the commercial value attached to it multiplies. A sourcing model optimized under one tariff environment may quietly accumulate sensitivity as geopolitical alignment shifts.

Nothing "fails." Nothing "breaks." Nothing triggers variance reporting. And yet the enterprise-level consequence changes.

This is the structural blind spot.

Governance systems are calibrated to detect error. They are rarely calibrated to interrogate scale.

As a result, executive confidence increases in direct proportion to operational stability. The longer a position operates without dispute, the more embedded it becomes in the enterprise. The more embedded it becomes, the less frequently it is reconsidered. Stability hardens into posture. This is how accumulation hides inside excellence.

The better the operational discipline, the more convincing the appearance of control. The more convincing the appearance of control, the less likely leadership is to question cumulative exposure absent disruption.

The visibility gap widens precisely when the organization appears strongest.

Growth intensifies the distortion in various ways. Volumes increase. Geographic reach expands. Sourcing models evolve. Transfer pricing adjustments shift duty concentration. Enforcement priorities change across jurisdictions.

Each development is strategic, and none signals noncompliance. Yet together, they reshape exposure.

Because reporting focuses on error, not accumulation, the board does not see this reshaping as it occurs. It sees confirmation of control.

The absence of findings reinforces confidence, and confidence reduces urgency.

Urgency narrows governance attention to disruption.

This is not negligence. It is structural design.

Most governance systems are built to respond to deviation. They are not built to interrogate scale.

A methodology that remains technically defensible does not trigger escalation merely because it now governs twice the volume. A classification approach validated years earlier does not surface simply because it now applies across additional jurisdictions. An origin strategy that once optimized duty may continue unchanged even as enforcement posture tightens.

Without structural triggers tied to accumulation, leadership visibility becomes episodic.

It activates under friction and quiets under stability. This is why the visibility gap often becomes apparent only after external reframing. Perhaps a regulator challenges an interpretation previously accepted. Maybe a geopolitical shift alters tariff exposure overnight or a cross-border investigation compares positions across jurisdictions.

Suddenly, the board must understand not only what the organization did but also how and why it sustained that position over time. The tone of the board's questions changes:

- When was this approach last reconsidered?
- Who reauthorized it as volumes expanded?
- How did we assess cumulative impact across regions?
- Where is the evidence of leadership awareness as exposure scaled?

These are governance questions that are rarely asked in stable periods.

Executives often experience surprise at the change in tone—not because they were uninvolved, but because the system never required them to see accumulation explicitly.

They saw execution. They did not see scale.

This is the leadership visibility gap.

It is not a failure of reporting. It is a limitation of architecture.

Governable organizations close this gap intentionally. They distinguish between operational metrics and exposure signals. They require periodic reconsideration of enduring positions—not because something broke, but because scale changed. They elevate accumulation as a governance matter, not just dispute as an operational one. They define review triggers tied to consequence, not only to error.

Without that design, leadership visibility remains reactive. It depends on enforcement, external framing, and friction. But friction is an unreliable governance tool.

Boards that close the leadership visibility gap do not see more slides. Instead, they see differently. They move from reviewing performance to owning exposure. They shift from asking whether controls work to asking whether cumulative position still fits. They recognize that stability does not equal safety.

That shift is subtle, but it is also transformative.

Because once leadership understands that visibility must include accumulation—not just activity—governance ceases to be assumed.

It becomes deliberate.

Distortion at depth does not occur because signals are false. It occurs because conditions change how signals are interpreted.

In diving, light behaves differently as depth increases. Colors fade, distance compresses, and objects appear closer than they are. The diver sees clearly, but perception shifts subtly under pressure. Nothing has been fabricated. Nothing is imaginary. The environment is real. It is the conditions that alter interpretation.

Governance distortion forms under similar physics.

Controls operate. Policies are documented. Audit findings are limited. Experts are competent. Regulators may even have previously accepted a methodology. These signals are real, not fabricated. They are not misleading in isolation.

But when those signals become the primary basis for leadership reassurance, perception shifts: Discipline is interpreted as governance. Stability is interpreted as alignment.

And absence of challenge is interpreted as ownership.

Exposure accumulates beneath that confidence, and distortion persists because nothing appears broken. There is no fraud. There is no concealment. There is no systemic collapse of controls. The organization is doing what responsible enterprises believe they should do: documenting methodology, applying policy consistently, responding to inquiries, passing audits.

In the meantime, posture the cumulative exposure created by sustained decisions at scale—hardens quietly. A valuation methodology applied consistently across jurisdictions becomes embedded in operating rhythm. A classification framework validated once becomes default practice. An origin strategy designed under earlier trade agreements persists as sourcing expands. Transfer pricing alignments interact with customs valuation in ways that amplify duty concentration over time.

Volume increases. Geographic reach expands. Business models evolve. Enforcement posture tightens. The signals remain stable, but the exposure changes.

Distortion at depth does not form because organizations lack intelligence. It forms because escalation is typically tied to disruption rather than accumulation. Leadership engagement is triggered by assessment, inquiry, penalty, or dispute—not by scale alone.

Then reframing occurs. A single reassessment challenges a methodology long considered defensible. A one-year calculation expands into multiple years of lookback.

A local inquiry reveals implications across jurisdictions. What appeared stable becomes material.

From leadership's perspective, exposure seems to surface suddenly. In reality, nothing sudden occurred. The exposure was present, and it had been compounding. It had been carried forward each year through consistent application. What changed was not the risk—it was visibility.

Distortion corrects when external pressure forces recalibration. Before then, the enterprise seems well controlled. Boards receive updates. Audit committees review reports. Trade leaders present metrics demonstrating discipline. The enterprise sees activity and interprets governance. Confidence rises because nothing indicates failure.

But confidence built on visible control alone is conditional. It holds only until scale alters consequence.

Structural distortion explains why intelligent executives, acting in good faith, can believe trade risk is governed—until exposure reframes the narrative. It explains why restructuring feels corrective, why reporting feels sufficient, and why stability feels safe.

The phenomenon is not rooted in incompetence. It is rooted in architecture. When leadership is not required to deliberately equalize cumulative exposure as conditions change, the system continues operating smoothly while consequence deepens beneath it.

Governable organizations do not eliminate complexity. They eliminate distortion, designing visibility so that exposure cannot scale without deliberate leadership reengagement.

Once distortion is understood, the question changes. It is no longer whether controls function. It is whether cumulative exposure remains structurally visible before enforcement reframes it.

That shift marks the end of assumed stability and the beginning of equalization.

Understanding distortion at depth is not academic. It is structural.

Once leadership recognizes that visible control can coexist with invisible accumulation, the obligation shifts. Governance can no longer rely on reporting intensity, organizational placement, or episodic vigilance. It must be embedded in how exposure is owned, how escalation is triggered, and how enduring decisions are reauthorized as depth increases.

That design—not energy, not movement, not structure alone—is what separates programs that appear governed from those that are governable.

SECTION IV

The Discipline of Equalization

Once distortion at depth is understood, responsibility changes.

The issue is no longer whether controls function. The issue is whether exposure can continue to grow without leadership deliberately choosing to carry it.

Equalization begins there—not with more slides, not with moving the function again, not with another audit cycle or revised dashboards.

It begins with ownership of exposure.

By exposure, I do not mean a single classification decision or one valuation methodology. I mean the cumulative trade exposure created by sustained decisions applied at scale across years, jurisdictions, and growing volume.

Someone at the leadership level must own that. Not observe it and not receive updates about it. Own it.

That ownership cannot depend on who happens to be in the role, how recently a regulator asked a question, or whether the last audit cycle was clean. Instead, it must be embedded.

Executive governance means that leadership accepts responsibility for the exposure the enterprise is carrying—not just whether individual transactions were processed correctly.

Governance requires structure, not vigilance. It requires clarity about when leadership is expected to look up and say, "We are still choosing to carry this."

Equalization requires defined exposure thresholds. Not thresholds tied only to error, but thresholds tied to accumulation:

- At what point does cumulative duty exposure become something leadership reviews directly?
- At what point does growth in volume or geographic expansion require stepping back and asking whether the approach still makes sense?
- At what point does a shift in enforcement climate require reconsidering assumptions that have been operating for years?

If those points are undefined, leadership involvement becomes inconsistent. It depends on what is visible at the moment, who is paying attention, or whether something has drawn scrutiny. And inconsistent involvement allows exposure to expand quietly.

Equalization also requires periodic reauthorization because trade programs rely on methodologies that endure. Valuation frameworks are applied year after year. Classification structures support expanding product lines. Origin strategies persist as sourcing evolves. Transfer pricing alignments influence duty concentration over time.

Many of these decisions are reasonable and defensible. But defensibility is not the same as deliberation. At scale, leadership must occasionally ask a simple question: whether the enterprise is still consciously choosing to carry the exposure created by its methodology at its current scale. Not because it failed, not because someone challenged it, but because the consequence attached to it has grown.

If that question is never asked, exposure continues under historical approval even though historical approval does not automatically align with present-day scale.

Escalation must also evolve. Most organizations escalate when something goes wrong—when a reassessment challenges a methodology, when a dispute recalculates prior years, when an inquiry expands beyond a single transaction.

Equalization requires escalation before something goes wrong: when volume increases materially, the business model changes, the company expands into new jurisdictions, or tariff exposure concentrates in ways it did not before.

These developments may not generate findings, but they still alter the exposure the enterprise is carrying.

If leadership engages only when something breaks, it is always responding to accumulated exposure rather than governing it. Equalization brings engagement forward.

Finally, exposure must be understandable beyond the people who manage it. Trade knowledge often lives in individuals. The reasoning behind decisions sits in conversations, in emails, in experience. Over time, that knowledge becomes assumed.

That is not governance. Leadership should be able to explain:

- Why this exposure exists.
- When it was last deliberately reconsidered.
- What assumptions it relies on.
- How large it has become.
- How it interacts with enterprise risk.

If the explanations depend entirely on institutional memory, then the enterprise is more fragile than it appears.

Together, these disciplines can help to shift trade from operational management to enterprise ownership:

- Operational oversight focuses on transaction accuracy and process adherence. It ensures discipline at the execution level.
- Executive governance focuses on cumulative exposure and enterprise consequence. It ensures alignment at scale.
- Operational excellence keeps transactions disciplined.
- Equalization ensures that the exposure those systems create remains deliberate.

Structure alone cannot create enterprise ownership. Reporting lines can clarify coordination, but they do not define when exposure must be reviewed. They do not require reauthorization. They do not force leadership to decide whether continued exposure is acceptable.

Only deliberate design accomplishes that.

> *"Exposure is not allowed to expand indefinitely with-out leadership consciously choosing to carry it."*

Equalization is not heavier management. It is disciplined reconsideration under growth. It requires leadership to accept that stability does not eliminate responsibility, that growth requires review, and that scale amplifies consequence even when discipline remains intact.

When equalization is embedded:

- Growth triggers review.
- Scale prompts conversation.
- Stability does not automatically equal comfort.
- Exposure is not allowed to expand indefinitely without leadership consciously choosing to carry it.

Trade risk will always be complex.

Complexity is manageable. Unexamined exposure is not.

Equalization does not eliminate risk. It ensures that the risk being carried is intentional.

And once exposure is intentional, governance stops being implied.

It becomes real.

SECTION V

The Architecture That Holds at Depth

A trade program does not become governable because it is disciplined. It becomes governable because it is designed to withstand depth.

In diving, equipment alone does not make a descent safe. Skill alone does not make it safe. What makes sustained descent survivable is architecture—pressure awareness, equalization discipline, and equipment configured for depth rather than surface comfort.

Governance is no different. A disciplined trade program can still accumulate exposure quietly if leadership has not designed how that exposure is owned, surfaced, and reconsidered as scale increases.

The architecture that holds at depth is not an operational enhancement. It is a structural requirement. Without it, the organization may appear stable while pressure builds beneath it. With it, exposure cannot expand without deliberate leadership engagement.

Three structural disciplines make that possible.

1. The first discipline is exposure ownership.

In a governable enterprise, leadership explicitly owns cumulative trade exposure. Not individual classifications, not transaction-level accuracy, not procedural compliance. Cumulative exposure.

Exposure is the sustained enterprise consequence created by valuation methodologies applied across jurisdictions, classification frameworks operating at scale, origin strategies supporting global sourcing, and transfer pricing alignments influencing duty concentration over time.

Those decisions do not belong solely to the trade team. They belong to the enterprise.

Exposure ownership means leadership has defined when cumulative duty impact requires its attention. It means enduring methodologies are deliberately reaffirmed as scale increases. It means the enterprise has consciously accepted the exposure it is carrying, not simply inherited it.

Without exposure ownership, expertise can become insulation. Discipline can create comfort. Comfort allows exposure to grow quietly beneath stable metrics.

Ownership collapses that insulation.

2. The second discipline is visibility architecture.

In diving, visibility changes with depth. Divers who rely only on what appears immediately in front of them can lose orientation.

Governance visibility behaves the same way.

Reporting confirms activity. It shows error rates, audit findings, and resolved disputes. Those signals are important, but they are not the same as visibility into accumulation.

A governable architecture does not wait for friction to surface exposure. It does not rely solely on reassessments, cross-jurisdictional inquiries, penalties, or disputes to bring exposure into leadership view. Instead, it ties visibility to scale. Scale can increase when volume expands materially, when jurisdictional reach grows, when enforcement posture tightens across regions, or when business transformation concentrates exposure in new ways.

These changes may not generate findings, but they still alter enterprise exposure.

Visibility architecture ensures those shifts become visible before external pressure forces the conversation. It consolidates exposure across jurisdictions and business units. It translates cumulative trade exposure into the same enterprise terms leadership already governs—capital, margin, continuity, and regulatory credibility.

Exposure must not scale invisibly. Depth must not increase unnoticed.

3. The third discipline is continuity design.

Divers do not depend on memory alone to manage pressure. Instead, gauges are visible and procedures are repeated. Equipment is configured so that equalization is continuous rather than improvised.

Governance requires the same discipline. Exposure cannot depend solely on institutional memory. The reasoning behind sustained methodologies cannot live only in conversations or in the experience of long-tenured individuals.

Continuity design makes exposure legible beyond any single leader. Leadership should be able to articulate:

- Why this exposure exists.
- When it was last deliberately reconsidered.
- What assumptions sustain it.
- How large it has become relative to enterprise consequence.

If those explanations disappear when personnel change, governance has not been embedded.

Continuity design ensures that exposure remains owned through restructuring, expansion, and turnover. Together, these disciplines shift trade from operational containment to enterprise durability:

- In operational oversight, stability is the objective.
- In governance at depth, alignment under pressure is the objective.
- Discipline at the transaction level ensures accuracy.
- Architecture ensures survivability.

Repeated restructuring does not solve exposure drift. Movement can sharpen attention temporarily, but it does not redesign how exposure becomes visible or how leadership reauthorizes enduring positions as scale increases. Architecture does that.

Equalization does not happen once. It happens repeatedly as depth changes.

Trade will remain complex when these disciplines are embedded:

- Growth triggers structured reconsideration.
- Scale prompts leadership engagement.
- Stability does not eliminate review.
- Exposure is not allowed to expand indefinitely without conscious ownership.

Complexity is navigable. Unexamined exposure at depth is not.

Architecture does not eliminate pressure. It ensures that pressure is managed deliberately.

Once embedded, restructuring loses urgency and surprise loses shock. Leadership conversation shifts from reaction to calibration.

Trade ceases to sit at the edge of governance and becomes integrated into it.

The difference is not semantic. It is structural.

And structure is what holds at depth.

SECTION VI

The Leadership Decision

Once distortion is understood and architecture is defined, neutrality disappears.

At depth, there is no such thing as remaining still. You are either descending with discipline or drifting under pressure.

The issue is no longer technical. It is no longer organizational. It is no longer about where trade reports or how many controls operate.

It is about whether leadership chooses to govern exposure—or allow it to persist by default.

Once equalization is understood, leadership faces a structural choice. Every executive team ultimately operates within one of two structural conditions.

In the first condition, trade functions effectively:

- Controls operate.
- Audit findings remain limited.
- Escalation occurs when required.
- Dashboards show stability.
- Reporting confirms discipline.

From the surface, the system appears controlled, but exposure accumulates beneath that stability.

When disruption occurs—a reassessment, a cross-border inquiry, a recalculation extending across years—leadership engages. Structure may shift. Oversight intensifies and attention sharpens.

For a period, the organization equalizes. Pressure is felt. Adjustments are made.

Over time, urgency recedes. Meetings return to routine, metrics stabilize, and the sense of depth fades. Calm reasserts itself, quietly and convincingly.

This condition can persist for years. It is not negligent, reckless, or inattentive. But it is structurally incomplete because engagement remains reactive. It is triggered by pressure rather than designed for it.

In the second condition, leadership makes a deliberate shift. Trade exposure is no longer treated as something the trade team manages quietly in the background. Rather, it is recognized as an enterprise-level responsibility.

Long-standing methodologies are not assumed to be permanent. They are deliberately reconsidered as the organization grows.

Escalation does not wait for something to break. It is triggered when exposure increases, even if operations appear stable.

The reasoning behind sustained positions does not disappear when people change roles.

It remains visible, documented, and understood.

Leadership does not wait for a regulator to redefine the risk. Instead, exposure is surfaced internally, before outside pressure forces the conversation. In this condition, disruption does not create awareness because awareness already exists.

The difference between these two conditions is not compliance maturity. It is governance design.

The organizations most vulnerable to structural distortion are often those that are operationally strong. Discipline creates credibility, credibility creates confidence, and confidence reduces structural interrogation.

When systems appear controlled and professionals appear capable, leadership feels justified in maintaining distance because that distance feels efficient, appropriate, and respectful of expertise—until scale changes consequence.

The danger is not visible disorder. It is earned stability that masks cumulative exposure.

The stronger the execution, the more persuasive the illusion of safety.

Executive governance requires leaders to question not weakness, but strength—to ask whether the very stability they trust has allowed exposure to deepen.

At depth, pressure does not announce itself with drama. It builds.

If a diver does not equalize repeatedly, injury does not occur immediately. Instead, it occurs as depth increases beyond what the body can absorb unconsciously.

Governance behaves the same way.

Most executive teams do not believe they are operating inside structural distortion. They believe they are operating responsibly. That belief allows exposure to persist without deliberate ownership.

When discipline is visible and disruption is absent, there is little incentive to question architecture. Confidence feels earned. But governance is not confirmed by the absence of friction. It is confirmed by deliberate ownership of cumulative exposure as the enterprise scales.

Organizations that remain structurally defaulted are not careless. They are relying on stability to substitute for architecture. Trade expertise operates effectively, controls function as designed, and reporting reassures. Yet leadership engagement remains reactive. The leadership decision is whether to leave that default intact.

Executives do not need to master customs valuation to govern trade. They do need to decide whether cumulative exposure will remain an operational byproduct—or an enterprise-level responsibility.

That decision does not require restructuring. It requires commitment. It requires accepting that depth demands equalization. It requires refusing to allow exposure to grow simply because nothing has broken.

Equalization at depth is not dramatic. It is disciplined and repetitive, and it is often invisible to observers at the surface. But it is what allows descent to continue safely.

Governability is not achieved through vigilance alone. It is achieved when leadership refuses to allow exposure to exist without deliberate ownership, even in periods of stability.

The choice is structural. The pressure is real.

And at depth, delay compounds consequence.

Chapter 9 will not ask whether exposure exists. It will ask whether leadership is prepared to own it.

CHAPTER 9

The Blue Hole: Governance at Depth

From the surface, the ocean appears stable. There is light, orientation, and air.

Expansion often feels the same way. Markets are growing. Revenue is increasing. Operations are disciplined. The enterprise appears in control.

But descent changes conditions. As depth increases, pressure builds gradually and without drama. The diver does not feel the shift immediately. There is no sudden alarm or visible fracture. Only quiet compression.

Governance behaves the same way.

As expansion accelerates—across jurisdictions, suppliers, regulatory regimes, and strategic initiatives—systemic exposure deepens. The enterprise may remain operationally disciplined. Controls may function effectively. Reporting may indicate stability. Yet structural pressure increases beneath the surface.

At depth, oxygen is not optional; it is monitored continuously. Limits are not advisory; they are absolute. Time becomes a governed variable.

Enterprise governance must operate under the same physics.

> *"The question is not whether the enterprise is performing well. The question is whether its governance system is engineered to function under increasing pressure."*

Surface calm does not eliminate pressure at depth. Stability at scale does not eliminate systemic exposure. The question is not whether the enterprise is performing well but whether its governance system is engineered to function under increasing pressure.

Expansion does not become dangerous because growth occurs. It becomes structurally dangerous when governance has not been engineered to function under increasing pressure.

At depth, oxygen is monitored before it is needed. Limits are defined before they are approached. Ascent is planned before descent begins. Enterprise governance must operate under the same discipline.

This chapter examines what governance requires once descent has begun.

SECTION I

Pre-Dive Assessment

No diver enters depth casually.

Before descent, equipment is verified, oxygen supply is calculated, environmental conditions are assessed, and limits are acknowledged. The decision to descend is not a reaction to curiosity. It is a commitment to operate under pressure.

From above, the Blue Hole appears perfectly contained—a deep indigo circle surrounded by bright reef. It looks finite, measured, and bounded.

It is not.

Its walls descend vertically. Light fades quickly. Pressure increases without visual drama. Divers who enter without preparation often misjudge how quickly depth overtakes perception.

Enterprise expansion behaves the same way.

Once leadership accepts responsibility for systemic trade exposure, the question is no longer whether the trade function is competent. It is whether governance has been deliberately positioned to function under increasing structural pressure.

That positioning begins with anchoring ownership.

Systemic trade exposure must be formally integrated into the governance body responsible for enterprise-level risk. In most organizations, that governance body is the Enterprise Risk Management (ERM) Committee. If exposure does not reside within that forum's mandate, it will remain operational by default—managed locally, absorbed silently, and escalated only when externally reframed.

Structural ownership is not symbolic. It requires explicit inclusion within the enterprise risk inventory reviewed by the ERM Committee. If systemic trade exposure is absent from that inventory, it is absent from disciplined oversight.

Anchoring ownership also requires defined parameters for review. The ERM Committee must approve the thresholds that require reassessment. These parameters must reflect scale, jurisdictional concentration, regulatory exposure, and strategic expansion—not transactional error rates or isolated findings. Governance at depth is concerned with systemic position, not isolated variance.

Without governance-approved thresholds, escalation remains optional. Optional escalation is not governance. It is reliance on judgment.

Pre-dive assessment further requires deliberate review intervals. Similarly, sustained trade methodologies cannot persist indefinitely without deliberate reconsideration. Expansion alters pressure, and pressure alters consequence. Governance must therefore recalibrate systemic exposure at defined intervals aligned with enterprise growth and strategic planning cycles.

Clarity about ownership, thresholds, and deliberate review intervals is not procedural detail. It is structural preparation.

Descent without preparation introduces avoidable risk. Expansion without anchored governance does the same.

Anchoring ownership within the Enterprise Risk Management Committee is conceptually straightforward, but in practice, it is often resisted. Why? Trade exposure has historically been classified as operational. It sits within supply chain, finance, or legal. It is managed by specialists. It is reviewed through audits. It is reported as compliance status. Reclassifying it as enterprise-level systemic exposure requires a shift in mindset.

Boards and executive committees are accustomed to reviewing strategic risks—geopolitical volatility, liquidity exposure, cyber threats, regulatory investigations, market contraction. Trade compliance is often perceived as a control function, not a structural exposure driver. This classification error weakens governance at depth.

Systemic trade exposure influences margin sustainability, capital allocation, geographic strategy, and reputational resilience. It can trigger multi-year reassessment, regulatory scrutiny across jurisdictions, and compressed decision cycles at the board level. These are enterprise consequences. If exposure has enterprise consequence, it requires enterprise anchoring.

Another source of resistance is performance alignment.

Operational leaders may perceive ERM integration as oversight expansion rather than structural protection. Risk committees may hesitate to assume responsibility for exposure mechanics they consider technical. Finance may treat exposure as contingent liability rather than strategic dependency.

Anchoring therefore requires clarity of definition. Systemic exposure must be described in enterprise language, not technical terminology. It must be translated into margin impact, liquidity sensitivity, geographic concentration, and strategic dependency.

If the Enterprise Risk Management Committee does not understand exposure in those terms, integration becomes symbolic. But symbolic anchoring does not protect at depth.

Formal integration also requires documented mandate. The ERM Committee charter should explicitly reference systemic trade exposure as an enterprise risk category. Review frequency should be defined. Threshold approval should be formalized. Board reporting pathways should be clarified. Without formalization, anchoring becomes conversational rather than structural.

Descent cannot rely on conversation. It requires architecture.

Finally, anchoring must extend beyond awareness to authority. If the ERM Committee identifies increasing systemic exposure but lacks authority to require reassessment, escalation remains informational. Governance authority must include the ability to mandate recalibration, request scenario modeling, and elevate matters to the board when structural limits approach.

Ownership without authority is surveillance.

Ownership with authority is governance.

*"Ownership without authority is surveillance.
Ownership with authority is governance."*

Pre-dive assessment therefore requires more than inclusion in risk inventory. It requires reclassification of systemic trade exposure as an enterprise-level determinant of strategic durability. Without that reclassification, descent begins with incomplete engineering.

Incomplete engineering does not create immediate instability. That is why anchoring failures persist. An organization can operate for years with systemic trade exposure classified as operational. Performance may remain strong, and audit findings may be minimal. Regulatory inquiries may not materialize. The absence of visible consequence reinforces the belief that existing placement is sufficient.

But classification determines visibility.

If systemic exposure remains within operational reporting lines, then leadership engagement becomes episodic. Review occurs during audit cycles or in response to inquiry. It does not occur in alignment with strategy. Depth increases silently when governance review is decoupled from expansion decisions.

Anchoring at the enterprise level ensures that systemic exposure is evaluated when strategic decisions are made—not after their effects compound. This distinction is subtle but decisive.

When acquisition strategy is reviewed by the board, geographic expansion plans are debated, capital allocation is approved, and market entry decisions are authorized, systemic trade exposure must be present in those discussions—not as technical compliance detail but as structural exposure affecting durability.

If exposure is reviewed separately from strategy, it becomes reactive by design.

Enterprise anchoring also changes the tone of governance. When systemic exposure is positioned as enterprise-level risk, recalibration becomes a leadership decision rather than an operational adjustment. It moves from technical debate to strategic evaluation.

That shift alters accountability. Operational leaders no longer carry exposure alone. The board shares responsibility for the depth at which the enterprise chooses to operate. At depth, shared responsibility is not dilution. It is clarity.

If systemic exposure is left within operational tiers, the organization effectively delegates depth monitoring to specialists while strategic leaders accelerate descent. That is not governance engineering. It is structural misalignment.

Pre-dive assessment therefore requires a leadership decision before any trigger is activated.

Will systemic exposure be governed where strategy is governed? Or will it remain where transactions are executed?

The answer determines whether descent begins with shared oxygen—or with isolation.

SECTION II

Descent Protocol

Descent is sustained by discipline, not by intention.

Once expansion begins, systemic trade exposure does not remain static. It deepens with scale, jurisdictional complexity, supplier concentration, regulatory shifts, and strategic acceleration. The organization may not feel immediate strain, and operational performance may remain stable. But structural pressure increases regardless of perception.

A diver tracks depth continuously. An enterprise must do the same.

Descent protocol in governance requires defined escalation triggers that operate independently of failure. Most organizations escalate when deviation occurs—an inquiry, a dispute, a penalty, a breakdown in controls. Those are surface-level alarms. They respond to consequence.

Governance at depth cannot rely on consequence as a signal. Systemic exposure must trigger structured review based on conditions, not disruption.

> *"Systemic exposure must trigger structured review based on conditions, not disruption."*

Three categories of triggers govern descent.

The first trigger is scale expansion. When import volume increases materially under a sustained methodology, when new jurisdictions are added, or when concentration intensifies in higher-scrutiny regions, systemic exposure changes. Even if execution remains precise, aggregate risk deepens.

The second trigger is environmental shift. Changes in enforcement intensity, interpretive guidance, tariff regimes, or sanctions landscapes alter structural risk without altering internal processes. Governance must respond to shifts in external pressure, not only internal variance.

The third trigger is strategic transformation. Acquisitions, product diversification, supply chain redesign, and market expansion reshape systemic exposure automatically. Strategy alters depth.

Triggers must be quantified and approved at the governance level. They must be embedded within the mandate of the Enterprise Risk Management Committee. Without formalized parameters, review remains discretionary. Discretion introduces delay, which in turn narrows margin.

Descent protocol is not about generating alerts. It is about defining inevitability: When defined conditions are met, review occurs. When scale increases, exposure is reassessed. When the external environment shifts, sustained positions are recalibrated.

Escalation is not a matter of preference. It is structural.

Structural Failure Modes

Descent protocol does not fail most often because triggers are absent, but because those triggers are neutralized.

In many enterprises, exposure thresholds are defined but set too high to activate meaningfully. Escalation criteria may exist on paper, yet they are calibrated in ways that favor stability over scrutiny. The intent is to avoid unnecessary disruption. The effect is delayed recognition.

Systemic exposure does not announce itself in absolute numbers alone. It expands through interaction effects—volume multiplied by jurisdictional complexity, multiplied by regulatory volatility, multiplied by concentration risk. When thresholds fail to account for interaction effects, governance reviews are postponed until external scrutiny forces recalibration.

Another common distortion occurs when exposure is fragmented across reporting lines. A regional increase may not appear material in isolation. A product-line shift may not appear consequential independently. Yet, when aggregated, these changes alter systemic position significantly. Without deliberate aggregation design, trigger activation becomes mathematically unlikely.

ERM Committees may also inadvertently suppress escalation by over-weighting historical stability. If a methodology has operated for years without challenge, it may be perceived as inherently stable. Yet stability in one enforcement environment does not guarantee resilience in another. Depth conditions change. Pressure does not remain constant.

Trigger discipline therefore requires periodic recalibration of thresholds themselves. As the enterprise scales, what once represented acceptable exposure may represent structural vulnerability. Governance must adapt not only to expansion, but to its own historical assumptions.

This is where many organizations miscalculate. They assume that competence at the surface guarantees survivability at depth.

It does not.

Without disciplined descent protocol, systemic exposure accumulates beneath the line of executive visibility. Review becomes reactive, correction becomes compressed, and margin narrows.

Governance at depth requires that escalation precede discomfort.

Without descent protocol, expansion proceeds without depth markers. With it, systemic exposure becomes visible before it becomes irreversible.

Escalation Ownership

Triggers do not function unless ownership is explicit.

In many enterprises, escalation pathways exist in theory but remain ambiguous in practice. Operational teams may recognize threshold movement, and risk functions may observe increasing exposure. Yet uncertainty persists regarding who carries authority to formally elevate concern to the enterprise tier.

Therefore, escalation ownership must be defined before descent accelerates.

First, responsibility to identify threshold movement must be assigned clearly. This identification is typically the responsibility of the operational or risk function.

Second, authority to elevate systemic exposure to the Enterprise Risk Management Committee must be explicit. If escalation requires consensus, comfort, or informal alignment before elevation, delay is introduced.

Third, response authority must be defined. Once systemic exposure is escalated, who determines whether recalibration is required? Who has the mandate to suspend expansion in a jurisdiction? Who can require reassessment of a sustained interpretive position? Who informs the board if necessary?

Without defined response authority, escalation becomes informational rather than structural.

In diving, a buddy does not request permission to signal low air. Nor does a diver debate whether ascent is appropriate once a limit has been reached. The signal itself carries authority.

Enterprise governance must operate under similar clarity.

If threshold movement requires negotiation rather than action, escalation ownership is weak. Weak escalation ownership consumes margin.

Another distortion occurs when escalation authority is placed too low in the organization. Operational leaders may recognize exposure but lack an enterprise-level mandate to intervene. Alternatively, escalation authority may sit too high, insulated from exposure mechanics and dependent on filtered reporting.

Governance engineering requires escalation pathways that are direct, time-bound, and insulated from performance incentives.

Escalation cannot be subordinate to revenue pressure. It must be structurally protected.

At depth, hesitation consumes air.

In enterprise expansion, hesitation consumes margin.

Escalation ownership is therefore not procedural detail.

It is oxygen discipline in practice.

SECTION III

Depth Recognition

In the Blue Hole, color disappears long before the diver realizes it. Red fades first. Then orange. Then yellow. The environment changes gradually, almost politely. Only instruments reveal how deep the descent has become.

Enterprise exposure behaves the same way.

At depth, perception changes before awareness does. Color fades gradually, distance distorts, and objects appear closer than they are. The diver may feel calm and capable, unaware that the environment is already operating under different physics.

From the surface, the Blue Hole appears contained—a perfect circle of indigo surrounded by reef. But once descent begins, depth increases rapidly. The walls drop away, and orientation narrows. There is no gradual shoreline transition to signal how far you have gone.

Enterprise expansion can create the same illusion of containment. As organizations scale across jurisdictions, suppliers, product lines, and regulatory environments, systemic trade exposure deepens in ways that are not immediately perceptible.

Each business unit appears stable. Each region reports compliance. Each methodology may function precisely as designed. From the surface, there is no disruption.

But systemic exposure deepens vertically, not horizontally. That distinction matters. And depth is not measured by local stability, but by systemic position.

Systemic exposure becomes difficult to recognize because it fragments. Regional teams assess their own activity. Product groups evaluate their own classifications. Finance monitors margin. Legal interprets regulatory change. Each view is accurate within its boundary, but none reflects total depth. Depth recognition requires aggregation beyond operational lines.

Without aggregation architecture, organizations mistake distribution for diversification. Exposure appears spread when, in reality, it may be concentrated—across valuation assumptions, origin determinations, tariff regimes, or geopolitical risk corridors.

At depth, pressure is uniform. It does not differentiate between regions.

Enterprise exposure behaves similarly. Enforcement authorities do not evaluate risk in fragments. They evaluate position in aggregate.

Another distortion at depth is time compression. A diver at significant depth cannot ascend instantly without consequence. The deeper the descent, the narrower the recovery window. In enterprise governance, systemic exposure may remain stable for years. Then an inquiry, audit, or regulatory shift reframes systemic position in compressed time, and the organization is forced to evaluate years of accumulated exposure within months.

That compression is not created by enforcement. It is created by depth unrecognized.

Recognition, therefore, is not reporting volume. It is understanding systemic interaction.

Volume multiplied by duration. Duration multiplied by jurisdictional intensity. Jurisdictional intensity multiplied by strategic reliance. These interaction effects determine depth.

Recognition also requires confronting comfort.

Long-standing methodologies often create institutional confidence. "We have always done it this way" becomes a stabilizing narrative. At the surface, that narrative feels rational. At depth, it becomes insulation.

Governance at depth requires the discipline to reassess systemic positions before external pressure forces reconsideration.

Recognition is not about discovering error. It is about acknowledging exposure before it hardens. The deeper the organization descends without structured recognition, the more constrained its eventual options become.

At depth, oxygen remains constant only if monitored. Systemic exposure remains governable only if seen in totality. Recognition is therefore not operational awareness. It is an understanding of systemic interaction.

Recognition must also confront concentration risk that hides inside apparent diversification.

In diving, the Blue Hole appears expansive and open from above. But with descent, that space narrows. The walls are vertical. The exit path is singular. What appears broad from the surface becomes structurally constrained at depth.

Enterprise exposure behaves similarly.

Organizations often interpret geographic spread as risk dispersion. Multiple jurisdictions, multiple suppliers, and multiple product lines all create a perception of diversification. Yet systemic exposure frequently concentrates around a limited number of interpretive assumptions, valuation methodologies, origin strategies, or tariff treatments applied consistently across the enterprise.

Breadth of footprint does not guarantee breadth of risk posture.

When a single valuation framework governs billions in imports, that is concentration. When a preferential origin assumption underpins global sourcing, that is concentration. When a tariff engineering approach is embedded across multiple divisions, that is concentration.

At depth, concentration determines consequence. Recognition therefore requires leadership to ask not only "Where are we operating?" but also "Where are our assumptions concentrated?"

Another distortion at depth is false redundancy.

Multiple review layers may exist—internal audit, regional compliance checks, finance oversight, external advisory validation. The presence of multiple reviewers creates a sense of structural reinforcement. Yet if all layers rely on the same underlying assumption, redundancy becomes illusion.

Independent review is not diversification if the foundational position remains unexamined. Depth recognition demands examination of underlying frameworks, not only confirmation of process execution.

Finally, recognition must occur at the enterprise tier.

Boards and executive committees frequently see assurance metrics, not systemic position. For example, operational dashboards often reflect transactional accuracy. Audit findings may reflect control effectiveness. Finance may track margin impact. None of these necessarily reflect systemic exposure in aggregate.

Depth recognition requires aggregation at the level where consequence resides, not at the level where activity occurs. Without this elevation, leadership operates at the surface while exposure deepens below.

Recognition is not alarm. It is clarity about structural depth. It is enterprise-level visibility into how deep the organization has already gone.

Depth becomes most dangerous when it becomes normal.

In diving, experienced divers grow comfortable at increasing depth. Confidence expands with familiarity. The environment may feel manageable. Procedures become routine. Yet comfort does not alter pressure physics, and familiarity does not eliminate absorption.

Enterprise growth produces similar normalization. As expansion succeeds, leadership recalibrates what feels acceptable. Increased exposure becomes part of operating rhythm. Interpretive dependency feels stable because it has not yet been challenged. Concentration in a high-return jurisdiction feels justified because performance reinforces it.

Success conditions perception, and recognition discipline weakens when stability reinforces confidence.

Organizations rarely misjudge depth during crisis. They misjudge it during sustained success.

Growth narratives compound this effect. When expansion is framed as strategic achievement, governance recalibration can feel counterproductive. Signals that margin is narrowing may be interpreted as hesitation. Exposure analysis may be perceived as obstruction.

At depth, ambition must yield to physics. In enterprise governance, ambition must remain subordinate to structural limits.

Depth recognition therefore requires counterbalancing success with scrutiny:

- If revenue has doubled, exposure must be reexamined.
- If geographic footprint has expanded, interpretive concentration must be reevaluated.
- If enforcement intensity has increased, sustained positions must be reauthorized.

Recognition must intensify when success accelerates because success accelerates descent.

Depth recognition also requires quantitative discipline.

In diving, depth is not estimated by sensation. It is measured by gauge. Air supply is not inferred by comfort. It is monitored numerically. In diving, time at depth is monitored because it varies. Air consumption changes with exertion, stress, equipment efficiency, and breathing discipline. A diver who remains controlled preserves margin. A diver who breathes rapidly shortens it.

Enterprise exposure behaves similarly. For example, two organizations may operate at comparable scale. One may consume governance margin quickly because exposure is concentrated, thresholds are undefined, or delay in visibility is high. The second may preserve margin because recognition is structured and recalibration occurs deliberately.

Depth is not defined solely by scale. It is defined by how margin is managed under pressure.

Enterprise governance must operate with similar clarity. Systemic exposure cannot be recognized solely through narrative updates or periodic reporting summaries. Instead, they enterprise requires structured aggregation models that quantify systemic position across jurisdictions, methodologies, and strategic dependencies.

Volume alone is insufficient. Duration alone is insufficient. Jurisdictional intensity alone is insufficient.

Depth is determined by interaction: volume multiplied by duration, duration multiplied by enforcement environment, enforcement environment multiplied by interpretive vulnerability, interpretive vulnerability multiplied by strategic reliance.

These multipliers compound quietly, and recognition requires modeling how they interact over time.

Most organizations measure activity. Fewer measure accumulation. Almost none measure interaction.

Without interaction modeling, leadership may see rising import volume without recognizing concentration in high-volatility jurisdictions. They may see stable margins without recognizing reliance on a single interpretive assumption. They may see compliance rates without recognizing that a regulatory shift could retroactively alter exposure across multiple fiscal years.

At depth, what matters is not isolated correctness. What matters is sensitivity:

- How sensitive is the enterprise to reinterpretation of a valuation framework?
- How sensitive is systemic exposure to a change in origin qualification?
- How sensitive is the organization to geopolitical reclassification or sanctions expansion?

Sensitivity analysis is depth awareness.

Another layer of distortion at depth is governance delay in visibility—specifically, the delay between exposure change and leadership recognition.

As organizations grow, delay in visibility increases unless architecture reduces it. Regional reporting cycles may not align. Business units may escalate at different thresholds. Audit reviews may lag operational change by quarters. By the time systemic exposure surfaces at the enterprise level, depth may already exceed prior assumptions.

Governance at depth demands reduction of delay in visibility. Recognition must occur while margin still exists.

Boards frequently miscalibrate depth because they see assurance, not exposure trajectory. Audit reports confirm controls are operating. Compliance attestations confirm policies are followed. Financial statements reflect current margin. None of these documents reflect how deep the enterprise has already descended.

Recognition at the board level must therefore include trajectory analysis:

- Are we deeper this year than last?
- Has systemic exposure expanded proportional to revenue growth?
- Has interpretive concentration increased?
- Has enforcement volatility intensified in our core jurisdictions?

If governance is oxygen at depth, recognition is the gauge.

Without a gauge, descent continues on assumption.

With it, leadership sees depth before depth dictates terms.

SECTION IV

No-Decompression Limits

In diving, no-decompression limits define how long a diver can remain at depth before ascent requires structured stops. These limits are not theoretical. They are derived from pressure physics. Exceed them, and ascent becomes dangerous.

What matters is not whether the diver feels fine. What matters is how long the body has been absorbing pressure.

Enterprise governance operates under similar constraints. Systemic exposure may remain manageable for extended periods. Operations may appear stable, revenue may grow, and enforcement may remain quiet. Yet exposure is being absorbed into the structure of the enterprise.

The longer exposure accumulates without structured reassessment, the narrower the margin for correction becomes. And margin is everything.

Two organizations at similar scale do not share identical margin. For example, one may have clear thresholds, structured review intervals, diversified interpretive assumptions, and defined escalation architecture. Another may operate on historical confidence, fragmented reporting, and informal reassessment.

The first preserves margin. The second consumes it, often without awareness.

In diving, breathing discipline affects how long a diver can safely remain at depth. Calm, controlled respiration extends available air. Exertion shortens it. Stress accelerates consumption.

Enterprise behavior affects governance margin in the same way:

- Aggressive expansion without review shortens margin.
- Concentrated methodologies shorten margin.
- Geographic reliance in volatile jurisdictions shortens margin.
- Unexamined interpretive assumptions shorten margin.

Margin does not disappear suddenly. Instead, it narrows gradually—until it does not exist at all.

No-decompression limits in governance are the structural thresholds beyond which correction becomes compressed, expensive, and externally dictated. These limits must be defined before they are crossed. They may include:

- Enterprise-wide exposure concentration thresholds.
- Duration limits on sustained methodologies without reassessment.
- Jurisdictional intensity thresholds.
- Strategic dependency ratios.

The specific metrics will vary by organization. The principle does not.

Limits are not advisory. They are structural boundaries protecting ascent.

Without defined limits, leadership assumes it has flexibility.

With defined limits, leadership understands when flexibility is diminishing.

No-decompression limits are not about restriction.

They are about preserving the ability to ascend deliberately.

A Practical Illustration of Accumulated Exposure

An enterprise relies on a single valuation methodology across multiple jurisdictions for more than a decade. The methodology was reviewed internally, and external advisors confirmed its reasonableness. Audit findings were minimal. Operational execution was disciplined.

Import volume increased steadily over that period. Geographic footprint expanded. Revenue doubled. The methodology did not change, and from the surface, nothing appeared unstable.

Then enforcement intensity shifted in one key jurisdiction. A reinterpretation of acceptable valuation treatment was issued. What had been considered reasonable became subject to challenge.

The organization was not facing a technical error. It was facing accumulated exposure. Years of systemic reliance on a single interpretive position were compressed into months of reassessment. Financial reserves were evaluated. Prior periods were examined. Board attention intensified. Margin for adjustment narrowed rapidly.

The issue was not that the methodology had been careless. It was that no-decompression limits had never been defined. No trigger had required reassessment as volume scaled. No structural boundary had required reauthorization as geographic intensity increased. Depth had increased gradually, but recognition had not kept pace.

In diving, exceeding no-decompression limits does not cause immediate distress. The diver may feel stable, but pressure had already been absorbed. Ascent can no longer be direct. Additional stops become mandatory. Margin has been consumed.

Enterprise exposure behaves the same way.

Ascent was no longer deliberate.

Instead, it was dictated by depth.

Understanding Absorption at Depth

No-decompression limits are often misunderstood as tolerance levels.

But they are not tolerance limits. Tolerance suggests flexibility. Limits suggest physics.

An organization may believe it can absorb exposure because financial performance is strong, liquidity is healthy, and reserves exist. External challenge has not materialized. These indicators create a perception of resilience. But resilience is not the same as absorption capacity.

Absorption capacity reflects how much structural recalibration the enterprise can sustain without destabilizing strategy, liquidity, reputation, or board confidence. It includes:

- The financial capacity to reassess prior positions.
- The operational capacity to reconfigure supply chains.
- The strategic flexibility to alter market commitments.
- The governance credibility to withstand external scrutiny.

Depth consumes absorption capacity gradually. Performance incentives accelerate that consumption. When growth targets are aggressive, margin pressure intensifies. Expansion into new jurisdictions may be rewarded without parallel governance recalibration. Strategic leaders may prioritize speed over structural reassessment. None of these decisions are irrational. They are often celebrated. But at depth, acceleration increases pressure.

In diving, exertion increases air consumption. Rapid movement shortens available time. The diver may feel strong, but margin decreases faster.

Enterprise growth behaves similarly.

Revenue acceleration without governance recalibration narrows structural flexibility. Interpretive assumptions may be stretched to support strategic objectives. Exposure concentration may increase in high-return markets. These decisions appear rational at the surface. At depth, they alter consequence.

Another misreading occurs at the board level. Stability in audit findings may be interpreted as stability in exposure. Strong compliance metrics may be interpreted as structural safety. Yet no-decompression limits are not measured by control accuracy alone. They are measured by systemic exposure duration and concentration. The absence of visible distress does not indicate structural margin.

At depth, the body absorbs pressure silently. Enterprise exposure does the same. Irreversibility is the final constraint. Once no-decompression limits are exceeded, ascent requires structured stops. Time is imposed. Flexibility decreases. The diver cannot choose immediacy.

Similarly, in a well-governed enterprise, corrective action becomes externally timed when systemic exposure exceeds structural limits. Regulatory scrutiny dictates pace. Financial disclosure obligations accelerate decision cycles. Strategic options narrow.

The organization is no longer choosing recalibration. It is managing consequence.

No-decompression limits exist to preserve leadership control.

When limits are respected, leadership retains room to maneuver. When they are ignored, depth dictates the terms.

SECTION V

The Buddy System

In diving, the buddy system is not optional. It is required.

Two divers descend together not because they lack competence but because depth alters perception. Each diver monitors their own oxygen supply. Each monitors the other's. Hand signals confirm air levels. A raised finger indicates remaining pressure. An "OK" sign confirms status. Line of sight is maintained continuously. Monitoring is mutual, and risk is contained because visibility is shared.

Enterprise governance at depth requires the same architecture. Trade cannot operate as a solitary technical function. Nor can the Enterprise Risk Management Committee operate as a detached oversight forum. Finance, audit, and legal cannot function as periodic reviewers disconnected from systemic exposure.

At depth, no function governs alone. The governance buddy system requires continuous visibility across structural exposure. The ERM Committee must see enterprise-wide trade exposure not as a compliance detail but as embedded risk. Trade must understand how its methodologies affect enterprise-level consequence. Finance must recognize how interpretive assumptions influence margin sustainability. Audit must test not only control execution but structural exposure concentration.

This is not about additional reporting layers. It is about shared monitoring discipline. Each function must understand:

- Current systemic exposure.
- Defined thresholds.
- Changes in jurisdictional intensity.
- Strategic shifts affecting position.

And each must have authority to signal when margin narrows.

In diving, air is not shared casually. Each diver carries independent supply. Redundant regulators exist for emergency use. Shared oxygen is a contingency, not a plan.

Enterprise governance must operate similarly. Each function maintains its own controls and accountability, but redundancy exists in the form of shared visibility and escalation authority. If exposure approaches defined limits, escalation is not confined to one reporting line. Instead, it becomes collective responsibility.

The buddy system also prevents isolation drift.

At depth, a diver who loses visual contact increases risk exponentially. Disorientation can occur quickly. Recovery becomes harder.

In enterprise expansion, isolation drift occurs when trade operates within operational silos, the ERM Committee reviews risk in aggregate without understanding exposure mechanics, and finance monitors margin without assessing structural interpretive dependency.

Without continuous line of sight, depth increases unnoticed. The buddy system reduces delay in recognition, and when one diver signals concern, both respond. When one governance function detects threshold movement, all responsible bodies reassess.

Shared oxygen is not the objective. Shared margin awareness is.

Governance at depth requires engineered interdependence. Not informal collaboration and not periodic review, but engineered visibility, shared thresholds, and mutual authority to intervene. That is how risk remains contained before ascent is dictated by depth.

The buddy system fails when visibility becomes hierarchical instead of mutual. In many enterprises, trade reports upward. ERM reviews laterally. Finance evaluates performance independently. Audit assesses retrospectively. Each function believes it is fulfilling its role, but depth monitoring is sequential rather than simultaneous.

Sequential visibility increases delay, and at depth, delay consumes margin.

Another point of failure is incentive distortion. When revenue targets, cost containment goals, or market expansion objectives dominate executive focus, governance signals may be interpreted as friction rather than protection. Trade may hesitate to elevate exposure that could slow expansion. Risk functions may temper language to avoid appearing obstructive. Finance may prioritize margin protection over structural reassessment.

In diving, a diver does not suppress a low-air signal to preserve pace. Instead, the signal is given immediately because consequence is shared.

Enterprise governance must operate under the same norm. Signals must be insulated from performance incentives.

If escalation creates career risk, the buddy system is compromised. Structural reinforcement therefore requires clarity of mandate. Each governance function must understand that identifying narrowing margin is not opposition to strategy but rather protection of strategy.

The buddy system also requires consistent line of sight at the governance tier.

In diving, partners remain within visual range. Separation increases risk exponentially. Reorientation consumes time and air. At depth, losing sight of a partner can be fatal. Similarly, in enterprise structures, separation occurs when exposure discussions are siloed within functional reporting lines: Trade discusses methodology within operations, ERM discusses risk posture in aggregate, finance reviews performance impact, and the board sees summaries.

Without shared forums, systemic exposure is filtered through function-specific language. The Enterprise Risk Management Committee must therefore function as the structured convergence point. It is the governance-level "line of sight" where systemic exposure, strategic objectives, and performance pressure are evaluated simultaneously.

If convergence occurs only during crisis, the buddy system has already failed.

Redundancy is the final reinforcement.

In diving, each diver carries redundant air supply—not because failure is expected, but because depth demands preparation for the unexpected.

Enterprise governance requires similar redundancy in monitoring and authority. Trade monitors exposure mechanics. ERM monitors enterprise risk alignment.

Finance monitors margin sustainability. Audit validates control reliability. None replaces the other.

Redundancy reduces blind spots.

Shared awareness reduces delay.

Mutual authority reduces hesitation.

At depth, survivability depends on disciplined interdependence.

Enterprise governance is no different.

SECTION VI

Controlled Ascent

In diving, ascent is planned before descent begins.

Depth determines limits, but ascent determines survivability. A diver does not surface abruptly from significant depth without consequence. Pressure must be released gradually. Structured stops allow the body to recalibrate. Time is not an inconvenience. It is protection.

Enterprise governance requires the same discipline.

Controlled ascent is not recovery from failure. It is deliberate recalibration before structural pressure dictates terms.

Once systemic exposure has been recognized and limits defined, leadership must determine how and when to reassess sustained positions. This may involve reauthorizing valuation methodologies, reevaluating origin strategies, reconsidering concentration in high-intensity jurisdictions, or adjusting strategic expansion pacing.

The discipline lies in timing. If reassessment occurs too late, flexibility narrows. If it occurs too early or too frequently, the organization destabilizes itself unnecessarily.

Controlled ascent therefore requires structured review cycles aligned with enterprise growth and strategic milestones. Expansion events—acquisitions, major sourcing shifts, jurisdictional entry, product diversification—should automatically trigger governance-level reassessment of systemic exposure. Not because error is suspected, but because depth has changed.

Strategic recalibration must also address interpretive dependency.

Many enterprises rely on sustained interpretive positions that underpin financial performance. These positions may be legally defensible and operationally consistent. Yet as scale increases, dependency intensifies. Controlled ascent asks an essential question: If external interpretation shifted tomorrow, how exposed are we?

That question must be asked *before* external shift occurs.

Recalibration may not always require structural change. Instead, it may confirm continued validity of sustained methodologies, refine thresholds, or adjust geographic exposure concentration. The point is not disruption. The point is preserved leadership control.

In diving, ascent includes safety stops even when the diver feels strong. The absence of discomfort does not eliminate absorbed pressure.

Enterprise leadership must adopt similar restraint.

Strong performance, favorable audits, and stable enforcement climate do not eliminate absorbed exposure.

Recalibration is not a signal of weakness. It is a signal of maturity.

Another dimension of controlled ascent is communication discipline.

When systemic exposure is reassessed, communication pathways must be clear. The Enterprise Risk Management Committee must understand the rationale for recalibration. The board must understand how exposure trajectory has evolved. Finance must understand margin implications. Operational leaders must understand strategic adjustments.

Silence during recalibration breeds speculation, but transparency reinforces structural confidence.

Finally, controlled ascent protects pace.

When reassessment is structured and deliberate, the organization retains authority over timing. Adjustments can be phased, strategic shifts can be sequenced, and market messaging can be managed.

When ascent is forced, timing is external. Regulatory scrutiny accelerates decision cycles. Financial disclosure compresses communication windows. Strategic options narrow rapidly.

At depth, panic ascent is dangerous. In enterprise governance, reactive recalibration is destabilizing.

Controlled ascent ensures that recalibration occurs while margin remains.

Governance is oxygen at depth. Controlled ascent is how leadership uses it.

However, strategic recalibration at depth often collides with executive momentum. Expansion initiatives carry internal champions. Market entry is celebrated. Cost efficiencies are defended. Revenue acceleration reinforces leadership confidence. Recalibration under these conditions requires restraint, but restraint is rarely incentivized.

Controlled ascent therefore demands structural discipline beyond individual judgment. When systemic exposure approaches defined limits, recalibration must not depend on the willingness of expansion leaders to slow pace voluntarily. Instead, it must be embedded in governance architecture.

This is where the Enterprise Risk Management Committee plays its most important role. Its mandate is not to suppress strategy but rather to evaluate strategy under pressure. If exposure concentration intensifies in high-volatility jurisdictions, pacing may require adjustment. If interpretive dependency deepens beyond acceptable limits, diversification may be required. If the enforcement climate shifts materially, sustained positions may require board-level reauthorization.

These decisions are not reactive. They are disciplined responses to depth.

Failure to recalibrate at this stage does not produce immediate consequence. It narrows future choice.

As depth increases, the cost of change rises. Supply chains become harder to reconfigure. Contracts become harder to renegotiate. Market commitments become harder to withdraw from. Investor expectations become harder to reset.

Controlled ascent preserves flexibility while it still exists. It is the difference between choosing adjustment and managing fallout.

Executive discipline is most fragile when performance is strong—when expansion momentum creates psychological reinforcement, growth targets are met, markets respond positively, internal champions of strategy gain influence, confidence increases, and risk signals appear manageable. At depth, this is precisely when discipline must intensify.

Executive teams often mistake absence of disruption for confirmation of structural soundness. Because no regulatory challenge has surfaced, exposure is presumed contained. Because audits remain stable, systemic position is presumed sustainable. Because prior decisions have not yet produced consequence, interpretive dependency feels validated.

These are cognitive errors. Depth does not signal distress in real time. Instead, pressure accumulates before perception adjusts. Executive discipline therefore requires deliberate interruption of momentum.

Recalibration conversations must occur even when no trigger has forced them. Assumptions must be stress-tested even when performance is accelerating. Strategic pacing must be questioned even when revenue supports continuation.

These activities feel uncomfortable because high-performing organizations are conditioned to accelerate when success appears stable. To pause voluntarily in that environment feels counterintuitive, yet controlled ascent demands exactly that restraint.

Another distortion emerges through incentive compression. Compensation structures tied to revenue growth, cost reduction, or market expansion may unintentionally discourage recalibration. Leaders responsible for delivering performance may resist adjustments that appear to slow trajectory. Governance signals may be interpreted as friction rather than structural preservation.

Executive discipline requires separating performance ambition from exposure discipline.

Ambition drives descent, but discipline preserves survivability. When those forces are not balanced intentionally, ambition dominates. At depth, dominance of ambition narrows margin rapidly.

Executive teams must therefore institutionalize recalibration cadence aligned with strategic milestones, not with crisis. Acquisition integration, jurisdictional expansion, major sourcing realignment, and capital investment cycles must automatically include systemic exposure reassessment at the executive tier. Not because error is suspected, but because depth has changed.

Discipline also requires tolerance for visible constraint. When leadership communicates recalibration, it must frame it as strength, not retreat. Adjustment in pace must be positioned as preservation of structural durability. Without that narrative discipline, recalibration will appear to be reactive rather than strategic.

Executive discipline at depth is not technical competence. It is psychological restraint under success.

The most dangerous moment is not when pressure is obvious.

It is when depth feels routine.

Controlled ascent demands leadership maturity strong enough to question momentum before physics enforces consequence.

Synthesis

Descent, Discipline, and What Comes Next

At the surface, the Blue Hole remains calm long after divers have returned.

Depth leaves no visible mark from above.

Enterprise exposure is equally discreet.

Depth does not reveal weakness. It reveals structure.

An enterprise may descend intentionally, pursuing growth, entering new jurisdictions, expanding product lines, and accelerating strategic objectives. Expansion is not the problem. Unengineered descent is.

This chapter has not argued against depth. It has argued for discipline within it.

- Pre-dive assessment anchors ownership before pressure increases.
- Descent protocol defines when exposure must be reassessed.
- Depth recognition ensures systemic position is seen in aggregate.
- No-decompression limits preserve leadership control before margin narrows.
- The buddy system ensures visibility is shared and authority is mutual.
- Controlled ascent preserves strategic pacing before consequence dictates it.

These are not merely compliance techniques. They are the components of governance architecture.

At depth, a diver does not argue with physics. The body absorbs pressure whether acknowledged or not. Air is consumed whether monitored or ignored. Limits apply whether understood or dismissed.

Enterprise exposure behaves no differently.

"Governance is oxygen at depth."

Governance is oxygen at depth—not because depth is dramatic, but because depth changes the rules.

The discipline described in this chapter protects leadership control while expansion continues.

But engineering alone is not enough. Sustained depth also requires durability.

The question is not how to descend properly. It is how to remain governable as depth becomes normal.

Chapter 10 describes that challenge.

CHAPTER 10

Sustained Depth: Strength Under Pressure

At 120 feet, light fades.

Color drains from the water column. Red disappears first. Then orange. Then yellow. What remains is a narrowing spectrum of blue and gray. Marine life thins. The reef ecosystem that once surrounded you no longer survives at this depth. It is replaced by massive limestone formations—stalactites and stalagmites formed thousands of years ago when this cavern was dry.

The environment feels monumental. It does not adjust to you.

Pressure at this depth is constant: Approximately 75 pounds per square inch press evenly against the body—more than five times the pressure at the surface. Air consumption increases dramatically. Every breath matters. Margin narrows faster than perception adjusts.

You cannot descend here casually.

You do not enter this environment because you are adventurous. You enter because you are trained. You enter with advanced certification, specialized preparation, and respect for the physics that govern the environment. Recreational skill and basic preparation are insufficient. Compressed air is insufficient. Advanced breathing mixtures, such as Nitrox—oxygen-enriched air that extends time at depth—extend survivability, but only if managed correctly.

Fear has no place at this depth.

Fear produces panic. Panic accelerates air consumption, narrows judgment, and disorients.

In contrast, respect produces discipline.

At sustained depth, breathing slows deliberately. Movement becomes measured. Instruments are monitored continuously. Position is maintained intentionally. You do not drift. You do not improvise. You do not rely on instinct alone. Your partner remains within sight. Signals are exchanged without hesitation. Discipline replaces impulse. There is no improvisation, distraction, or ego.

You are not trying to escape the depth. You are operating within it. And that distinction is everything.

Most divers are trained for recreational depths—forty to seventy feet. At those levels, margin is wider. Surface access is close, and environmental feedback is visible. The reef is alive. Mistakes are often survivable. The environment provides cues. The physics are manageable with standard preparation.

At 120 feet, the environment provides nothing. There is no reef ecosystem to distract you. No visible life to reassure you. No margin for casual adjustment. The physics are constant and indifferent.

Air is consumed faster. Decompression discipline becomes non-negotiable. Light diminishes. Error compounds quickly. Small miscalculations produce disproportionate consequence. The environment demands maturity.

Enterprise leadership at global scale exists in this same environment.

At smaller scale, governance is active and visible. Signals surface quickly, issues are loud, and margin is forgiving. Exposure is often compartmentalized. Leaders can rely on operational teams to manage risk locally.

At sustained enterprise depth, governance cannot be event-driven. It cannot be reactive. It cannot rely on historical comfort or isolated technical expertise.

At sustained enterprise depth, that operating model fails. Pressure becomes constant rather than episodic. Margin compresses faster than leaders accustomed to mid-scale governance may recognize. Surface indicators—stable audits, steady margins, absence of inquiry—provide limited assurance. The reef ecosystem of smaller scale no longer applies.

Exposure is systemic. Interpretive positions accumulate over years. Jurisdictional concentration deepens gradually. Transfer pricing alignments intertwine with valuation methodology. Supply-chain decisions harden into structural dependencies. Margin compresses faster than leadership recognizes.

Surface calm is meaningless.

Stable audit findings do not reduce pressure. Strong quarterly performance does not widen margin. The absence of inquiry does not eliminate embedded exposure.

Pressure remains constant.

At this level, governance cannot be episodic. It cannot be delegated quietly to technical specialists. It cannot be satisfied with historical comfort or procedural adequacy. Instead, it requires executive discipline equal to the depth chosen.

This is where many organizations falter. They scale revenue without scaling governance architecture. They expand geographic footprint without recalibrating exposure thresholds. They reward acceleration without reinforcing discipline. They assume past survival validates future durability.

It does not. At sustained depth, survival is not accidental. It is engineered.

> *"At sustained depth, survival is not accidental. It is engineered."*

This chapter is not about how to descend safely. It is about how to remain at depth without consuming margin recklessly, without allowing ambition to override discipline, and without permitting complexity to cloud judgment.

Operating at sustained depth is not dramatic. It is deliberate. It is strength under pressure. And strength at this level is quiet.

If you are leading at enterprise scale, you are already operating at depth—whether you acknowledge it or not.

Revenue size does not determine depth. Structural exposure does. So do jurisdictional footprint, interpretive dependency, supply-chain concentration, and multi-year assumptions embedded in financial performance.

You may feel steady. You may feel experienced. You may feel insulated by history or size. But depth does not adjust for confidence. It responds only to discipline.

Many organizations believe they are operating at enterprise maturity because revenue has grown, global footprint has expanded, and technical compliance programs are in place. However, scale is not maturity.

> *"Scale, however, is not maturity."*

At mid-scale, exposure is often compartmentalized: a limited number of jurisdictions, concentrated product lines, fewer interpretive positions, shorter assumption chains. Margin may be tighter, but complexity is still visible.

At sustained enterprise depth, exposure embeds across layers. Interpretive positions stack across jurisdictions. Transfer pricing decisions intertwine with valuation methodologies. Origin strategies affect duty planning across multiple markets. Supplier dependencies span continents. What once appeared isolated becomes interconnected.

The risk profile changes from transactional to structural.

This is where executive miscalculation most often occurs. Leadership assumes that prior success validates current durability. Because the organization has navigated audits, disputes, and growth phases before, leaders believe the enterprise can continue to operate under the same governance model.

But governance does not scale automatically. It must evolve intentionally.

Operating at sustained depth without advanced governance architecture is equivalent to descending to 120 feet with recreational training. You may survive for a time, but margin will narrow faster than you recognize.

The question is not whether your organization has control. It is whether your leadership operates with the composure and structural discipline required at sustained depth:

- Have exposure thresholds been formally reauthorized as scale increased?
- Has interpretive dependency been stress-tested against enforcement volatility?
- Has geographic concentration been evaluated at the enterprise tier rather than within operational silos?
- Has escalation authority been insulated from performance pressure?

At depth, these are not compliance questions. They are survivability questions. And survivability at scale is not dramatic. It is methodical.

Governance at sustained depth demands more than competence. It demands maturity.

Maturity at this level is measurable. It is visible in how exposure is aggregated and reviewed by the Enterprise Risk Management Committee. It is evident when systemic interpretive positions are periodically reauthorized at the executive tier. It is reflected when escalation authority is protected from performance incentives. It appears when geographic concentration is stress-tested before expansion accelerates.

These are not operational refinements. They are executive decisions.

Organizations that operate successfully at sustained depth do not rely on technical excellence alone. They require leadership that understands structural exposure as a strategic determinant, not as a downstream compliance matter.

Without that recognition, complexity outpaces discipline.

And at depth, discipline is the difference between strength and fragility.

SECTION I

Respect at Sustained Depth

At sustained depth, isolation and clarity exist at the same time. Respect at depth is not emotional. It is structural.

Visibility narrows, but what remains is sharp. When you descend to 120 feet, you do not feel overwhelmed. You feel alert, focused, and deliberate. The reef environment is gone and marine life has diminished. The familiar color and motion of reef ecosystems disappear. What surrounds you instead are massive limestone walls, stalactites, and stalagmites— ancient, immovable, unsympathetic—formed thousands of years ago when the cave was dry. The environment is older than your presence within it and does not adapt to your confidence. Instead, you adapt to it.

An experienced diver notices that difference immediately: The reef is alive, dynamic, forgiving. Depth is structural, primal, and indifferent.

Enterprise leadership at sustained scale must recognize the same environmental shift.

At smaller scale, governance feels active. Issues surface quickly and activity is high. Teams debate interpretations openly and adjustments are often tactical. Margin, though narrower, still allows for recovery. Mistakes are often recoverable.

At sustained enterprise depth, signals diminish. Not because exposure disappears, but because it embeds. Interpretive decisions made years ago become structural dependencies. Geographic concentration increases gradually. Supply-chain efficiencies harden into inflexible commitments. Tax alignment decisions intertwine with customs valuation positions. What once appeared as discrete decisions accumulate into systemic exposure.

Respect begins with recognizing that you are no longer operating in a dynamic reef. Instead, you are operating inside formation. At this point, executive overconfidence becomes dangerous.

Success at mid-scale can create the illusion that governance maturity has scaled proportionally. Revenue growth reinforces confidence. Clean audits reinforce comfort. Prior disputes resolved without catastrophic impact reinforce belief in durability.

But scale changes physics. Exposure that was once compartmentalized becomes interconnected. A reinterpretation in one jurisdiction can ripple across transfer-pricing alignment. A supply-chain realignment can alter origin strategy and valuation methodology simultaneously. Margin sensitivity increases. Response windows shorten.

Respect at sustained depth requires acknowledging that complexity has crossed a threshold. It requires leaders to ask: Are we governing exposure as an enterprise system, or are we still managing it as a collection of technical domains?

The difference is material. Technical management assumes exposure can be handled within functional silos. Enterprise governance recognizes that exposure aggregates across those silos and must be evaluated collectively.

Respect also requires discipline under success. At 120 feet, you do not relax because you feel stable. Stability is the expectation. Breathing remains deliberate even when your gauges read comfortably. Your partner remains within sight even when nothing appears wrong. Monitoring does not cease because nothing has failed.

Enterprise leadership must adopt similar restraint.

Strong performance is not evidence of sufficient governance. It may simply mean that pressure has not yet surfaced visibly.

Respect at sustained depth means assuming that exposure exists—not waiting for it to announce itself. It also requires clarity of capability.

You are not surviving at 120 feet because you are "a PADI-certified diver (trained through a global recreational diving certification program)." You are surviving because you have undergone the prerequisites for advanced certification and have completed a Nitrox certification course to understand how to use it safely and manage the increased oxygen levels for deeper dives. Specialized preparation allows you to operate safely where others cannot.

Enterprise governance must reflect similar capability thresholds.

If exposure modeling remains basic, if interpretive positions are not stress-tested against enforcement volatility, if systemic aggregation is not reviewed by the Enterprise Risk Management Committee, the organization is operating at depth without advanced certification. It may function temporarily, but it is not operating with respect.

Respect demands insulation of escalation from ego. At sustained depth, you do not suppress a low-air signal to preserve your pride. You do not drift from your partner because you feel capable of doing so. You do not accelerate because the cavern is beautiful. Instead, your judgment must remain clear because consequence compounds quickly.

In enterprise leadership, ambition and performance incentives can distort that clarity. As organizations scale, performance expectations rise. Revenue targets increase, and expansion becomes part of the identity of the enterprise. In that environment, it becomes uncomfortable to question the structural positions that support financial success. Recalibration feels disruptive and slowing feels countercultural. Yet at sustained depth, avoiding recalibration because performance is strong allows exposure to embed quietly.

Respect at sustained depth means that discipline overrides ego. It means acknowledging that physics—not confidence—govern survivability.

Finally, respect means defining boundaries before they are tested. Experienced divers know there are depths they do not enter—not because they are fearful, but because they understand that the environment beyond those thresholds is beyond a recoverable range.

Enterprise governance must define similar boundaries. There are exposure levels that, once reached, become increasingly difficult to unwind without consequence. Geographic concentration can reach a point where your room to maneuver narrows. Long-standing interpretive positions can harden to the point that revisiting them becomes disruptive rather than routine. Supplier or jurisdictional dependency can quietly reduce flexibility. Respect at sustained depth means identifying these boundaries before they are tested, not after they are crossed.

Respect is not caution. It is control. And control at sustained depth is what separates organizations that endure from those that drift into fragility.

Respect at sustained depth also requires recalibrating instinct. At the reef, instinct serves you well. You adjust easily, navigating by color and movement. The environment gives feedback continuously. Small corrections are often enough.

At 120 feet, instinct alone is insufficient. The visual cues are reduced. The environment is quiet. Movement must be intentional. Monitoring replaces intuition. You do not "feel" your way through depth. You operate by instrument, training, and protocol.

Enterprise leadership at sustained scale must make the same shift. Experience remains valuable, and instinct remains important. But instinct untested by systemic review becomes overconfidence. Familiarity with growth does not equal mastery of structural exposure.

One of the most common violations of respect at enterprise depth is assuming that operational familiarity translates into governance maturity. It does not. Instead, revenue growth conditions leaders to move quickly. Market success reinforces confidence. Repeated survival of minor disputes builds resilience. These experiences create comfort.

But comfort at depth is dangerous. Comfort reduces vigilance, and vigilance is not fear. It is disciplined awareness.

At sustained depth, a diver does not stop checking gauges because nothing feels wrong. Air consumption does not pause because the environment feels stable. Partnership does not dissolve because the cavern appears beautiful. In other words, the absence of visible threat does not eliminate structural risk.

Enterprise governance requires the same vigilance. Exposure must be monitored even when performance is strong. Interpretive positions must be revisited even when no inquiry is active. Concentration must be evaluated even when margin remains intact.

Respect means assuming that complexity compounds quietly. It also means acknowledging that leadership psychology shifts at scale. Expansion should not occur on autopilot. Each additional jurisdiction, each acquisition, each new interpretive alignment alters the exposure profile of the enterprise. Respect at sustained depth means pausing long enough to understand how those layers interact before adding another. Growth is not the risk. Unexamined accumulation is.

All of this affects decision-making.

At depth, if a diver allows excitement or distraction to alter breathing rhythm, air depletes rapidly. The physics do not care about enthusiasm.

Enterprise exposure behaves the same way. If growth velocity outpaces governance recalibration, systemic exposure accumulates faster than leadership awareness adjusts.

Respect at sustained depth demands something few organizations prioritize: intentional slowing.

Slowing is not hesitation. It is recalibration.

Growth is not the risk. Unexamined accumulation is.

At depth, movement is deliberate. You do not rush. Instead, you respect your surroundings and protect your margin.

Respect means refusing to let ambition outrun discipline. And at sustained enterprise scale, discipline is the only thing that preserves strength.

There is another danger at depth that is rarely discussed openly: overconfidence.

As pressure increases, nitrogen dissolves into the bloodstream and can affect the central nervous system. Divers call this process nitrogen narcosis or the "Martini Effect." It does not feel like fear. It can feel like mild euphoria. Judgment softens. Reaction time slows. Confidence increases while clarity decreases. The most dangerous part is that it often goes unnoticed.

At sustained enterprise depth, a similar distortion can occur. Success can create a sense of insulation. Repeated survival of enforcement cycles can create comfort. Strong performance can produce confidence that structural exposure is under control.

But pressure compounds quietly. Over time, interpretive decisions do not stay isolated. They build. Geographic concentration increases. Strategic commitments that once felt manageable become fixed into the way the enterprise operates.

Judgment does not usually fail loudly; instead, it drifts. Respect at sustained depth means guarding against that drift. It means recognizing that strength is proven by composure, not by acceleration. It means intentionally slowing the pace of decision-making even when performance is strong. It means stepping back to evaluate the full exposure picture before layering on additional complexity even when nothing appears wrong.

You must not panic at depth, but you must also not become intoxicated by stability. The physics do not care how confident you feel.

At depth, the paradox is clear. Air is being consumed faster. Time feels limited. The instinct is to move efficiently, to conserve, to finish what you came to do.

But discipline demands the opposite. You must slow down. You must regulate your breathing. You must move deliberately. You must monitor your instruments even more carefully than before. You must pay attention to what your body is telling you and how you are responding to the pressure.

Rushing at depth increases risk. Enterprise leadership faces the same tension. As organizations scale, time pressure increases. Markets move quickly. Investors expect momentum. Strategic windows feel narrow. The instinct is to accelerate decision-making and maintain pace.

Respect at sustained depth requires the discipline to do the opposite.

It requires leaders to slow the pace of structural decisions precisely when expansion feels urgent. It requires stepping back to evaluate the full exposure picture even when performance suggests momentum. It requires composure when everything around you signals acceleration.

Strength at depth is not speed.

It is control under pressure.

SECTION II

Pressure Is Constant

At 120 feet, pressure is not an event. It is the environment.

> *"Pressure is not an event.*
> *It is the environment."*

You feel it constantly. Approximately 75 pounds per square inch press evenly against your body. That pressure does not spike or fluctuate. It does not announce itself. It simply exists because of depth. And it increases exponentially.

For every 33 feet of descent, pressure increases by one atmosphere. A few feet may feel insignificant but can double the force exerted on the body.

Depth does not negotiate. It compounds.

The only way to manage that pressure is through continuous equalization. You pinch your nostrils and blow gently, forcing air into the middle ear. You do so deliberately as pressure dictates. You do not wait for discomfort. You anticipate pressure before it becomes pain.

Equalization is not optional. It is continuous management of an unavoidable force.

Enterprise governance at sustained scale requires the same discipline. Pressure does not begin when a regulator issues an inquiry. It does not begin when a dispute is filed. It does not begin when a penalty is assessed. Instead, pressure exists because of scale: multi-jurisdictional exposure, layered interpretive positions, supply-chain dependency, and duration.

The force exerted on the organization increases with depth—whether leadership feels it or not. And just as in diving, that pressure increases exponentially.

An additional jurisdiction may appear incremental. A new acquisition may feel manageable. An additional interpretive position layered onto existing structure may seem minor. But depth compounds, and what feels like "just a few more feet" can double the force applied to the enterprise.

The most dangerous misunderstanding among newer divers is not fear. It is overestimation of capability. Just because one diver can safely operate at 90 feet does not mean another diver, certified only to 60 feet, can handle that depth. The difference may appear small. The experience may feel similar. But the physics are not the same, and each diver's body responds differently. Air consumption accelerates. Pressure intensifies. Equalization becomes more demanding.

Enterprise leadership faces a similar risk. Organizations that have operated comfortably at one level of complexity may assume that incremental expansion remains within tolerance. They may see competitors operating deeper and assume they have similar capability. They may follow opportunity without monitoring structural depth.

But personal and organizational limits matter. When divers exceed their current capability, the consequences can be immediate. Equalization fails. Pain intensifies. Hemorrhage becomes possible. A ruptured eardrum is not a theoretical risk; it is a structural response to unmanaged pressure.

Enterprise rupture follows a similar path. When systemic exposure is not acknowledged, pressure accumulates. Interpretive positions become increasingly difficult to unwind. Geographic concentration reduces room to maneuver. Structural commitments narrow flexibility. The organization may feel stable—until it does not.

There is another pattern at depth that is subtle but dangerous.

You are underwater. Visibility is clear enough. You see other divers slightly below you, perhaps with a different guide. They appear calm and comfortable. You see something extraordinary—a spotted ray, a manatee—and they have the better vantage point.

You were already at your planned maximum depth, but you move toward them. It is only a few feet, and it does not feel significant. You do not check your gauge immediately because you are focused on the moment. You are following position, not monitoring depth. What began as 60 feet becomes 70. Then 80. Then 90.

The difference between 60 and 90 feet does not feel dramatic, but the pressure has nearly doubled. Air consumption increases rapidly. Equalization becomes more difficult. The body responds immediately even if the mind has not yet recalibrated.

The surrounding pressure does not negotiate. Discomfort becomes pain. Pain can become rupture. A hemorrhage in the ear is not theoretical. It is physics responding to unmanaged depth.

The most dangerous assumption is believing that because someone else can operate safely at a certain depth, you can as well. But personal limits matter.

Enterprise leadership is not immune to this pattern as competitors expand, peers acquire, markets reward acceleration, and industry narratives celebrate scale. It becomes tempting to match depth without recalibrating structural capacity.

Following momentum without monitoring your own exposure profile is enterprise depth drift, and what appears incremental can become exponential.

A new jurisdiction is layered onto existing complexity. An acquisition is added before integration is stabilized. An interpretive position is extended because performance supports it.

It may not feel like much, but physics do not adjust to confidence. When expansion outpaces capability, pressure intensifies faster than governance recalibrates.

And rupture does not require catastrophe. It requires unmanaged force.

Pressure cannot be removed at depth. It can only be managed.

The water above you determines the force exerted on your body. Complaining does not reduce it. Ignoring it does not reduce it. Confidence does not reduce it. Management is the only option.

Enterprise leadership cannot remove regulatory pressure. It cannot eliminate jurisdictional complexity, prevent enforcement volatility, or erase the structural consequences of global scale. It can only manage the force created by its chosen depth.

Equalization in governance terms is continuous structural review. It is the periodic re-examination of the enterprise exposure profile. It is executive-level aggregation of systemic exposure. It is reassessment of concentration before additional layering occurs. It is discipline applied before discomfort becomes visible. Instead of waiting for pain to equalize, you anticipate it.

At sustained depth, failure to equalize is not gradual. It is abrupt.

And at enterprise scale, structural rupture is rarely sudden. It is the accumulated result of unmanaged pressure.

Pressure is constant, and maturity lies in managing it before it demands attention.

When a diver exceeds their personal limit and feels acute pressure, the response is not debate. It is immediate adjustment. You ascend slightly. You re-establish equalization. You regain control. You do not attempt to force your body to tolerate pressure it is not prepared to handle. Forcing it does not demonstrate strength. It demonstrates misunderstanding of physics.

Enterprise leadership must apply the same discipline. When expansion, complexity, or structural layering begins to outpace governance capacity, the response cannot be denial. It cannot be optimism. It cannot be reliance on past resilience. It must be recalibration.

That may mean slowing expansion or pausing acquisition velocity. It may mean revisiting long-standing interpretive positions or reinforcing executive oversight where operational autonomy has expanded too quickly.

Immediate adjustment is not retreat. It is control.

Pressure at sustained depth will not disappear. It cannot be negotiated away. It is inherent to the scale chosen.

The key question is whether leadership manages that pressure deliberately—or waits until discomfort becomes damage.

Governance at sustained depth is continuous equalization.

Not because something has failed, but because pressure is constant. At sustained depth, the challenge becomes not simply execution, but managing the limits of capacity, capability, and constraint.

CHAPTER 11

Managing at Depth: Capacity, Capability, and Constraint

At sustained depth, stability is no longer achieved through effort alone. Conditions have already shifted, pressure is constant, and the margin for error has narrowed in ways that are not always visible but are always present. What once could be managed through responsiveness must now be supported by capability, and what once felt manageable must now be evaluated against the limits of what can be sustained over time.

In these conditions, performance is not defined by how well activity is executed, but by how well that activity is supported. Capacity becomes finite. Attention must be directed. Judgment must be exercised with greater precision, and decisions that once operated independently begin to interact in ways that require coordination rather than reaction. The system itself begins to matter more than the effort applied within it.

Constraint is not a signal of weakness at depth. It is a defining condition. It determines how long an organization can operate effectively, how quickly it must adjust, and how deliberately it must move. Without recognizing those limits, even well-executed activity begins to accumulate pressure faster than it can be absorbed.

What follows examines how organizations operate within these conditions—how capability must evolve, how constraint must be understood, and how governance must shift from supporting execution to sustaining performance under pressure.

SECTION I

Air Consumption Multiplies

At depth, air consumption increases whether you are anxious or not.

It increases because of physics. As you descend, the air in your tank becomes denser. Each breath requires more volume. The body works harder. Its metabolic rate adjusts. Buoyancy shifts. You must compensate continuously.

Air does not last at 120 feet the way it lasts at 40 feet. The difference is not emotional. It is structural.

Enterprise scale behaves the same way. Exposure accelerates not because leadership is reckless, but because structural complexity increases. Additional jurisdictions, layered interpretive positions, supply-chain dependencies, and strategic commitments create density within the enterprise. Every decision carries more weight, every assumption compounds, and every adjustment requires more review.

Governance margin does not last as long at enterprise depth. At enterprise scale, "air" is not literal oxygen. It is capacity. Specifically, it is the capacity of the organization to absorb inquiry without destabilizing operations. It is the capacity of leadership to respond to regulatory interpretation shifts without triggering restructuring. It is the capacity of capital structure to withstand reassessment. It is the capacity of governance mechanisms to function under stress.

That capacity is finite, just as air volume in a tank is finite.

When organizations scale, they often assume capacity scales proportionally, revenue increases, geographic presence expands, and headcount grows. It appears that the enterprise has more air.

But capacity does not expand automatically. In fact, complexity increases faster than governance capability in many organizations. Each additional layer of structure consumes review time. Each additional jurisdiction consumes interpretive bandwidth. Each additional acquisition consumes integration capacity.

Air consumption multiplies not because leadership is careless—but because scale increases structural density and margin narrows quietly.

> *"Air consumption multiplies at depth. Margin compresses."*

At this point executive discipline becomes visible.

Experienced divers do not monitor their tank only when it feels low. They monitor continuously. They know their baseline consumption rate and how quickly that rate increases under stress. They understand how effort, current, and depth affect burn rate.

Enterprise leadership must develop the same awareness by answering important questions:

- What is the organization's baseline exposure capacity?
- How much interpretive layering can be absorbed before review cycles compress?
- How much geographic concentration reduces room to maneuver?
- How much integration load can be added before oversight begins to fragment?

These are not theoretical questions. They determine endurance.

Air management is not about fear of depletion. It is about intentional pacing. At depth, you adjust breathing to conserve margin. You avoid unnecessary exertion. You maintain neutral buoyancy to prevent wasted energy. You stay close to your partner to prevent correction effort.

Enterprise governance requires similar conservation discipline because unnecessary structural layering burns oversight capacity. Reactive restructuring burns executive focus. Uncalibrated expansion burns integration bandwidth. Performance-driven urgency burns review margin.

These burns may not be visible immediately. But like air depletion, they compound.

Fatigue is another indicator. An over-weighted diver working constantly to maintain buoyancy tires quickly. An under-weighted diver fighting to descend wastes energy. Both conditions accelerate depletion.

In enterprise terms, miscalibrated governance structure creates organizational fatigue. Too little architecture forces constant correction. Too much architecture creates drag and bureaucracy. In both cases, energy is consumed inefficiently.

Air consumption multiplies at depth because physics demand it. Enterprise depletion multiplies at scale because complexity demands it.

Management is not optional. It is survival.

And just as in diving, panic accelerates depletion. When a diver becomes anxious, breathing intensifies. Short, rapid breaths burn through air quickly. The body consumes more oxygen. Judgment narrows and efficiency declines. The problem is not fear alone. It is uncontrolled response.

Enterprise leadership under pressure can exhibit similar patterns. For example, an inquiry triggers rapid restructuring. A regulatory shift produces reactive policy layering. Performance volatility leads to sudden governance redesign. Resources are redirected quickly and without integration.

These responses feel decisive, but they can also consume margin rapidly.

Air management at depth is not about conserving air obsessively. It is about controlled breathing: slow, measured, and deliberate.

Enterprise governance at sustained scale requires similar discipline. Not overreaction, not paralysis, but controlled response.

But air consumption management alone is not sufficient. Neutral buoyancy must also be achieved.

This is where weights matter.

The purpose of weights in diving is not to sink. It is to stabilize. Without proper weighting, a diver expends energy unnecessarily. Under-weighted divers struggle to descend and fight constantly to remain submerged. Over-weighted divers work harder to control ascent and burn air compensating for excess mass. Both conditions waste energy and increase risk.

In contrast, proper weighting allows neutral buoyancy. Neutral buoyancy conserves air, reduces unnecessary movement, and stabilizes the diver within the water column.

Enterprise governance requires equivalent stabilization.

Too little governance architecture—underweighting—forces leadership to fight for control. Exposure drifts, escalation becomes chaotic, and teams expend energy reacting to surface indicators.

Too much governance layering—overweighting—creates drag. Decision-making slows unnecessarily. Bureaucracy increases. Air is burned managing structure rather than managing exposure.

Neutral governance does not mean minimal governance. It means calibrated governance; structure aligned with depth.

And like diving weights, calibration must be tested regularly as gear, water conditions, and personal comfort change. In each case, divers adjust weights accordingly.

Enterprise conditions change as well: Market expansion alters exposure profile. Acquisitions alter integration load. Regulatory interpretation shifts. Incentive structures evolve.

In each case, governance calibration cannot be static. It must be adjusted deliberately.

Equipment integrity is equally non-negotiable.

Before entering the water, a diver checks the regulator, the tank pressure, the buoyancy compensator, the gauges, and the hoses. A small leak in a breathing hose may appear minor at the surface. At depth, it can become fatal.

A faulty gauge can provide false confidence. A faulty gauge underwater is dangerous not because it immediately fails but because it provides inaccurate assurance.

A malfunctioning regulator can fail under pressure. A diver who believes there is more air remaining than there actually is operates under false confidence. The error may not reveal itself until margin is already compromised.

Enterprise governance systems can suffer similar distortion. If exposure aggregation is incomplete, leadership may believe concentration is lower than it is. If reporting frameworks do not capture duration of interpretive positions, leaders may assume that positions are more recent and flexible than they are. If escalation pathways are unclear, then warning signals may not surface at the appropriate tier.

Governance instrumentation must be trusted. To be trusted, it must be tested, and it must function under pressure. Pre-dive safety checks are not administrative rituals. They are structural verification before entering an environment that will amplify weakness.

Enterprise governance reviews must serve the same function. They must be structural, not ceremonial or performative. Their goal is to ensure survival.

Enterprise governance mechanisms require the same inspection. Escalation pathways must be clear. Aggregation mechanisms must function. Reporting integrity must be reliable. Executive review structures must operate without distortion from performance incentives.

A governance gauge that reads incorrectly creates false assurance. For example, a structural leak—an unreviewed interpretive assumption, an unmonitored concentration ratio, an untested integration layer—may appear insignificant. But at depth, insignificance compounds and air consumption multiplies. Margin narrows. Stability depends on calibration, inspection, and disciplined breathing.

Governable organizations do not wait for discomfort to confirm depletion. Instead, they monitor continuously and adjust deliberately. They preserve margin intentionally.

Air management at depth is not casual. When your tank reaches a defined threshold—1,000 psi, for example—you do not ignore it because there is still "some air left." You signal your buddy. You begin planning ascent. You adjust position. You maintain decompression discipline.

You do not wait for urgency. Rather, you respond to threshold.

Enterprise governance requires the same clarity. There must be defined exposure thresholds that trigger review—not because something has failed, but because depth demands it. Review can be triggered by concentration levels that require executive discussion, duration limits on interpretive positions that trigger formal reauthorization, and/or integration loads that require reassessment before additional layering occurs.

Escalation must be tied to threshold, not discomfort. And when recalibration is required, it must be deliberate.

A diver does not sprint toward the surface when air is low. A rapid ascent creates new risk. Instead, decompression discipline must be maintained. Control is preserved through measured movement.

Enterprise recalibration operates the same way.

When exposure reaches defined limits, leadership must adjust deliberately, not reactively. Rapid restructuring driven by urgency can introduce instability. In contrast, disciplined reassessment preserves structural integrity.

Air consumption multiplies at depth.

Margin compresses.

Stability depends on disciplined monitoring, calibrated structure, and controlled response.

Strength at scale is not demonstrated by how long an organization can remain at depth.

It is demonstrated by how intentionally it manages its air.

SECTION II

Advanced Certification Required

No two dive sites are the same.

Some reefs are forgiving. Some currents are strong. Some wrecks are confined and disorienting. Some caves narrow into spaces where only one diver can pass at a time. Conditions vary across the globe. Visibility changes. Temperature shifts. Depth profiles differ.

Because of that diversity, not every certification qualifies you to dive in every environment. If you want to wreck dive in tight spaces, you must hold advanced certification. If you want to dive deep beyond recreational limits, you must have training specific to depth. If you want to explore caves, navigate at night, or dive with enriched air, specialty training is required, not optional. The environment determines the qualification threshold.

Enterprise leadership operates in equally diverse environments. A domestic organization operating within one regulatory framework does not face the same structural demands as a multinational enterprise operating across layered jurisdictions. A company managing simple product lines does not encounter the same interpretive complexity as one balancing valuation, origin, transfer pricing, and multi-tiered supply chains.

Depth and diversity change qualification requirements.

Entry-level certification allows a diver to operate independently with a buddy in standard conditions. It builds foundational skills: buoyancy control, air management, emergency procedures. Advanced certification then builds on that foundation. It introduces navigation in reduced visibility. It teaches depth discipline and trains divers to operate in confined spaces. It prepares them for drift currents, night environments, and enriched air management.

Logging dives alone does not equal advanced qualification; a diver can accumulate many standard dives and still not be certified for a specific environment in which the rules are different and enforced.

You cannot fake advanced certification. You must present proof. Your PADI certification must be verifiable. If you are not qualified, you do not dive.

Depth exposes incompetence immediately.

Enterprise governance operates under similar principles, though enforcement may appear slower.

Organizations often assume that longevity equals capability. Years of operation can create comfort. Repeated navigation of audits can create confidence. Experience can build credibility.

But enterprise-scale governance requires more than repetition. It requires specialization.

Managing systemic exposure across multiple jurisdictions requires more than operational competence. It requires structured aggregation at the executive tier. It also requires integration of trade exposure into enterprise risk review, formal reauthorization of interpretive positions as scale evolves, and escalation insulation from performance pressure. These are specialty disciplines, not extensions of entry-level compliance.

Just as enriched air requires understanding gas mixtures and oxygen exposure limits, enterprise governance requires understanding concentration thresholds and systemic exposure layering. Just as cave diving requires navigation discipline and contingency planning, enterprise-scale strategy requires structural clarity before entering confined regulatory environments.

Advanced certification is not about prestige. It is about preparation for the environment you choose.

Operating at enterprise depth without advanced governance architecture is equivalent to entering a cave without training. You may navigate open water comfortably, but the rules change inside.

Enterprise leaders must ask themselves uncomfortable questions:

- Are we certified for the environment we are operating in?
- Do our governance mechanisms reflect advanced capability?
- Are we relying on foundational compliance practices designed for less complex conditions?

Certification is not symbolic. It is demonstrated structurally in how exposure is aggregated, thresholds are defined, escalation is insulated, interpretive positions are revisited, and concentration is monitored before expansion accelerates.

Depth does not care how many dives you have logged. It responds to whether you are trained for the environment.

Advanced certification is structural, but advanced maturity is behavioral. A truly advanced diver is not distinguished only by the card they carry. It is visible in how they enter the water, plan the dive, respond when conditions shift, and remain composed when the environment becomes unfamiliar.

Composure is not optional at advanced depth.

Wreck diving requires navigating tight passages where visibility can change quickly. Cave diving introduces confined spaces where disorientation can occur without warning. The Blue Hole demands vertical descent into an environment that is monumental and indifferent.

Advanced divers do not enter these environments casually. Instead, they enter prepared.

Precision is essential. At depth, small errors compound. A few feet too deep changes pressure dramatically. An imprecise ascent risks decompression violation. A misjudged turn in a confined space creates unnecessary exposure.

Advanced divers execute deliberately, maintaining situational awareness at all times. Underwater environments are dynamic. Currents shift. Visibility changes. Depth creeps subtly. A diver who loses awareness of surroundings loses margin quickly.

Enterprise leadership operating at sustained scale must demonstrate the same qualities: composure when regulatory interpretation shifts, precision in structural recalibration, situational awareness across jurisdictions and integration layers.

Ego has no place at advanced depth. Underwater, ego isolates. It discourages signaling and suppresses acknowledgment of discomfort. It creates distance between partners. No experienced diver will choose a buddy who prioritizes pride over shared safety.

In other words, diving is collaborative. Your buddy is not optional support. Your buddy is your partner in survival. You monitor each other's air. You exchange signals continuously. You remain within sight of each other.

Enterprise governance at scale requires similar partnership. Trade exposure cannot be isolated from finance. Regulatory interpretation cannot be siloed from enterprise risk review. Integration capacity cannot be separated from acquisition strategy.

Advanced governance is collaborative.

Communication discipline is equally critical.

Underwater, speech is impossible. Communication occurs through signals that are precise, intentional, and unambiguous. A diver must communicate air level, discomfort, equalization difficulty, ascent planning, and environmental hazards clearly.

Because miscommunication at depth is dangerous, enterprise governance requires clarity of escalation signals. Exposure thresholds must be understood at the executive tier. Escalation authority must be defined. Interpretation shifts must be communicated accurately. Structural exposure must be visible beyond operational silos.

Advanced certification in governance is not symbolic. It is demonstrated in composure, precision, situational awareness, ego discipline, collaboration, and communication clarity.

Depth reveals whether those qualities exist. It does not reward pretense.

Advanced certification also implies preparation for stress. At depth, emergency drills are not theoretical exercises. Divers rehearse air-sharing procedures. They practice controlled ascents. They simulate equipment failure. They train for conditions they hope never occur. In short, preparation is built before stress occurs.

Enterprise governance must demonstrate similar rehearsal discipline. It must ask these important questions:

- Has the organization stress-tested systemic exposure under enforcement volatility?
- Has it modeled the ripple effect of reinterpretation across multiple jurisdictions?
- Has it simulated concentration shock within a core supply-chain region?
- Has it examined integration strain under simultaneous acquisition layering?

Advanced governance is not measured by absence of crisis. It is measured by readiness for it.

Entry-level compliance focuses on transaction accuracy. It ensures classifications are correct, documentation is complete, and procedures exist.

Advanced governance focuses on structural endurance. It examines whether exposure aggregates across time and geography in ways that compress margin. It evaluates whether interpretive positions have hardened beyond routine review. It asks whether escalation remains insulated from performance pressure.

This distinction matters.

Many organizations are compliant, but fewer are governable at depth.

Just as certification in diving is verifiable, certification in governance is visible in architecture:

- Does exposure reach the executive tier systematically?
- Are structural thresholds defined and honored?
- Is recalibration tied to defined triggers rather than discomfort?
- Is concentration monitored before flexibility narrows?

These are not operational questions. They are qualification markers.

Depth will reveal the difference.

Operating at sustained enterprise depth without advanced governance capability is not reckless in intent. It is misaligned in preparation.

Depth does not punish ambition. It exposes insufficiency.

Advanced certification is not about prestige.

It is about ensuring that the environment you choose does not exceed the discipline you possess.

SECTION III

Illumination at Depth

Light does not disappear abruptly at depth. Instead, it fades.

At 120 feet during the day, it is not dark. You can see your surroundings. You are not blind. But color filters out gradually, leaving only a narrowing spectrum of blue and gray.

You do not feel the loss immediately. The environment still appears stable, but detail diminishes before awareness does.

That distinction matters.

An inexperienced diver may not recognize the shift in contrast. The cavern walls remain visible. The descent feels controlled, the water calm. Nothing dramatic signals change, but subtlety is gone. Edges soften. Contours blur. Distance becomes harder to judge precisely. Depth reduces clarity gradually.

Gradual visibility loss is dangerous because it does not provoke alarm. Sudden darkness triggers immediate response. Gradual filtering produces adaptation. The eye adjusts and the brain compensates. The diver believes visibility is adequate. But detail continues to diminish.

Enterprise governance experiences similar adaptation.

As organizations scale, leaders adapt to complexity. They become accustomed to layered reporting. They grow comfortable with dashboards summarizing exposure in aggregate. They normalize the absence of noise.

Adaptation feels like control, but it is not always clarity.

At enterprise depth, the absence of visible disruption can mask structural accumulation. A clean audit cycle may conceal duration risk. Stable financial performance may obscure geographic concentration. Routine reporting may fail to capture interpretive dependency across jurisdictions. The organization sees activity, but it may not see exposure density.

Illumination at sustained depth requires intentional contrast.

Divers use artificial light not simply to see farther—but also to restore what filtering has removed. A flashlight reveals color that ambient light has muted, sharpening edges and exposing texture. Without it, surfaces appear smooth when they are not.

Enterprise governance must restore structural contrast in similar ways: aggregation across jurisdictions, duration analysis of interpretive positions, concentration mapping at the enterprise tier, dependency assessment across supply chain layers.

These are not additional reports. They are instruments.

Visibility also depends on conditions. Clear summer water may extend ambient light. Overcast conditions reduce penetration. Different dive sites produce different visibility ranges.

Enterprise conditions vary as well.

Regulatory enforcement intensity fluctuates. Market stability can create comfort. Industry peers may operate quietly. Strong revenue performance can mask structural stress.

Favorable conditions can produce overconfidence.

Ambient light in favorable water does not eliminate the need for illumination. Just as advanced divers carry lights regardless of conditions, advanced leaders design visibility architecture regardless of current stability.

There is another layer to illumination that is often overlooked: Distance distorts perception.

Underwater, objects appear closer than they are. Light refraction alters scale. What seems within reach may require greater movement than anticipated. Misjudging distance consumes energy and margin.

Enterprise leadership can misjudge exposure distance similarly. An interpretive position adopted years ago may feel distant from current strategy—until reinterpretation reveals embedded dependency. A geographic concentration may feel manageable—until external conditions change rapidly.

Illumination reduces misjudgment. Not by eliminating risk, but by revealing proximity.

Visibility at depth is not about brightness. It is about accuracy. Boards do not require more data. They require more accurate contrast.

Illumination at sustained enterprise depth means ensuring that structural exposure is visible at the level where decisions are made, not buried within operational summaries.

Without deliberate illumination, organizations operate in muted environments: stable, functional, and gradually less precise. And imprecision at depth compounds.

Enterprise governance at sustained scale behaves the same way.

Visibility does not collapse suddenly. It filters.

Operational dashboards continue to function. Financial reporting remains precise. Audit cycles may appear routine. Regulatory communication may be quiet. Leadership sees data. Leadership sees activity.

But structural exposure detail can fade without announcement.

Interpretive positions extend in duration quietly. Geographic concentration shifts incrementally. Supply-chain compression increases gradually. Integration layering deepens over time.

No single event signals loss of clarity. That is what makes it dangerous.

Illumination at depth is not about reacting to darkness. It is about preserving precision before distortion becomes structural.

Divers carry flashlights at depth not because it is pitch black, but because ambient light is insufficient for detail. Flashlights restore contrast, revealing edges, exposing boundaries, and illuminating confined spaces.

In wrecks and caves, illumination is essential for navigation. Without it, passages appear wider than they are. Turns appear clearer than they are. Hazards remain partially concealed. Light is an instrument of precision.

Enterprise governance requires deliberate illumination. Relying solely on functional reporting is ambient light. It shows activity. It shows output. It shows motion. It does not always reveal structural layering.

Deliberate illumination in governance means aggregating exposure across functions, reviewing duration alongside concentration, and examining dependency across jurisdictions rather than within silos. It means restoring contrast.

There is another reason divers carry lights at depth: Visibility is not only environmental. It is also relational.

Maintaining visual contact with a dive buddy becomes more difficult as light filters and conditions shift. A flashlight beam cuts through muted water and signals position. It communicates location, stability, and readiness. It reinforces connection.

At sustained depth, losing sight of your buddy is not dramatic at first. It is gradual. They drift slightly out of your peripheral vision. You assume they are close. You continue forward. By the time you look deliberately, distance has widened.

Enterprise governance experiences similar relational drift. Trade exposure can drift away from finance visibility. Regulatory interpretation can drift away from enterprise risk review. Integration strain can drift outside executive focus. No alarm sounds, and the distance increases gradually.

At the enterprise level, deliberate illumination restores connection through governance flashlights that ensure that partners remain within sight: structured executive aggregation meetings, clear escalation pathways, defined threshold communication, cross-functional review discipline.

Underwater, communication occurs through signals. You do not shout. You do not improvise. You use established hand signals to communicate air levels, discomfort, ascent planning, and direction. Precision matters.

Enterprise governance communication must be equally precise. Exposure thresholds must be communicated clearly. Escalation triggers must be understood. Interpretive shifts must be articulated accurately. Structural concerns must reach decision-makers without distortion. Ambient light is insufficient for these types of communication. Instead, deliberate illumination is required.

Because visibility at depth decreases gradually, discipline must increase deliberately.

Advanced divers do not wait for darkness to deploy light. Advanced leaders do not wait for crisis to increase clarity.

Illumination is part of preparation. It is not a response to fear.

At sustained enterprise depth, clarity does not maintain itself. It must be engineered.

There is a final dimension to illumination.

Divers who rely solely on ambient conditions often believe they see enough. The environment appears calm, and movement feels controlled. The absence of immediate hazard reinforces confidence. But depth is indifferent to perception.

Enterprise leadership must guard against similar self-assurance. If visibility is limited to functional reporting, if aggregation does not reach the executive tier, if duration and concentration are not deliberately mapped, leadership may believe clarity exists simply because disruption has not occurred.

Illumination at sustained depth is not reactive. It is structural.

It is engineered into governance design before distortion becomes consequential.

Depth does not reduce light suddenly. It filters it.

Leadership must choose whether to compensate for that filtering—or operate within it. At sustained depth, the challenge becomes understanding the limits within which strength remains reliable, where distortion begins, and how governance must adapt before boundaries are exceeded.

CHAPTER 12

The Limits of Depth: Boundaries, Distortion, and Strength

At sustained depth, the question is no longer whether an organization can operate effectively. It is whether it understands the limits within which that effectiveness can be sustained and how those limits change as conditions continue to evolve. Depth does not fail suddenly. It reveals itself gradually—through pressure that is absorbed without recognition, through signals that are interpreted within the context of past stability, and through decisions that continue to function even as the conditions surrounding them shift.

As organizations move deeper into complexity, boundaries become less visible. What once defined the limits of acceptable exposure begins to blur, not because those limits have changed but because the conditions under which they were established no longer apply in the same way. Accumulation continues, but the mechanisms used to interpret it remain static. What appears stable is often only familiar. What appears controlled is often only understood within a context that no longer exists.

Distortion begins in subtle ways. Information remains available, but its meaning changes. Signals continue to surface, but they are interpreted through assumptions formed at a different level of depth. Activity continues to perform, and because it performs, it reinforces confidence. That confidence delays reassessment, and delay allows accumulation to continue without interruption. By the time conditions require a different response, the system has already adapted in ways that make that response more difficult to execute.

There is also a point at which calm becomes deceptive. The absence of disruption is interpreted as evidence of control, when in reality it may reflect the system's ability to absorb pressure without signaling it. At depth, the absence of visible stress is not always a positive condition. It can indicate that exposure has moved beyond the point at which it is actively governed and into a state where it is simply being carried.

Understanding these conditions requires more than awareness. It requires a way to assess whether governance remains aligned with the environment in which it is operating. It requires a method for determining whether the structures that once supported performance are still sufficient to sustain it under current conditions.

The Governance Depth Index (GDI) provides that method. It is not a measure of activity, and it is not a reflection of performance in isolation. It is a structured way to evaluate whether governance has evolved with exposure—whether ownership, escalation, and decision authority remain aligned with the level of depth at which the organization is operating. It distinguishes between systems that continue to function and systems that are designed to sustain alignment as conditions change.

What follows examines the conditions that define the limits of depth—how accumulation becomes toxic, how complexity distorts perception, how calm can conceal misalignment, and how organizations that operate effectively at depth do so not through reaction, but through deliberate design and disciplined awareness of the boundaries within which they operate.

SECTION I

Toxic Layers and Accumulation

Below 300 feet, the environment changes fundamentally.

Oxygen disappears. A dense hydrogen sulfide layer settles like a cloud. Below it, organic matter does not decompose. Remains are preserved. The environment becomes silent and undisturbed.

Advanced divers do not approach this layer casually. In most cases, they do not approach it at all. Standard descent ranges in the Blue Hole reach 120 to 150 feet. That depth already demands composure, monitoring, and control.

Three hundred feet is not an incremental extension. It is a categorical shift.

Risk at that depth is not admired, encouraged, or aspirational. It is acknowledged as a space beyond operational boundary.

Safeguards exist for a reason. Dive masters establish depth limits. Certification levels restrict access. Training thresholds define capability. No responsible professional guide permits descent beyond structural safety limits.

These boundaries are not arbitrary. They are protective.

Enterprise governance requires similar recognition of toxic layers. There are levels of systemic exposure beyond which correction becomes destabilizing rather than adaptive. Concentration can reach thresholds where flexibility disappears. Duration can extend to the point where reinterpretation triggers cascading consequence. Dependency can intensify until diversification is no longer feasible without disruption.

These layers are not visible at the surface. Instead, they accumulate beneath operational depth. They do not signal loudly; they settle.

Just as hydrogen sulfide forms a dense layer beneath oxygenated water, structural exposure can settle beneath active reporting, remaining present, quiet, and preserved. And below certain thresholds, intervention becomes increasingly complex.

The most important discipline at depth is not curiosity. It is boundary recognition.

Advanced divers do not test the toxic layer to see what happens. Enterprise leaders must demonstrate similar restraint. Growth pressure may intensify. Market opportunity may expand. Acquisition prospects may multiply. Interpretive positions may harden under performance incentive. But not all depth is meant to be explored, and not all exposure should be absorbed. Structural boundaries must be defined before ambition accelerates.

There is another dimension to toxic layers: They are not dramatic when observed from above. The water appears continuous, and the boundary is not obvious until you reach it.

Enterprise governance often misjudges structural limits the same way. Leaders may believe additional layering is manageable. They may assume one more acquisition, one more jurisdictional expansion, one more interpretive extension is tolerable. Until it is not.

At depth, oxygen sustains life. Below the toxic layer, oxygen disappears.

In enterprise systems, transparency sustains flexibility. Below structural thresholds, transparency diminishes. Decisions become constrained by accumulated dependency. Correction becomes reputationally expensive. Recalibration becomes financially disruptive.

The discipline is not fear. It is recognition. You do not go to 300 feet because you understand physics: Pressure multiplies. Air compresses. Gas behavior changes. The margin for recovery narrows. The descent becomes more and more dangerous.

Enterprise leadership must understand structural physics as well. Exposure compounds. Duration entrenches. Concentration compresses optional flexibility. Dependency reduces maneuverability. Beyond certain points, adjustment is no longer iterative; it is corrective. And corrective action at sustained depth is destabilizing. Two divers would have to choose to exceed safe limits, but in practice, safeguards prevent that decision from occurring.

Enterprise governance requires similar safeguard architecture, not as suggestions, but as boundaries. These boundaries include defined exposure ceilings, concentration thresholds, duration review triggers, and escalation authority.

The most sophisticated organizations are not those that push deepest. They are those that know where depth ends. The hydrogen sulfide layer is not a mystery. It is a line. Enterprise governance must define its own boundary line.

A final truth about the toxic layer is rarely discussed. Below it, nothing decomposes. Organic material remains intact. Time does not correct what has settled there. Instead, it preserves.

In enterprise systems, there are forms of exposure that behave similarly. Once duration extends beyond structural review, once concentration compresses beyond diversification flexibility, once dependency embeds across strategic decisions, those positions do not dissolve naturally. They persist.

Correction requires excavation, and excavation is disruptive.

At sustained depth, the difference between reversible strain and irreversible accumulation matters. At 120 feet, if air consumption accelerates, you ascend deliberately. You equalize. You adjust. You recover. At 300 feet, recovery is not incremental. It is extreme.

Enterprise governance must recognize the difference between manageable exposure and structural entrenchment. Many organizations believe exposure corrects itself through operational vigilance. They believe that interpretive strain will ease, concentration will rebalance, and market conditions will normalize.

Sometimes they do. Sometimes they do not.

Below certain thresholds, systems preserve and harden risk. Duration becomes precedent. Concentration becomes dependence. Dependency becomes constraint. The danger is not dramatic collapse. It is quiet entrenchment.

From the surface, the water above the toxic layer appears continuous: calm, blue, and undisturbed. The boundary is not visible until you approach it.

Likewise, enterprise leadership can operate for years within narrowing margin without recognizing that flexibility has diminished. Strong performance can obscure structural compression. Stability can reinforce belief that limits have not been approached. But limits do not announce themselves loudly; they accumulate quietly.

The reason advanced divers do not descend toward 300 feet is not fear. It is physics. Beyond a certain depth, gas behavior changes. Pressure compresses margin dramatically. Decompression requirements become complex. The pathway back narrows. There is no operational benefit that justifies the structural risk.

Enterprise governance must apply the same discipline: Not every expansion opportunity should be pursued. Not every interpretive position should be extended. Not every concentration should be tolerated.

Maturity is not measured by how deep you can go. It is measured by knowing when depth becomes destabilizing.

There is another dimension to the toxic layer: It is silent. No marine life survives below it. The reef ecosystem disappears. Motion diminishes. The environment becomes still. Silence can be mistaken for stability.

Enterprise systems experience similar silence when structural exposure has become entrenched. Dissent reduces, questions diminish, and assumptions go unchallenged. Review cycles become routine. But calm does not always indicate safety. Sometimes it indicates oxygen absence.

The most dangerous governance failures are not loud. They are preserved.

Safeguards exist in diving because depth is indifferent to human safety. For this simple reason dive masters establish limits. Simultaneously, certification defines capability and equipment calibrates exposure.

Enterprise governance must define equivalent structural guardrails before ambition approaches irreversible layers, because you do not test the toxic layer. Instead, you must respect it.

There is a subtler failure that precedes irreversible exposure. It occurs not at 300 feet but at 180 feet. It occurs when leaders become accustomed to sustained depth and mistake endurance for capacity.

At 120 feet, discipline is active. Monitoring is constant and equalization is deliberate. Air consumption is tracked with focus.

But as familiarity grows, the psychological tension softens. The environment feels manageable, the systems are functioning, and the body adapts to pressure. The diver begins to believe that the margin is wider than it is.

Enterprise governance encounters the same drift. Organizations operating successfully at sustained complexity begin to believe they have mastered depth. Regulatory environments may remain stable. Performance may be strong. Audits may be clean. Integration may appear smooth. Success reduces tension, narrowing vigilance.

In other words, structural exposure may increase not through recklessness, but through confidence.

The step from disciplined depth to overextension is rarely dramatic. Rather, it is incremental: one more acquisition layered onto an already concentrated footprint, one more interpretive extension relied upon for competitive advantage, one more dependency embedded into a supply-chain architecture.

None of these decisions appear catastrophic. In isolation, they are defensible. But in aggregate, they compress margin.

The toxic layer is not reached through one bold decision. It is approached through accumulated permission.

Advanced divers understand that the most dangerous emotion at depth is not panic. It is complacency. Enterprise leaders must recognize the same inflection point.

Boundaries must be defined and reaffirmed before comfort reduces discipline, because the distance between 150 feet and 300 feet is not simply 150 more feet. It is a structural shift in survivability.

Organizations that define and honor structural boundaries do not limit growth.

They protect survivability.

SECTION II

Disorientation Under Complexity

There is a phenomenon at depth that divers respect but do not dramatize: nitrogen narcosis. As depth increases, nitrogen dissolves into the bloodstream under pressure. The effect on the central nervous system can resemble alcohol intoxication, though it does not present the same way for every diver: euphoria, slowed cognition, impaired judgment, false confidence.

It does not feel like panic. In fact, it can feel pleasant. That is what makes it dangerous.

A diver experiencing mild narcosis may feel relaxed and invincible. Risk may seem distant. But reaction time is slowing subtly. Fine motor skills are diminishing. Situational awareness is narrowing.

The diver may not immediately recognize the impairment because judgment distortion does not announce itself. Instead, it feels normal.

Enterprise leadership operating at sustained complexity experiences similar cognitive compression. As organizations scale, executives become accustomed to layered systems, multi-jurisdictional interpretation, integration stacking, regulatory nuance, and performance volatility. Complexity becomes the norm.

Familiarity reduces perceived threat, but cognitive bandwidth remains finite. Decision cycles compress. Information density increases. Trade-offs become layered.

Under sustained pressure, leaders can experience a form of governance narcosis: overconfidence in institutional control, an assumption that prior success guarantees stability, a belief that structural exposure is manageable now because it has been manageable before.

The most dangerous distortion is not fear. It is confidence.

At depth, a diver experiencing narcosis may underestimate risk, drifting deeper than intended or delaying ascent because nothing feels urgent. The effect is not uniform. Symptoms vary by individual—ranging from mild euphoria to confusion, reduced dexterity, and impaired problem-solving.

But the solution is universal: Ascend deliberately. Reduce pressure. Restore clarity.

Enterprise governance must design equivalent corrective mechanisms. If cognitive distortion is suspected—if overextension is detected, if confidence exceeds structural capacity, if complexity begins to cloud decision quality—the organization must recalibrate deliberately, not abruptly. It must slow strategic velocity, reassess systemic exposure, reaffirm structural thresholds, and re-examine dependency concentration.

Advanced divers are trained to recognize subtle symptoms. Enterprise leaders must cultivate similar awareness.

Under sustained performance, confidence can mask impairment. Strong revenue can obscure concentration risk. Stable audit cycles can reinforce belief that interpretive layering is safe. Familiar complexity can dull vigilance.

Narcosis alters cognition. The key is recognizing it early. At depth, if impairment intensifies, the pathway back narrows. Reaction slows further and judgment degrades. Delay compounds risk.

Enterprise systems experience similar compounding. When cognitive distortion intersects with structural accumulation, recalibration becomes more difficult. Correction costs increase. Margin tightens and reputation risk expands.

The solution is not paranoia. It is humility.

Advanced divers do not assume immunity from narcosis. They monitor themselves. They remain attentive to subtle shifts in perception. They trust their training enough to ascend when clarity diminishes.

Enterprise governance must build similar humility into decision architecture. Complexity does not make leaders invincible, but it makes clarity harder.

There is another dimension to disorientation at depth: perceptual error.

Hallucination is rare, but subtle perceptual error is common. Shapes can appear closer than they are. Distance can be misjudged. Motion can be interpreted incorrectly.

Enterprise leaders can misjudge exposure proximity in similar ways. For example, an interpretive risk may feel distant until enforcement reclassifies it. A dependency may feel manageable until geopolitical disruption exposes fragility. A concentration may appear diversified until correlation reveals overlap.

Disorientation under complexity is rarely dramatic. It is gradual. And it is correctable—if it is recognized.

The solution is not bravado. It is ascent.

There is another truth about nitrogen narcosis that divers understand: It does not always affect every diver equally. One diver may feel clear. Another may feel euphoric. Another may feel subtly impaired.

This variation is dangerous in group settings. If a diver begins to feel overconfident while their buddy remains composed, misalignment can occur. If both divers experience mild euphoria simultaneously, neither may immediately recognize the distortion. And shared distortion is more dangerous than individual impairment.

Enterprise leadership teams are not immune to this dynamic. Performance success can create collective confidence. Market dominance can reinforce belief in structural superiority. Years of operating at sustained complexity can produce an executive culture that normalizes depth.

When confidence becomes shared, questioning decreases. Escalation softens, assumptions go unchallenged, and interpretive positions harden. The organization begins to believe it sees clearly because it has seen clearly before. This is governance narcosis. It feels strong, capable, and earned, not reckless.

But depth does not respond to confidence. It responds to physics. As pressure increases, gas behavior changes regardless of experience. As systemic exposure compounds, margin compresses regardless of past success. There is a moment at depth when an experienced diver recognizes subtle impairment: Reaction time slows, focus narrows, and decision-making becomes less sharp.

The correct response is not to push further. It is to ascend slightly. Even a small ascent reduces pressure meaningfully. Clarity returns. Symptoms diminish. Control is restored.

Enterprise governance requires equivalent micro-ascents—not full retreat, and not abandonment of strategy, but deliberate recalibration.

Deliberate recalibration means:

- Slowing expansion temporarily.
- Pausing interpretive extension.
- Rebalancing concentration before further layering.
- Re-examining integration capacity before accelerating acquisition.

These are not signs of weakness. They are signs of cognitive discipline.

Narcosis also impairs risk perception. A diver under its influence may misjudge distance. A descent may continue a few feet beyond intention because nothing feels urgent.

Enterprise systems behave similarly under sustained complexity. The next layer does not feel dangerous. The next jurisdiction does not feel destabilizing. The next dependency does not feel constraining. Until accumulation reveals compression.

The most dangerous dimension of disorientation under complexity is not dramatic failure. It is delayed recognition. By the time impairment is obvious, correction becomes harder. Enterprise governance must therefore design self-check mechanisms that operate even when confidence is high. These mechanisms include:

- Independent review layers.
- Rotating structural audits.
- External perspective infusion.
- Formalized reauthorization cycles.

These mechanisms are not bureaucratic excess. They are anti-narcosis protocols.

Advanced divers respect their vulnerability to nitrogen narcosis regardless of experience level. Enterprise leaders must demonstrate similar humility. Complexity alters cognition; depth rewards discipline. Confidence without recalibration is distortion.

> *"Confidence without recalibration is distortion."*

And distortion at sustained enterprise depth is rarely isolated. It compounds. To regain clarity, the enterprise must:

- Reduce depth.
- Reestablish clarity.
- Recalibrate positioning.
- Restore margin.

At sustained enterprise depth, cognitive discipline must match structural discipline.

Without it, confidence becomes distortion.

And distortion at depth compounds silently.

SECTION III

Deceptive Calm

From the surface, the Blue Hole does not look dangerous. Instead, it appears serene.

A perfect circle of sapphire blue surrounded by turquoise reef. The water is calm. There is no turbulence, no visible warning, no dramatic signal that what lies beneath requires advanced skill and disciplined preparation. The Blue Hole is a geological formation created by the collapse of a limestone cave system thousands of years ago. It is surrounded by vibrant coral reef. From the surface, it appears like part of that ecosystem—alive, colorful, familiar.

Standing on the boat before descent, the emotional state is layered.

There is excitement—because the Blue Hole is extraordinary.

There is quiet focus—because it is unforgiving.

There is reverence—because not many descend to that depth.

There is confidence—because the diver has trained for this.

And there is humility—because training does not eliminate risk.

All of those emotions exist simultaneously, but none of them reduce discipline. Excitement does not override briefing. Confidence does not replace protocol. Reverence does not suspend calibration. Humility sharpens attention.

The calm surface does not create casualness. It creates seriousness.

Enterprise leadership often misreads calm differently: Stable quarters generate optimism. Clean audits reinforce belief in control. Strong earnings create momentum. Peer normalization reduces urgency.

Excitement can morph into acceleration. Confidence can morph into expansion. Reverence for past success can morph into entitlement.

Humility disappears first. The most dangerous interpretation of calm is this: "If nothing is wrong, nothing needs adjusting."

Divers do not approach the Blue Hole with that mindset. They do not wait for turbulence to prepare. They brief deliberately:

- They review depth limits.
- They confirm air mixtures.
- They recheck equipment.
- They clarify buddy signals.
- They define ascent parameters before entering the water.

Enterprise governance must demonstrate similar discipline. Calm conditions are not a reason to reduce review cycles. Strong performance is not a signal to extend interpretive boundaries. Stable regulatory cycles are not evidence that exposure has diminished.

The absence of visible disturbance does not eliminate vertical depth. It conceals it. And that is the deception.

The reef is vibrant. Marine life is active. The water is calm. Nothing signals that beneath that circular blue lies vertical descent, pressure compression, oxygen management, and strict protocol.

The surface ecosystem gives reassurance, but the depth demands discipline.

Enterprise environments operate the same way. Strong performance, healthy industry peers, routine reporting, stable regulatory cycles—these form the surrounding reef. They create vibrancy. They suggest familiarity. They imply normalcy.

But depth is not visible from the reef. Depth sits inside the system. It is vertical, not horizontal.

It does not create turbulence at the surface because its pressure is structural.

That distinction matters.

A diver who assesses risk only from the surface misjudges the environment.

A leader who assesses risk only from performance misjudges complexity.

The reef is real. The depth is also real. But they are not the same.

The surrounding reef reinforces reassurance.

Color. Movement. Life. Nothing about the surface suggests risk. That is what makes it deceptive.

Enterprise systems experience similar periods of calm: Regulatory enforcement quiets. Audits conclude without material findings. Revenue remains strong. Integration appears stable. Market conditions are favorable.

From the surface, expansion looks manageable. There is no turbulence.

Performance stability creates reassurance. The surrounding ecosystem—strong earnings, clean reporting, peer normalization—reinforces confidence.

Nothing suggests that sustained depth beneath the surface demands disciplined recalibration. But depth does not announce itself at the surface.

Pressure increases gradually below. Air consumption multiplies below. Light filters gradually below. Cognitive distortion begins below. The surface does not signal any of it. That is the danger of deceptive calm.

Leaders can interpret absence of disruption as evidence of control. They can interpret stable reporting as confirmation of structural resilience. They can assume that because the water is smooth, the environment is simple.

It is not. The Blue Hole does not create turbulence at the surface because its depth is vertical.

Enterprise exposure can behave the same way. Systemic concentration can deepen vertically without disturbing horizontal performance. Interpretive dependency can harden beneath stable revenue. Integration strain can accumulate beneath smooth operational metrics.

The surface remains calm, but the depth intensifies. The most disciplined divers do not rely on surface conditions to assess risk.

They brief before descent. They review equipment. They confirm certification. They define limits. They respect what they cannot see.

Enterprise leadership must adopt the same posture toward calm conditions because stable enforcement cycles do not eliminate exposure. Strong performance does not dissolve concentration. And favorable market conditions do not reduce systemic layering.

Calm can create overconfidence. Overconfidence reduces vigilance, which in turns accelerates accumulation.

The reef surrounding the Blue Hole is alive and vibrant. It signals familiarity. It suggests that the environment is typical. But the circular darkness at its center is not reef. It is depth.

Enterprise systems often sit inside familiar industries, surrounded by peer behavior, normalized practices, shared assumptions. That ecosystem can create collective reassurance. The enterprise assumes: If competitors operate similarly, the exposure must be manageable.

That assumption is flawed. Calm is not validation. It is condition. And conditions change.

*"Calm is not validation.
It is condition."*

Disciplined leaders do not wait for turbulence to reassess depth. Instead, they recognize that the absence of visible disruption is not proof of safety. They plan for descent even when the surface is still.

The reef surrounding the Blue Hole teems with life—movement, color, familiar patterns—all reassuring to the inexperienced eye. But the circular void at its center is not reef. It is depth.

Enterprise systems often sit inside vibrant industries with active markets and visible success. The ecosystem appears healthy. The environment feels alive. But depth is not horizontal. It is vertical, and performance may flourish across the surface while structural exposure intensifies beneath it.

Disciplined leaders do not mistake vibrancy for stability. They distinguish reef from depth. They respect both.

There is a pattern that repeats in enterprise environments during prolonged stability. Risk becomes normalized. When regulatory cycles remain quiet for several years, leadership begins to assume that exposure is structurally managed. When enforcement appears selective or distant, interpretive positions feel less urgent to revisit. When performance metrics trend upward, recalibration conversations feel inconvenient.

Calm conditions create momentum.

Momentum discourages interruption.

The discipline required during calm is greater than the discipline required during turbulence. In contrast, during crisis, organizations mobilize naturally. Escalation sharpens. Review intensifies. Boards demand visibility. Leaders convene rapidly.

Crisis forces vigilance.

Calm requires chosen vigilance.

This is the inflection point most organizations miss. The absence of disruption does not signal structural safety. It signals opportunity for disciplined review.

Divers do not wait for water movement to confirm depth. They do not rely on surface texture to infer conditions below. They respect what they know lies beneath regardless of what they see above.

Enterprise leaders must adopt the same posture:

- When markets are strong, they must reassess concentration.
- When audits are clean, they must review duration.
- When performance is stable, they must evaluate dependency layering.
- When expansion accelerates, they must re-equalize exposure discipline.

Calm is not a reward. It is a responsibility.

There is another subtle danger in deceptive calm: It reduces perceived urgency across teams. Escalation thresholds soften, questioning decreases, and assumptions harden. No one feels pressure to challenge. The water is still. But still water above depth does not mean absence of force. It means the force is vertical.

Enterprise exposure behaves similarly.

Pressure accumulates below performance lines. Dependency hardens beneath stable integration. Duration extends beneath routine reporting.

The leader who waits for visible disturbance before recalibrating has already descended too far.

SECTION IV

Operating with Respect

Respect at depth is visible in behavior. It is controlled, not loud or dramatic.

A diver who respects depth descends deliberately. Movements are measured. Breathing is steady. Equipment checks are habitual, not reactive. Attention does not drift. Awareness remains wide but focused.

Respect is not fear. It is composure under pressure. The diver relies on training without becoming rigid. He monitors his gauges without obsession. He remains aware of his surroundings without distraction. He maintains visual contact with his buddy without crowding them.

Control is constant, and respect looks like discipline in motion.

Enterprise leadership operating at sustained complexity must demonstrate similar presence: structure without rigidity, control without paralysis, confidence without ego, vigilance without panic.

Operating with respect means understanding that expansion increases consequence. It means recognizing that exposure compounds even when performance is strong. It means acknowledging that sustained depth demands sustained awareness.

Respect alters decision cadence:

- It slows impulsive expansion.
- It reinforces review before layering.
- It insists on reauthorization before extension.
- It requires confirmation before acceleration.

Not because growth is dangerous, but because unmanaged growth is destabilizing.

Divers who respect depth does not descend quickly simply because others are below. They do not chase movement impulsively. They do not abandon their depth plan to capture a better angle or a fleeting moment.

Instead, they hold position. They confirm air. They equalize deliberately. They descend only as intended.

Enterprise leaders must operate with the same intentionality: They do not chase every opportunity. They do not extend every interpretive advantage. They do not assume that because capacity exists, margin does.

Respect introduces restraint without hesitation. It also reinforces partnership.

Divers do not operate independently at depth. They remain within sight of their buddy. They monitor each other continuously. They signal intentionally. They adjust together.

Enterprise governance at sustained scale requires similar interdependence. Risk oversight must remain connected to strategy. Finance must remain connected to regulatory exposure. Expansion must remain connected to integration capacity. Board visibility must remain connected to operational depth.

Respect prevents isolation. It also prevents complacency.

Even after successful dives, respect does not diminish. Each descent is briefed as if it matters—because it does. Prior success does not eliminate preparation.

Enterprise leadership must maintain similar humility because past stability does not remove present obligation, previous compliance does not eliminate current review, and strong quarters do not suspend structural vigilance.

Respect at depth is not reactive. It is chosen, quiet, disciplined, and sustainable.

Organizations that operate with respect at sustained complexity do not fear depth. They thrive within it because they never forget what it requires.

Respect is not hesitation. It is not retreat. It is not risk avoidance.

Divers who respect depth still descend. They still explore. They still engage the environment. But every movement is intentional, every adjustment conscious, every signal deliberate. There is no impulsive motion at sustained depth.

Enterprise leadership often confuses respect with conservatism. It is neither.

Respect does not slow growth arbitrarily. It does not discourage ambition. It does not reject expansion. Instead, it disciplines it.

Operating with respect means expansion is accompanied by recalibration. It also means that acceleration triggers review and performance strength prompts re-evaluation, not complacency.

There is a physical dimension to respect underwater. You never rush descent. You never chase movement impulsively. You never ignore discomfort. You never override your gauges because you feel fine. Feeling fine is not data. Gauges are data.

Enterprise governance requires similar discipline.

Momentum is not data.
Confidence is not data.
Historical success is not data.
Exposure thresholds are data.
Concentration metrics are data.
Duration analysis is data.
Dependency mapping is data.

Respect means that decisions are anchored to structural indicators, not emotion.

There is also a cultural dimension to respect. Underwater, ego is dangerous. No one dives with a partner who ignores signals. No one trusts a diver who refuses to acknowledge discomfort. No one tolerates recklessness at sustained depth.

Enterprise cultures that reward unchecked acceleration, dismiss dissent, or equate questioning with weakness erode respect structurally.

Respect welcomes scrutiny and invites recalibration. It assumes that complexity demands humility.

Divers who respects depth never treat a successful dive as proof of invulnerability. Instead, they debrief, evaluate, and adjust.

Enterprise governance operating with respect institutionalizes similar behavior:

- After successful expansion, exposure is reviewed.
- After stable quarters, concentration is reassessed.
- After clean audits, interpretive positions are reauthorized.

Success does not suspend vigilance. It heightens responsibility.

Operating with respect is not emotional. It is architectural:

- It embeds discipline into decision structures.
- It defines boundaries before ambition reaches them.
- It maintains connection across governance tiers.
- It reinforces visibility before distortion sets in.

Respect is strength under control. It is composure under pressure. It is confidence without arrogance. And at sustained enterprise depth, it is the difference between survivability and fragility.

There is another dimension to operating with respect that becomes visible only at scale: External pressure does not disappear at depth. Instead, investor expectations intensify. Growth targets expand. Market comparison accelerates. Competitive positioning sharpens.

In those conditions, discipline is tested. Respect requires leaders to maintain structural review even when acceleration feels rewarded. It requires recalibration even when momentum is celebrated. It requires restraint even when opportunity appears abundant.

The disciplined diver does not accelerate descent because others are watching.

Enterprise leadership must demonstrate similar independence from external tempo.

Respect must be embedded institutionally. It cannot rely solely on individual temperament. If respect depends on a single disciplined executive, it disappears when leadership rotates. If vigilance depends on personality rather than architecture, it erodes under succession.

Sustained enterprise depth requires structural respect:

- Defined review intervals.
- Mandated reauthorization cycles.
- Escalation pathways that function regardless of performance strength.
- Cross-functional visibility that persists beyond personalities.

Respect becomes durable when it is designed.

There is also a temporal dimension. At depth, time matters. You monitor not only air, but also duration. You understand how long you have been operating under pressure. You know that prolonged exposure requires deliberate ascent planning.

Enterprise governance must track duration similarly:

- How long has this interpretive position been extended?
- How long has this concentration been sustained?
- How long has dependency remained unchallenged?

Duration without review hardens exposure. Respect requires time-bound recalibration.

Operating with respect also demands self-awareness. Underwater, you constantly assess your own composure. You check your breathing rate. You feel for subtle tension. You remain attentive to small changes in comfort.

Enterprise leaders must cultivate similar internal discipline, asking themselves:

- Are decisions accelerating beyond review capacity?
- Is dissent being reduced?
- Are escalation conversations shortening?
- Is integration strain being normalized?

Respect invites those questions before disruption forces them.

Finally, respect preserves partnership.

You do not abandon your buddy at depth. You do not drift without signaling. You do not prioritize your perspective over shared survival.

Enterprise governance operating with respect ensures that risk oversight, finance, strategy, and operations remain connected at decision level.

Isolation erodes respect.

Integration reinforces it.

Operating with respect is not conservative. It is controlled strength.

It is the discipline to expand while recalibrating.
It is the ability to accelerate while monitoring.
It is the maturity to pause without losing momentum.

At sustained enterprise depth, respect is not optional.

It is the operating condition that makes depth survivable.

SECTION V

Measuring Alignment at Depth

At sustained depth, the question is no longer whether governance exists. It is whether it remains aligned with the conditions it is expected to withstand. Activity continues. Controls function. Reporting persists. But none of these, on their own, confirm that governance is operating at the level required by the exposure it is meant to contain.

What becomes necessary is not additional oversight, but a way to determine whether the structure itself has kept pace.

The Governance Depth Index (GDI) provides that determination.

It does not measure performance in isolation, and it does not evaluate activity for its own sake. Instead, it assesses alignment—whether ownership, escalation, and decision authority have evolved in proportion to the depth at which the organization is operating. It makes visible the difference between systems that continue to function and systems that are designed to sustain control as conditions change.

The distinction is not academic. Organizations rarely fail because they lack activity. They fail because activity continues within structures that were never recalibrated for the level of exposure they ultimately reached.

The GDI captures that condition.

It evaluates governance across the dimensions that determine whether alignment is being maintained or quietly lost—clarity of ownership across boundaries, consistency of decision-making under changing conditions, and the presence of escalation structures that reflect not only current activity, but accumulated consequence.

At lower levels of depth, these elements are often sufficient by default. At sustained depth, they must be deliberate.

The result is not a score for its own sake, but a position—a clear indication of whether governance is aligned, compressing, or approaching failure under conditions it was never designed to support.

That position matters.

Because at depth, the difference between control and misalignment is rarely visible in the moment. It is revealed only when pressure demands explanation.

The GDI makes that visibility possible before that moment arrives.

The Governance Depth Index is designed to be applied deliberately—not read passively.

A full assessment, scoring model, and executive interpretation guide are provided at the end of this book, allowing leaders to evaluate their own alignment against the conditions described here.

What matters in this moment is not the score, but the recognition of where governance may no longer reflect the depth at which the organization is operating.

SECTION VI

Quiet Strength

When you surface from sustained depth and climb back onto the boat, the energy is not loud. There is no celebration or bravado.

There is quiet.

You sit for a moment.

You replay the descent. You evaluate your positioning. You remember the pressure. You acknowledge how many variables could have shifted.

You are aware that you made it back, and you are aware that depth did not owe you that outcome.

Quiet strength is not the confidence of invincibility. It is the composure that comes from disciplined execution under pressure.

After a successful deep dive, you do not feel reckless. You feel measured. You are more aware of your vulnerability, not less.

You recognize that pressure was real. That air consumption was constant. That clarity required intention. That partnership mattered.

You return stronger—not because you conquered depth, but because you respected it.

Enterprise leadership operating at sustained complexity should feel the same after disciplined recalibration. Not inflated, but grounded. Not triumphant, but aware.

Aware that systemic exposure remains dynamic.

Aware that complexity remains layered.

Aware that pressure remains constant.

Quiet strength in governance is not the absence of risk. It is the presence of discipline.

It is the ability to expand without losing calibration.

It is the ability to accelerate without surrendering review.

It is the capacity to operate under pressure without cognitive distortion.

It is the humility to define boundaries before they are forced.

Organizations that cultivate quiet strength do not announce their maturity. They demonstrate it through consistent review, deliberate recalibration, structured visibility, disciplined escalation, and partnership across governance tiers.

They do not wait for turbulence to prove resilience. They operate as if depth always matters.

There is a final distinction that separates fragile growth from governable growth.

Fragile systems celebrate survival.

Governable systems institutionalize discipline.

Divers who return from depth do not assume the next dive will require less preparation. Each time they dive, they brief, inspect equipment, confirm air, and respect the environment.

Enterprise leaders who understand sustained complexity behave similarly. They do not treat successful quarters as validation of permanent stability. Instead, they treat them as confirmation that discipline must continue.

Quiet strength is legacy. It is not loud or dramatic, and it does not depend on crisis for validation. It is the steady posture of an organization that understands depth—and chooses to operate within it with control.

Governance at depth is not about descending farther than others. It is about returning consistently and with discipline intact.

And that is what distinguishes maturity from momentum.

Celebration exists, but it is quiet—a nod, a brief smile, a silent acknowledgment between partners.

The ocean at that depth is unforgiving. It does not reward ego, tolerate improvisation, or adjust to your confidence.

Therefore, you must enter with reverence.

You must leave with the same reverence.

The Blue Hole is never routine. No matter how many times you descend, it remains unfamiliar terrain. Conditions shift. Visibility changes. Current patterns adjust. The dive master differs. Your partner's composure varies. Your own breathing rate changes. The environment is never identical. Depth is dynamic.

Enterprise complexity behaves the same way.

No two quarters are identical. No two integrations are identical. No two regulatory environments are identical. No two leadership teams are identical.

Assuming familiarity reduces vigilance.

Quiet strength recognizes variability without dramatizing it.

After surfacing, you sit quietly because you understand what could have gone wrong. Equalization could have failed. Air consumption could have accelerated. Cognitive distortion could have intensified. Communication could have faltered.

None of that happened. Not because depth was gentle, but because discipline held. That awareness humbles.

Enterprise leadership operating at sustained scale must cultivate similar humility. Success does not imply safety. Stability does not eliminate volatility. Growth does not remove exposure.

The absence of failure does not mean the absence of risk. Quiet strength acknowledges this without theatrics. Instead of declaring mastery, it reinforces discipline.

There is a visible difference between fragile expansion and governable expansion.

Fragile expansion celebrates momentum. Governable expansion reinforces calibration.

Fragile systems measure achievement. Governable systems measure survivability.

Fragile leadership equates scale with capability. Disciplined leadership equates capability with restraint.

When you return from sustained depth, you do not feel invincible. You feel sharpened—more aware, more measured, and more attentive. You understand that depth did not yield to you. You operated within its laws.

Enterprise governance at sustained scale requires the same posture.

You do not conquer complexity. You navigate it.

You do not eliminate pressure. You manage it.

You do not avoid risk. You calibrate it.

Quiet strength is the steady discipline of leaders who understand that operating at depth is not an event. It is an ongoing act, not a heroic act or a condition. It is not loud, but it is visible in architecture, review, recalibration, and restraint.

Governance at depth is not about descending farther than competitors. It is about building systems capable of returning—repeatedly—with discipline intact. It is about leading in complexity without distortion. It is about growing without breaching structural limits. It is about recognizing that the environment is ever evolving—and responding with equal discipline.

You enter with reverence. You leave with reverence.

That is maturity.

That is advisory strength.

That is governance at depth.

There are two final distinctions that separate leaders who operate at sustained complexity from those who merely survive it:

Survival is reactive. Governance is deliberate.

Survival celebrates the absence of catastrophe. Governance designs against its inevitability.

Organizations that lack quiet strength depend on favorable conditions. They rely on stable enforcement cycles, strong market performance, and institutional memory to carry exposure forward.

Organizations that operate with quiet strength do not depend on conditions. They depend on architecture:

- They embed recalibration before acceleration.
- They define thresholds before layering.
- They integrate visibility before expansion.
- They institutionalize review before vulnerability compounds.

They do not wait for disruption to validate discipline. They assume depth is real—whether it is visible or not.

This book has not argued that growth is dangerous. It has argued that unmanaged depth is.

It has not suggested that complexity should be avoided. It has insisted that complexity must be governed.

It has not glorified risk. It has disciplined it.

Governance at depth is not about fear.

It is about strength under constraint.

It is about leaders who understand that pressure is constant, visibility must be engineered, boundaries must be respected, distortion must be recognized, and calm must not be misread.

It is about designing organizations that remain clear when light filters, disciplined when air consumption accelerates, humble when success accumulates, and deliberate when momentum intensifies.

The Blue Hole does not change for you. Depth does not adjust to ambition. Enterprise complexity does not soften for optimism.

Leaders who operate with quiet strength understand all of this.

They do not chase depth to prove capability. They build capability before entering depth.

They do not celebrate survival loudly. They institutionalize discipline quietly.

And when they return to the surface—measured, reflective, aware—they brief again. Because sustained enterprise depth is not a single descent. It is a condition of modern leadership.

Governance is oxygen at depth. Without it, distortion sets in, accumulation hardens, boundaries blur, and calm deceives.

With it, organizations can descend deliberately, operate under pressure, recalibrate with discipline, and return with strength intact.

That is not metaphor.

That is architecture. That is maturity. That is advisory leadership.

Clarity does not eliminate depth. It defines how to operate within it.

Ownership does not remove pressure. It accepts responsibility for managing it.

Resolve is what transforms discipline from theory into architecture.

EPILOGUE

The Descent Is Deliberate

When you stand at the edge of the boat, you are not unaware of the ocean's depth. You simply cannot feel it yet.

From above, the water looks calm. The surface reflects light. The horizon appears steady. The entry is controlled. The descent is voluntary.

Nothing forces you into the water. You choose it.

Governance is no different.

Most organizations do not begin in disorder. They begin with structure, discipline, expertise, reporting, and confidence. They believe—reasonably—that trade risk is being managed. And often, it is.

But depth does not announce itself. It accumulates. It builds beneath stability and growth. It builds beneath consistency and professional competence. The stronger the execution, the less visible the accumulation.

This book is not about compliance failure. It is about structural illusion and about the difference between managing transactions and governing exposure, the difference between visible activity and deliberate ownership, and the difference between reacting to pressure and designing for it.

Depth is not the problem. Unacknowledged depth is.

The Descent Protocol is not a warning against growth. It is not an argument against complexity. It is not a critique of trade professionals. It is a structural reframe.

Governability does not require more intensity. It requires clarity:

- Clarity about what leadership owns.
- Clarity about when exposure must be reconsidered.
- Clarity about how scale changes consequence.
- Clarity about the difference between stability and alignment.

In diving, equalization is not dramatic. It is quiet, repetitive, and disciplined.

It is required. You cannot delegate it, ignore it, or wait until pain forces you to act. You do it because depth demands it.

Governance works the same way.

The organizations that endure at depth are not those that avoid pressure. Instead, they anticipate it and design for it. They accept that growth magnifies consequence. They refuse to allow exposure to accumulate without deliberate ownership.

They do not wait for enforcement to redefine their risk. They see it.

And once they see it, they cannot return to the surface unchanged.

That has been this book's journey. It has taken you beneath the visible controls and into the structure that determines whether governance holds. It has shown you where illusion forms, where accumulation hides, where stability persuades, and where leadership must decide.

The Descent Protocol is not a theory.

It is a choice.

You can continue to rely on discipline and assume alignment.

Or you can design governability—deliberately, structurally, and at scale.

The water will not grow shallower. Scale will not slow. Enforcement will not soften permanently. Depth is not temporary. The only question is whether your governance is.

The descent is voluntary, and once you understand depth, remaining at the surface is no longer an option.

And that is where governability begins.

TOOLS FOR APPLICATION

The following tools translate governance at depth into structured application.

They are designed to assess, interpret, and operationalize exposure across your organization.

Governance Depth Index™ (GDI) Toolkit

Pre-Assessment: Exposure Mapping
Scoring Model (0–5)
Executive Readout & Action Guide

Governance Depth Index™ (GDI) Assessment

Assessment
Interpretation Guide

Glossary of Terms and Concepts

GOVERNANCE DEPTH INDEX™

Executive Assessment & Alignment Framework

Assessing whether governance is aligned to the depth of exposure your organization creates.

This assessment is not designed to evaluate activity.

It is designed to evaluate alignment.

The Governance Depth Index™ measures whether governance exists where exposure is created—and whether it remains sufficient as conditions change. It distinguishes between systems that continue to function and systems that are designed to sustain control at depth.

Complete this assessment deliberately. The value is not in the score alone, but in what the score reveals.

Governance Depth Index™ (GDI) Toolkit: Pre-Assessment

Before scoring, identify where exposure is created and where governance is expected to exist.

GOVERNANCE DEPTH INDEX™
PRE-ASSESSMENT: EXPOSURE MAPPING

PAGE 1 OF 3
Before the GDI

Map where exposure is created—and where governance is expected to exist.

1 WHERE EXPOSURE IS CREATED

Identify where trade-impacting decisions are made across your organization.
Add any others specific to your organization.

Pricing decisions · Sourcing / supplier selection · Entity structure / legal · Tax strategy · Finance / transfer pricing · Contracting / commercial terms · Market entry / expansion · Operations / fulfillment · Other ______

2 WHERE GOVERNANCE ACTUALLY EXISTS

For each area above, indicate how governance currently shows up.

FUNCTION / DECISION AREA	GOVERNANCE EXISTS?	HOW IT SHOWS UP	OWNED BY
	☐ Yes ☐ Partial ☐ No		
	☐ Yes ☐ Partial ☐ No		
	☐ Yes ☐ Partial ☐ No		
	☐ Yes ☐ Partial ☐ No		
	☐ Yes ☐ Partial ☐ No		
	☐ Yes ☐ Partial ☐ No		
	☐ Yes ☐ Partial ☐ No		
	☐ Yes ☐ Partial ☐ No		

3 DISCONNECT IDENTIFICATION

Where does exposure exist without aligned governance?
List the most significant gaps.

1. ______
2. ______
3. ______
4. ______
5. ______

4 OWNERSHIP REALITY CHECK

Who believes they own governance in these areas?

Trade team: ______
Tax / Finance: ______
Operations: ______
Legal: ______
Other: ______

Where ownership is unclear, fragmented, or assumed, note it.

5 ESCALATION VISIBILITY

When risk emerges in these areas, how consistently is it escalated?

☐ Always ☐ Sometimes ☐ Rarely ☐ Never

- Who receives it? ______
- At what stage? ______
- What typically happens next? ______

Governance does not fail because it is absent.
It fails because it is present in the *wrong* places.

Why this matters:
Scoring without understanding where exposure lives and governance (does not) exist leads to false confidence. Complete this map before moving to the GDI.

→ **Next: Scoring Model** *(Page 2)*

Governance at Depth™ · The Descent Protocol™ · Darlene Waters-Colon

Governance Depth Index™ (GDI) Toolkit: Scoring Model (0-5)

GOVERNANCE DEPTH INDEX™
SCORING MODEL (0–5)

PAGE 2 OF 3
Before the GDI

How to Score Governance at Depth

Each condition is scored from 0–5 based on how consistently governance exists where exposure is actually created.

SCORE	LEVEL	WHAT IT MEANS	WHAT IT LOOKS LIKE
0	NOT PRESENT	Governance does not exist where exposure is created.	• No policies, process, or oversight • Decisions made without governance input • Risk is not considered
1	KNOWN, UNMANAGED	Exposure is visible, but governance is not applied.	• Exposure is known but not governed • Ad hoc responses to issues • No accountability or follow-through
2	INFORMAL / INCONSISTENT	Governance appears in pockets, but is not reliable or repeatable.	• Informal practices vary by person or function • Inconsistent application • Reliant on individuals, not structure
3	DEFINED, UNEVEN	Structures exist, but break under cross-functional pressure.	• Documented governance exists • Gaps in coverage or enforcement • Breaks down as complexity increases
4	ENFORCED ACROSS FUNCTIONS	Governance is applied beyond trade, but not fully integrated.	• Consistent application across most functions • Clear ownership and accountability • Some integration gaps remain
5	FULLY INTEGRATED	Governance is embedded where exposure is created and adapts as conditions change.	• Embedded in decision points • Real-time visibility and responsiveness • Scales with complexity and change

CALIBRATION PRINCIPLES

- ✓ Score based on observed behavior—not intended design.
- ✓ If governance depends on individuals, escalation, or exception handling, it is not fully integrated.
- ✓ Apply the same standard across all functions.
- ✓ When in doubt, score lower.

WHAT YOU ARE ACTUALLY MEASURING

- Where decisions create exposure
- Whether governance exists at that point
- Whether it holds under complexity

WHAT THIS IS NOT

- ⊗ Not a measure of documentation
- ⊗ Not a measure of control design
- ⊗ Not a measure of trade team capability
- ⊗ Not a maturity model
- ⊗ Not a one-time certification

The score reflects not how governance is designed—
but *how it behaves* under real operating conditions.

NEXT STEPS: (1) Score the 10 conditions on the GDI page. → (2) View your total score on the GDI gauge. → (3) Use the Interpretation Guide to understand your result.

Governance at Depth™ • The Descent Protocol™ • Darlene Waters-Colon

Score based on how governance behaves under real operating conditions—not how it is designed.

Governance Depth Index™ (GDI) Toolkit: Executive Readout and Action Guide

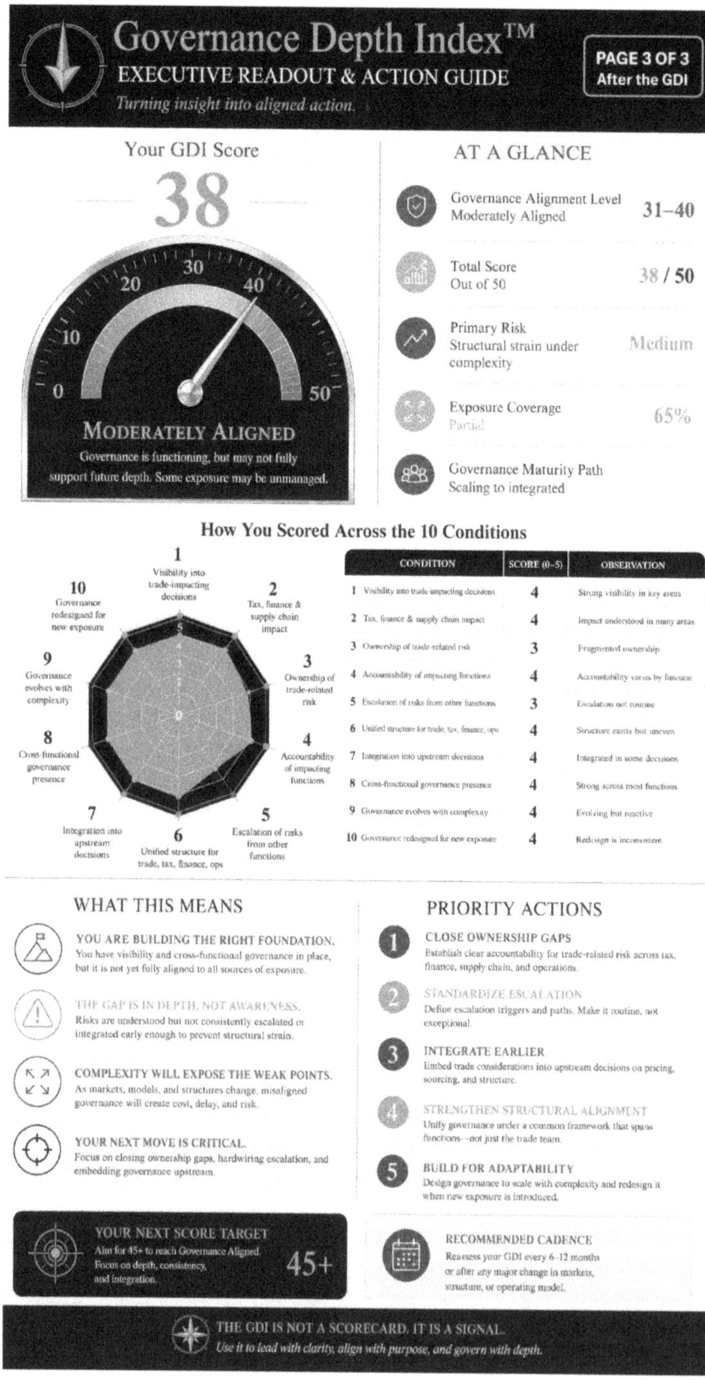

Governance Depth Index™

EXECUTIVE READOUT & ACTION GUIDE

Turning insight into aligned action.

PAGE 3 OF 3
After the GDI

Your GDI Score

38

MODERATELY ALIGNED

Governance is functioning, but may not fully support future depth. Some exposure may be unmanaged.

AT A GLANCE

Governance Alignment Level — Moderately Aligned — 31–40

Total Score — Out of 50 — 38 / 50

Primary Risk — Structural strain under complexity — Medium

Exposure Coverage — Partial — 65%

Governance Maturity Path — Scaling to integrated

How You Scored Across the 10 Conditions

CONDITION	SCORE (0–5)	OBSERVATION
1 Visibility into trade-impacting decisions	4	Strong visibility in key areas
2 Tax, finance & supply chain impact	4	Impact understood in many areas
3 Ownership of trade-related risk	3	Fragmented ownership
4 Accountability of impacting functions	4	Accountability varies by function
5 Escalation of risks from other functions	3	Escalation not routine
6 Unified structure for trade, tax, finance, ops	4	Structure exists but uneven
7 Integration into upstream decisions	4	Integrated in some decisions
8 Cross-functional governance presence	4	Strong across most functions
9 Governance evolves with complexity	4	Evolving but reactive
10 Governance redesigned for new exposure	4	Redesign is inconsistent

WHAT THIS MEANS

YOU ARE BUILDING THE RIGHT FOUNDATION.
You have visibility and cross-functional governance in place, but it is not yet fully aligned to all sources of exposure.

THE GAP IS IN DEPTH, NOT AWARENESS.
Risks are understood but not consistently escalated or integrated early enough to prevent structural strain.

COMPLEXITY WILL EXPOSE THE WEAK POINTS.
As markets, models, and structures change, misaligned governance will create cost, delay, and risk.

YOUR NEXT MOVE IS CRITICAL.
Focus on closing ownership gaps, hardwiring escalation, and embedding governance upstream.

PRIORITY ACTIONS

1. CLOSE OWNERSHIP GAPS
Establish clear accountability for trade-related risk across tax, finance, supply chain, and operations.

2. STANDARDIZE ESCALATION
Define escalation triggers and paths. Make it routine, not exceptional.

3. INTEGRATE EARLIER
Embed trade considerations into upstream decisions on pricing, sourcing, and structure.

4. STRENGTHEN STRUCTURAL ALIGNMENT
Unify governance under a common framework that spans functions—not just the trade team.

5. BUILD FOR ADAPTABILITY
Design governance to scale with complexity and redesign it when new exposure is introduced.

YOUR NEXT SCORE TARGET
Aim for 45+ to reach Governance Aligned.
Focus on depth, consistency, and integration.
45+

RECOMMENDED CADENCE
Reassess your GDI every 6–12 months or after any major change in markets, structure, or operating model.

THE GDI IS NOT A SCORECARD. IT IS A SIGNAL.
Use it to lead with clarity, align with purpose, and govern with depth.

Governance Depth Index™ Assessment

GOVERNANCE DEPTH INDEX™

Assessing Governance Alignment with Operational Depth

GOVERNANCE FAILURE	COMPRESSION PRESENT	COMPRESSION EMERGING	MODERATE ALIGNMENT	GOVERNANCE ALIGNED
0 – 10	11 – 20	21 – 30	31 – 40	41 – 50

Total Score: _____ / 50

1. Leadership has visibility into trade-impacting decisions made outside the trade function 0 1 2 3 4 5
2. Leadership understands how tax, finance, and supply chain decisions impact trade exposure 0 1 2 3 4 5
3. Ownership of trade-related risk is defined across all functions *(not just trade)* 0 1 2 3 4 5
4. Functions creating trade impact (tax, finance, sourcing) are accountable for that impact 0 1 2 3 4 5
5. Trade-related risks originating in other functions are consistently escalated 0 1 2 3 4 5
6. Escalation connects trade, tax, finance, and operations into a unified structure 0 1 2 3 4 5
7. Trade considerations are integrated into upstream decisions (pricing, sourcing, entity structure) 0 1 2 3 4 5
8. Governance exists across functions, not only within the trade team 0 1 2 3 4 5
9. Governance evolves as cross-functional complexity increases 0 1 2 3 4 5
10. Governance is redesigned when new exposure is introduced (markets, pricing, restructuring) 0 1 2 3 4 5

"The question is no longer whether governance exists – but whether it exists where exposure is created."

Interpretation Guide: Governance Alignment at Depth

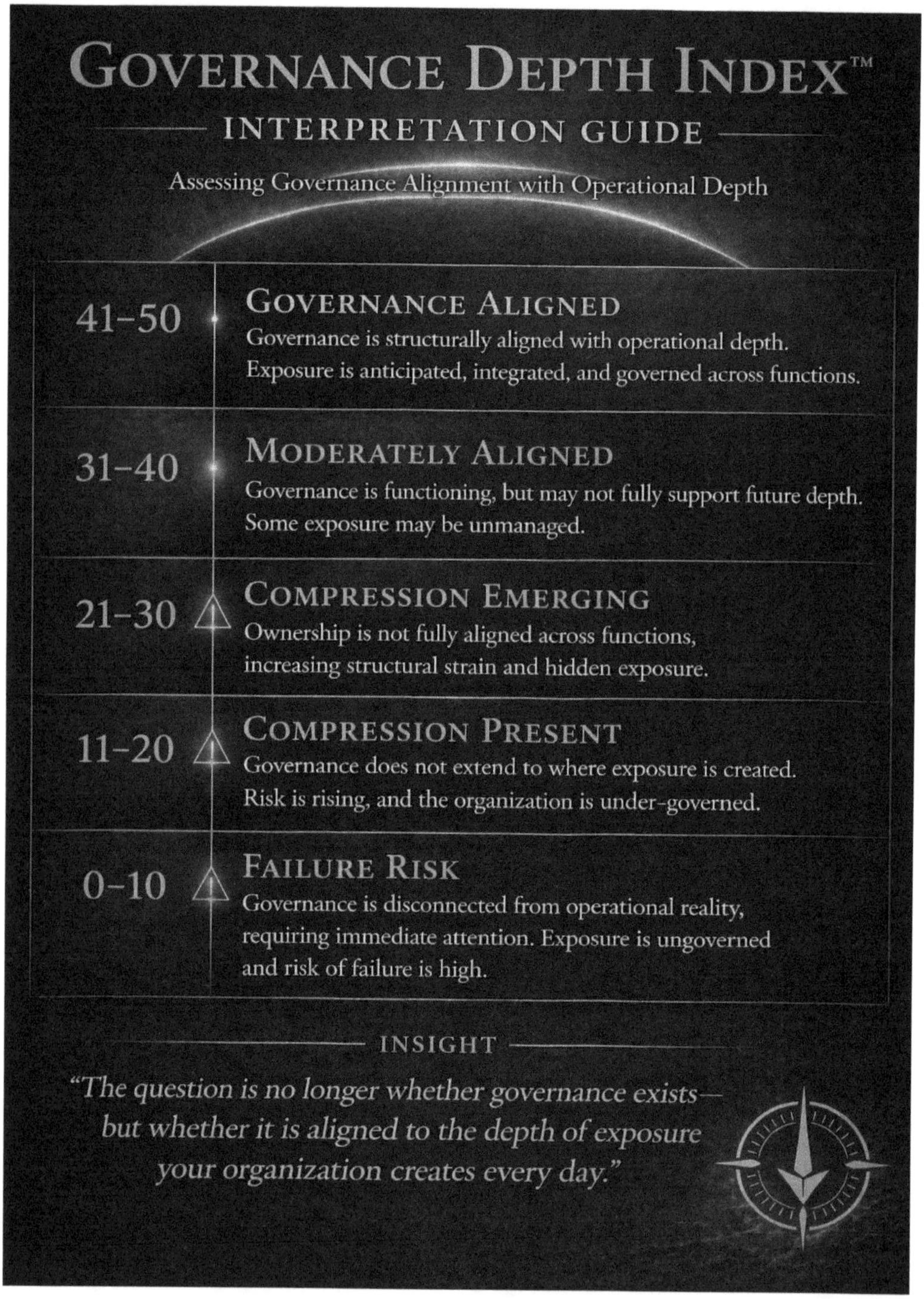

GLOSSARY OF TERMS AND CONCEPTS

The following terms define the conceptual language of diving and are intended primarily to explain the diving metaphor used throughout this book. Terms are presented in order of progression—from surface-level conditions to governance at depth.

Signature Language

The Descent Protocol

A structured approach for moving from surface-level governance to deliberate governance at depth. It defines how organizations recognize, assess, and realign decision-making authority, accountability, and exposure as complexity increases, enabling governance to operate effectively within real operational environments.

Governance must be designed to operate where exposure is created.

Governance Depth Index (GDI)™

A structured framework used to assess how governance is designed to operate relative to an organization's complexity, scale, and exposure. The GDI evaluates alignment between decision-making authority, accountability, and accumulated exposure, providing a clear view of whether governance is operating effectively at depth or remaining at the surface.

Alignment is measured at the point of decision—not in design.

Governance at Depth

A state in which governance is deliberately designed to operate within the complexity, scale, and pressure of real operational environments, rather than at the surface level of policy and oversight.

Depth is where governance is tested—and revealed.

Surface Governance

Governance that appears structured and effective but operates primarily at a policy or compliance level, without alignment to how decisions actually occur within the organization.

What appears controlled may not be connected.

Pre-Dive Assessment

The deliberate evaluation of governance structures, decision rights, and exposure before entering complex operational environments.

Clarity before entry determines stability at depth.

The First Few Feet

The early stage of operational activity where initial decisions are made and exposure begins to accumulate, often without visibility or deliberate governance design.

Exposure begins before governance is noticed.

Exposure Accumulation

The process by which risk builds over time through repeated decisions across functions, geographies, and systems, often without visibility or ownership.

Risk builds quietly—until it doesn't.

Drift

The gradual deviation between intended governance structures and actual decision-making behavior over time.

Misalignment rarely happens all at once.

Design Silence

The absence of deliberate governance design in areas where exposure is actively being created; often mistaken for stability.

Silence is not stability—it is absence.

Surface Illusion

The perception that governance is effective based on visible controls and compliance indicators, while underlying exposure continues to accumulate unnoticed.

Visibility can create false confidence.

Equalization (Governance Context)

The deliberate alignment of decision-making authority, accountability, and exposure to maintain balance as complexity increases.

Balance must be maintained as pressure rises.

Compression at Depth

The increasing pressure created by accumulated exposure as organizations operate at scale, often without corresponding governance design.

Pressure reveals what structure cannot support.

Governance Compression Curve

The increasing strain placed on governance structures as operational depth expands. As organizations move from surface-level activity to complex global exposure, structural capacity is compressed by rising regulatory, operational, and financial pressures—until governance either adapts or fails.

Capacity and complexity must move together.

The $10M Moment

A defining point at which accumulated exposure becomes visible and consequential, forcing recognition of governance misalignment.

Recognition arrives when consequence becomes unavoidable.

Depth of Exposure

The extent to which accumulated exposure is embedded within operational systems, decision-making structures, and enterprise processes, often beyond immediate visibility.

What is embedded is hardest to see—and hardest to unwind.

Controlled Ascent

The structured process of unwinding accumulated exposure in a deliberate and staged manner to prevent disruption or unintended consequences.

Recovery requires as much structure as descent.

Diving Terminology Glossary

Blue Hole, The

A vertical underwater sinkhole representing depth, complexity, and exposure. In this book, it symbolizes the environment where governance design is truly tested.

Buddy System, The

A principle in diving where individuals operate with shared awareness and mutual accountability. In the governance context, it reflects the need for aligned decision-making and shared responsibility across functions to manage exposure effectively.

Controlled Ascent

The deliberate and structured process of reducing accumulated exposure in a staged manner, ensuring that governance realignment occurs without creating additional instability or risk.

Decompression

A staged ascent allowing pressure to equalize safely. In this book, it represents the careful unwinding of complex risk exposure.

Depth

The operational environment where real risk exists. In governance terms, depth is where decisions, systems, and controls are tested under pressure.

Descent

The controlled process of moving from the surface to operational depth. In this book, descent represents the transition from surface governance to operational exposure.

Dive Computer

A device that tracks depth, time, and decompression requirements. In governance, this device parallels data visibility and monitoring systems.

Dive Plan

The predetermined strategy for depth, time, and route. Equivalent to governance architecture designed before exposure occurs.

Equipment Check

Pre-dive verification that systems are functioning. Analogous to internal control validation.

No-Decompression Limit (NDL)

The maximum time a diver can remain at a given depth without requiring decompression stops. In governance, the NDL parallels risk thresholds that organizations unknowingly exceed.

Surface Interval

Time spent above water between dives. Used metaphorically to describe reflection or evaluation periods between operational cycles.

Governance and Industry Concepts

Customs Valuation

The method used to determine the value of imported goods for duty assessment.

Decision Rights

Defined authority specifying who is permitted to make which decisions under what conditions.

Depth Recognition

The point at which an organization becomes aware that its operations have moved beyond surface-level governance, requiring deliberate alignment of decision-making, accountability, and exposure.

Dutiable

Goods whose value must be included in the customs valuation base for calculating import duties.

Escalation Architecture

The structured design that determines when and how decisions are elevated within the organization based on exposure, ensuring that increasing risk is matched by appropriate levels of authority and oversight.

Escalation Threshold

Predefined criteria that trigger elevation of decisions based on exposure, not discretion.

Exposure

The cumulative impact of decisions across time, geography, and scale—not just individual risk events.

Governability

The enterprise's ability to demonstrate deliberate ownership of its accumulated exposure.

Governance

The system by which decision-making authority, accountability, and oversight are deliberately designed to manage exposure as it scales.

Governance Architecture

The integrated system of structures, decision rights, escalation paths, and accountability mechanisms that determine how governance operates across the enterprise.

Operational Excellence

The ability to execute consistently and effectively within defined processes—distinct from governance, which determines how decisions are structured and owned.

PO-to-Payment

The full commercial transaction lifecycle from purchase order through final financial settlement.

Post-Entry Audit

A regulatory review conducted after goods have been imported to verify compliance with customs laws.

Posture

The aggregate position an organization assumes through repeated decisions, whether deliberately designed or not.

Structural Drift

The gradual misalignment between decision-making authority and accumulated exposure over time.

Structural Pressure

The force created when accumulated exposure exceeds the capacity of existing governance structures, resulting in misalignment between how decisions are made and how risk is carried within the organization.

System Visibility

The ability to observe, measure, and understand how decisions and data move across systems, enabling informed governance at scale.

Systemic Risk

Risk that emerges from interconnected decisions across functions, regions, or time—not from isolated events.

Technical and Regulatory Terms

Assists (Valuation)

Goods, services, or intellectual property provided by the buyer that must be included in the customs value of imported merchandise.

Enforcement Posture

The level of regulatory scrutiny, aggressiveness, and prioritization applied by authorities in monitoring and enforcing compliance.

Enterprise Risk Tolerance

The level of exposure an organization is willing to accept in pursuit of its strategic objectives, whether explicitly defined or implicitly assumed.

Governance Ownership (Exposure Ownership)

The explicit assignment of accountability for accumulated exposure across the enterprise, rather than isolated responsibility for individual compliance activities.

Royalties (Valuation)

Payments related to imported goods that may be required to be included in customs value depending on their relationship to the transaction.

Tariff Sensitivity

The degree to which product classification or valuation changes materially impact duty liability.

Trade Remedy Exposure

Risk arising from anti-dumping, countervailing duties, or safeguard measures that may be triggered by sourcing decisions, pricing, or country of origin.

Transfer Pricing (Customs Context)

The intersection of intercompany pricing and customs valuation, where declared values must satisfy both tax and customs regulatory requirements.

www.ingramcontent.com/pod-product-compliance
Lightning Source LLC
LaVergne TN
LVHW071411210926
848486LV00004B/248
* 9 7 9 8 9 9 5 4 1 7 8 0 4 *